EXECUTIVE COACHING

EXECUTIVE COACHING

Systems-Psychodynamic Perspective

Edited by

Halina Brunning

KARNAC
LONDON   NEW YORK

First published in 2006 by
H. Karnac (Books) Ltd.
6 Pembroke Buildings, London NW10 6RE

British Library Cataloguing in Publication Data

A C.I.P. for this book is available from the British Library

ISBN 978-1-85575-327-3

Edited, designed and produced by The Studio Publishing Services Ltd,
www.studiopublishingservicesuk.co.uk
e-mail: studio@publishingservices.co.uk

Printed in Great Britain

10 9 8 7 6 5 4 3 2 1

www.karnacbooks.com

CONTENTS

To Basia and Adam

ACKNOWLEDGEMENTS

I wish to acknowledge and thank the following:

The International Society for the Psychoanalytic Study of Organizations (ISPSO) for its intellectual inspiration.

The contributors to this book for their professionalism, high quality of collaboration and creative writing.

Mark Stein and Larry Gould for their comments on my chapters.

All my coaching clients for allowing me to learn from them and with them.

Karen Partridge for our conversations about models and meaning.

Simon and Robert Brunning for the technical help, Freya Bass and Rosie B. for their assistance, my friends and family for their support.

And above all, to Clare Huffington, for our fascinating conversations that led to the integration of all of the above.

Miranda Alcock is an independent organizational consultant who works with whole organisations, teams and individuals. She is a specialist in executive coaching and mentoring. She works in the public and private sectors, including the National Health Service (NHS), central and local government, as well as with charities and NGOs. She is the Organizing Tutor for the Certificate in Counselling for Refugees at the Tavistock Centre. She has many years' experience in Group Relations work as Staff Consultant and as Director. She is a member of the Society of Analytic Psychology, Birkbeck Counselling Association, and the International Society for the Psychoanalytic Study of Organizations. She is an associate of OPUS and a Fellow of the Bayswater Institute.

Halina Brunning is a Chartered Clinical Psychologist, organizational consultant and executive coach. She has worked in the British and Polish National Health Service as a clinician, therapist, supervisor, manager, and consultant. She has published extensively on clinical and organizational issues, has co-written three books and over twenty articles on these subjects. In parallel with her NHS career, Halina has worked as an organizational consultant and coach. Her approach to coaching is psychological and psychodynamic and is informed by the Tavistock Clinic systems-psychodynamic training. She is an Associate Fellow of the British Psychological Society, member of the International Society for the Psychoanalytic Study of Organizations, OPUS, Association of Coaching, and founder member of the Coaching Psychology Forum. She presents papers, lectures, and runs professional development workshops in the UK, Poland, France, Holland, and Italy.

Angela Eden works as an independent organizational consultant from her own practice EDENevolution. She has worked in a wide range of employment sectors: health, education, community work, social welfare, probation, agriculture, local and central government, construction and telecommunications. Working in so many settings gives her a greater understanding of management and organization issues. She consolidated her group and consultancy experience at the Tavistock Clinic and the London Institute of Group Analysis. She has associate relationships with the Work Foundation and Tavistock Institute as a leadership consultant. Her focus with individuals, teams, and groups is on the issues of power, diversity, and leadership, and as a mediator in conflict resolution.

Clare Huffington has a Master's degree in Educational Psychology, is a Chartered Psychologist and an Associate Fellow of the British Psychological Society. She is a qualified teacher, systemic therapist with Membership of the Tavistock Society of Psychotherapists. She has over twenty years' experience in education, health, and business. She is currently Director of The Tavistock Consultancy Service. She works with individuals and top teams in a variety of organizations in the private, public, and voluntary sectors. She is a board member of the International Society for the Psychoanalytic Study of Organizations. She is also on the faculty of "Organizational Psychodynamics and Transformations", a professional development programme for managers based in Coesfeld, Germany. She acted as a staff member on many group relations events. She offers supervision to executive coaches for Right Management Consulting in the UK. Clare has written twelve books and a variety of articles on organizations, consultancy, coaching, and the management of change.

Laurence J. Gould, PhD, is a Former Professor and Director of the Clinical Psychology Doctoral Programme, The City University of New York, and Director of the Socio-Psychoanalytic Training Programme, The Institute for Psychoanalytic Training and Research (IPTAR). He is also the founding Co-Director of the Programme in Organizational Development and Consultation, a Research Fellow of the Sigmund Freud Centre, Hebrew University, and a founding member of International Society for the Psychoanalytic Study of Organizations (ISPSO). Dr Gould is the recipient of the American Psychological Association's Levinson Award for outstanding contributions to the theory and practice of organizational consultation. He has written numerous articles, and is a Co-Editor of *The Systems Psychodynamics of Organizations* (Karnac, 2001) and *Experiential Learning in Organizations* (Karnac, 2004). In addition, he is the Co-Editor of *Organizational and Social Dynamics*, an international journal for the integration of psychoanalytic, systemic and group relations perspectives. He practises psychoanalysis and organizational consultation in New York City.

Michael Jarrett, PhD, is an Adjunct Associate Professor in Organizational Behaviour at London Business School and a managing partner of Ilyas Jarrett Consulting (www.ilyasjarrett.com), a strategic management consultancy. He works with a team of experienced consultants who specialize in implementing organizational change. Their work is underpinned by innovative approaches to change as well as leading-edge research. Michael was formerly the Managing Director of the London office at Personnel Decisions International, and a Director with the Alexander Corporation. Michael's consultancy experience has been complemented with several academic posts, including faculty positions at a number of leading universities. He has been a staff consultant with the Tavistock Group Relations Conference. Clients have included the BBC, United Nations, Cap Gemini, Ernst & Young, Lloyds TSB, Barclays, and media companies. Michael has written books and several articles on the dynamics of strategic management groups, the difficulties of change, the psychodynamics of consulting, and the strategic role of management information systems.

Richard Kwiatkowski works mostly as a Senior Lecturer in Organizational Psychology at Cranfield School of Management, where he redesigned the Organizational Behaviour Programme, which is ranked fourth in the world by the *Financial Times*. He is a Chartered Occupational and Chartered Counselling Psychologist, Chartered member of the Institute of Personnel and Development, founder member of the Special Group in Coaching Psychology, and Associate Fellow of the British Psychological Society (BPS). Richard has worked in psychiatry, psychotherapy, stress management, and as a psychologist and manager in industry. He set up and was the director of the first UK Doctorate in Organizational Psychology. He is former Chair of the BPS Division of Occupational Psychology, elected to the BPS Council and the Board of Directors. Currently he is the Chair elect of the BPS Ethics Committee. He has consulted to numerous individuals, companies, and consultancies. He has published on a wide range of psychological topics, is a reviewer for several journals and associate editor of *The Psychologist*. He combines psychological approaches to his work with a realistic understanding of contemporary organization.

W. Gordon Lawrence is a graduate of Aberdeen University and Bergische Universität (Wuppertal) where he obtained a doctorate in economics. Currently he is a visiting professor at the New Bulgarian University, Sofia, and the University of Northumberland, Newcastle. He is a fellow of AISA, Australia, a former board member of ISPSO, and sits on the editorial advisory boards of the *Journal of Organizational and Social Dynamics*, *Free Associations*, and *Freie Assoziation*. He has written over seventy articles and six books, including *Introduction to Social Dreaming: Transforming Thinking* (Karnac, 2005). After working in the army and in commercial and educational organizations in the 1970s, he joined the Tavistock Institute where he worked for eleven years. He resigned to join Shell International, followed by Presidency of the International Foundation for Social Innovation, Paris. Currently, he is a managing partner of Social Dreaming Ltd, London. He works mainly as an organizational consultant, and offers Creative Role Synthesis. He also mentors organizational consultants and researchers.

Anton Obholzer has been a senior faculty member of Insead Global Leadership Centre, Paris, for the past five years. He is a Fellow of the Exeter University Strategic Leadership Centre; and was a

Founder/Director, Tavistock Centre Consulting to Institutions Workshop 1980–2002; Director/Chief Executive of the Tavistock Centre, London 1985–2002. Dr Obholzer has been a Visiting Professor, Universities of Vienna, Graz and Innsbruck, since 1990. By training, he is an MD, psychiatrist, psychoanalyst, and group and organizational consultant. Anton Obholzer has increasingly moved into the application of psychological understanding in the management of organisations. His consultancy experience covers a wide range of commercial, banking and public sector organisations with the main emphasis of work and publications being on "beneath-the-surface"/unconscious factors causing resistance to change. He is currently engaged in projects in the USA, UK, Scandinavia, Germany, Austria, Holland, France, Italy, Spain, and South Africa. His work with chief executives and senior management staff takes the form of mentoring, coaching, and role consultancy. The emphasis is on the multiplicity of factors playing a role in personal and institutional creativity.

Jane Pooley is a Principal Consultant at the Tavistock Consultancy Service (TCS) and runs her own organizational consultancy practice. She has fifteen years' experience in organizational and management development and training. Jane is Director of the Executive Coaching Training programme at TCS. (See "Directory of resources" in this book for further information on the course.) Jane is currently working with clients in global business enterprises, and in the public and voluntary sectors of UK, Spain, South Africa, and South America. Jane is a qualified family psychotherapist and member of the Tavistock Society of Psychotherapists, The Institute of Family Therapy and OPUS. Jane specializes in consulting to senior executives and their teams in the areas of leadership development, executive performance, and interpersonal and influencing skills. She works with organizations to develop and implement guiding principles based on corporate values. Jane facilitates executive, management, and team-building sessions, and supervises coaching practitioners. Her publications and contributions to a number of books reflect her interest in organizational and social development initiatives.

Vega Roberts trained originally as a psychiatrist and psychotherapist in the USA. She came to the UK in 1984 as a Fellow of the

Action Research Training Programme at the Tavistock Institute of Human Relations, and since then has worked as a consultant to individuals, teams and organizations. Currently, Vega works as a Senior Organisational Analyst at The Grubb Institute. She is also Director of the Management and Leadership Programme in Mental Health Services in the West London Mental Health Trust, a Senior Associate of the Health Service Management Centre at the University of Birmingham, and adviser to FRC Consultants, of which she was a founding member. She supervises consultants and researchers in both the private and public sectors, and is an accredited coach (Law Society) working with middle and senior managers. Special interests include working across organizational boundaries to enhance collaboration and partnership working, and developing leadership potential in people at all levels of an organization. She has lectured and run workshops on leadership and change in the United States, France, Switzerland, and Italy, has contributed to books and professional journals, is co-editor of *The Unconscious at Work: Individual and Organisational Stress in the Human Services*, and of *Managing Mental Health in the Community*, and is a member of the editorial board of the journal *Organisational and Social Dynamics*.

Marlene Spero read sociology and gained a PhD at the London School of Economics. She is a Member of the Institute of Group Analysis, an Associate Member of the British Association of Psychotherapy, and a Chartered Member of the Institute of Personnel and Development. She consults to individuals, groups, and organizations in transition, using a socio-psychological approach. She works as an executive coach and has a particular interest in intercultural issues and leadership development and assessment. Her clients include those in retail, finance, banking, health, education, and IT. She teaches on management and psychotherapy programmes in the UK and abroad and has run conferences on group dynamics and leadership. She was a founder member and past Chair of the Consultancy Services of the Institute of Group Analysis, a Board member of the International Society for the Psychoanalytic Study of Organizations and the European Association for Trans-cultural Group Analysis. She has her own practice and is also an associate of the Bayswater Institute.

Lionel F. Stapley, PhD, is the Director of OPUS (an Organisation for Promoting Understanding of Society) and an organizational consultant. He has worked as a staff member of several international Group Relations Conferences. His consultancy clients include a variety of organizations, including the football industry. He is the author of *The Personality of the Organisation: A Psychodynamic Explanation of Culture and Change* (Free Association, 1996) and *It's an Emotional Game: Learning About Leadership from the Experience of Football* (Karnac, 2002); and co-editor with Larry Gould and Mark Stein of *The Systems Psychodynamics of Organisations* (Other Press, 2001), and *Applied Experiential Learning: The Group Relations Training Approach* (Karnac, 2004). He is the Chair of the Editorial Management Committee of the OPUS international journal, *Organisational & Social Dynamics*, a Fellow of the Chartered Institute of Personnel and Development, a Fellow of the Chartered Institute of Management, and a Member of the International Society for the Psychoanalytic Study of Organizations.

Foreword

Anton Obholzer

This book aims for an ambitious goal and successfully achieves it. It not only documents a particular approach to understanding individuals and organizations with a view to improving their effectiveness and creativity, but it also illustrates the application of this approach in a wide range of settings. This is a field that has been relatively sparsely covered to date. Thus, the contribution of this book is in the area of giving a structure and body to an increasingly important approach in the field of executive coaching. This approach has previously found expression in a variety of places: individual papers, conferences, and so on, but not to date in a clearly co-ordinated and coherent way such as is represented by this book. With its publication the field of systems-psychodynamic coaching will acquire the necessary foundation on which the individual reader can build his or her professional coaching experience. The approach as outlined in this book will also provide a basis on which authors of subsequent publications can build.

The book sets out to address the age-old question of how to improve the performance of both individuals and organizations. The two are intimately interlinked. The pursuit of excellence is a standing quest and has generally followed the "stick and carrot" pathway that consists in setting ambitious goals and then attempting to reach them through a series of persecutory and incentivizing measures. This approach has been refined over the years and comes in a variety of permutations, all with some degree of success. In recent years it has become clear that this approach has exhausted its potential. Something new or something extra is required. Inevitably, what is heralded as a new idea turns out to be the old idea represented in a new fashion, rather than fresh thinking that provides a way beyond the limitations of the traditional approach.

However, there is something else available. It would be a misnomer to call it "new", as it is not a recent creation. It is an approach that has been in the public domain for centuries in a simple form, that developed enormously in the twentieth century, and has now attained the maturity and experience to make a significant contribution to the achievement of excellence in the personal, organizational, and business realm. This is the systems-psychodynamic approach. It makes no claim to dethrone the managerial, goal-orientated incentives model. It should be seen instead as augmenting and facilitating the effectiveness of the traditional model, not replacing it.

What does the systems-psychodynamic model bring? As the name implies, it has two components: first, it places the question or problem in a systemic context. That might be anything from the personal family system, the work group and colleagues system, the whole business, the wider industrial situation, and the national climate. In this way a broad range of systems perspectives are considered. Second, the psychodynamic aspect of the model consists in examining the emotional "weighting" of the various parts of the system. This activity investigates and emphasizes issues, both *personal* and *organizational*, that are unspoken, not thought about, denied, and repressed. The systems-psychodynamic approach therefore brings in the "soft" human relations component that is missing from the conventional overall equation. Just as in a family, it is helpful to have both a masculine and a feminine presence (not necessarily carried by the named gender person) so that in managing the individual and the organization it is the combination of *both* approaches that allows for the most effective headway.

This systems-psychodynamic approach to understanding individuals and groups, in a simpler form, has a long history. Plato understood both individuals and the city-state in terms of similarly related structures of parts. In the twentieth century, grounded in the work of Sigmund Freud and his theoretical explanations of psychological disturbance, a deeper understanding of psychological functioning has become widespread. This more comprehensive grasp of the mental economy has not only been further developed in relation to understanding the individual, but has also had application, in the work of Kurt Lewin and others, in exploring group and institutional processes.

In the latter half of the twentieth century there was a huge push to improve personal and organizational performance. As mentioned, this was done by ever-clearer goal setting and attempts at motivation. However, what became clear is that it is often not the lack of clear goals or of motivating factors that hinders growth and advancement, but that it is more hidden personal and institutional factors that stall and sabotage development. These "under the carpet" factors are now increasingly recognized as key elements that need to be addressed if the best possible outcome is to be achieved. It would be wrong to call it the maximum achievement, because that would imply that all obstacles could be removed and a clear pathway to success and creativity achieved. This is not possible in personal life, or in business. What is possible is to create a climate of greater awareness of difficulties ahead, difficulties coming towards one. Once the monster ahead is recognized, then there are ways of overcoming it or sidestepping it, or at least of drawing some of its teeth.

The systems-psychodynamic approach is essentially about charting the various overt and covert issues on the road ahead; finding a way of mitigating them and, most importantly, establishing an awareness and a monitoring system that can alert one to the presence of the sabotaging elements before they arrive.

How is this achieved? It is recognized that most individuals do not reach anywhere near their full potential. For those lucky enough, education and socialization, as well as work related training, goes some way to improving the situation. It is now acknowledged that emotional intelligence is at least as important as the traditional measure known as IQ. So what does emotional intelligence mean? It means the capacity to read personal, interpersonal, group, and institutional interactions in a way that gets as near as possible to what they are really like, as opposed to seeing them as we would like to see them. Emotional intelligence, therefore, is a capacity to relate to the world and to see it through a series of emotional "lenses" that are as accurate as can be. In other words, it is the capacity to understand the specific distortions of one's own particular way of seeing things and to modify one's "lenses" to discount one's bias and take greater account of things as they are.

It is the distortion of our personal way of seeing things that makes for the problems we encounter in our relationships. The same problems that hold us back in our personal relationships also tend to hold us back in our professional careers. It is to be hoped that the process of growing up and learning from experience plays a major role in our adapting our way of seeing and relating to our environment towards a greater recognition of how things actually are, but there are inevitably blocks and blind spots in our development. A relative absence of these makes for emotional intelligence: the capacity to see and respond to the world as it is. A substantial presence of blocks and blind spots makes for poor emotional intelligence, to the detriment of the individual and those around him at home or at work.

A systemic psycho-social approach contributes to growth and development by helping people towards a more insightful and realistic grasp of both their inner world in their minds and the external world. The two worlds are connected for, to an extent, it is the inner world that determines how we see the external world and determines how we "invite" the external world of other people to respond to us. Equally, experiences in the outer world deeply influence our inner world perceptions and configurations.

The systemic aspect of the model therefore attempts to create an understanding—one could say that it conducts an "ecological survey"—of human relationships. It is there to provide insight into the character of everyday human interactions, how groups and clusters of human beings innately behave, and to provide an insight into the spectrum of human behaviour. Put another way, the systemic component focuses on the stage, the props, and the backcloth of human interaction, whether the setting is personal or work related.

The psychodynamic aspect of the model, by contrast, is focused on the players on the stage, with emphasis on the self as character and all the responses, both positive and negative, that the other players on the stage trigger in the particular self and in each other. The goal is for the individual to be in touch with his feelings and have time to think about them, to assess their relevance to the present moment and, in that light, judge how best to deal with the situation at hand, here and now, on this stage. In other words, the psychodynamic component aims to create a thinking space in which the meaning of the situation, both personally and interpersonally, can be understood, to create the capacity to respond thoughtfully, while at the same time keeping future relationships in mind.

So, a systemic-psychodynamic view works towards a mature and task-orientated approach in addressing a problem. It is a way of overcoming resistance, both conscious and unconscious, that is fruitful and satisfying for the individual and the organization. "You can take a horse to water but you can't make it drink" goes the expression. Setting goals, leadership, management, and incentives can very often lead the horse to water, but if it won't drink, an approach that includes thinking about the problem is required. One can, of course, fire the horse or beat it, but most organizations have by now learnt that such measures are not necessarily the solution.

As far as the application of the systemic-psychodynamic model to everyday life goes, counselling or therapy are the best way forward for problems that are essentially *personal*. The focus would then be on the inner world and the effect of one's personal make-up on one's family, friends, etc. It may be that benefits would also accrue to one's work situation. For problems that are essentially in the area of work the most suitable approach would obviously be a work-focused one. Following a "diagnostic" phase, which might take some time, a decision would need to be made about the best way forward. This decision should be jointly made between the client and consultant, should be time limited with a built-in review, and should be embarked on with an awareness of the systemic context. The decision to proceed would then be either on the basis of an institutional consultative intervention, the exact format of which would be negotiated, or else on the basis of coaching.

This book focused particularly on the coaching applications of systemic-psychodynamic theory in the context of organizational life that is both goal-orientated and held in a managerial/leadership context, however flat or steep the pyramid. In this context, coaching provides a confidential, bounded, secure space in which issues might arise from the unspoken, the semi-dark, the peripheral vision, and from under the carpet. The issues might have a *personal* or an *organizational* provenance. It is usually a combination of the two. It is the interplay of these factors, the triggering mechanisms they release in each other, that make for the rich material that is to be looked at, spoken about, and moved in the direction of better understanding that results in improved management of the self and of the organization.

The various chapters of this book give excellent examples of how this might be done. The clients vary, the organizations and problems vary, and the approach of the coach/authors also varies. What all contributors have in common is the pursuit of understanding and the application of this understanding to fill in, or at least partially fill in, the potholes on the rutted road to improvement, creativity, and relative contentment.

Introduction

Halina Brunning

Executive coaching has recently become the approach of choice in management and leadership development, having established itself as standard practice in some industries. A lot has also been written recently about the rationale and process of coaching.

In a world where one internet search will reveal over one million practitioners of coaching, all trying to promote and sell their particular approach or technique, there is clearly a need for caution and some scepticism. One can, for example, locate a paper by Loh and Kay (2003) containing a sobering warning under the title "The coaching menace". The authors claim that the popularity of coaching owes much to the modern craze for quick fixes, saying that in an alarming number of situations, coaches, who lack rigorous psychological training, do more harm than good.

In recognition of the fact that an increasing number of practitioners with varying degrees of qualification operate in the field of coaching, there has been a corresponding effort to professionalize the coaching industry. Leading the way is the European Mentoring and Coaching Council (EMCC), a not-for-profit organization, and professional bodies such as the British Psychological Society, the Association of Coaching, and several other institutes and training organizations. Basic competency frameworks are being proposed and ethical codes of conduct agreed with the membership. This is a significant and welcome development, particularly as effective coaching is a complex, multi-dimensional process, like psychotherapy or counselling, that should not be practised by untrained or poorly trained practitioners.

It is against this particular background that I am pleased to present this book on executive coaching. It is an attempt to define executive coaching framed within a clear theoretical perspective of systems-psychodynamics, which has, both with regard to theory and praxis, a long and well developed history.

First, we need to broadly define the systems-psychodynamic approach and how it can contribute to the field of coaching. The development of this interdisciplinary field and its defining perspectives have, for example, been outlined by Gould, Stapley, and Stein (2001) in their edited book entitled *Systems Psychodynamics of Organizations*, who offer the following:

> At least in a formal sense, the field of systems psychodynamics had its birth with the publication of Miller and Rice's seminal volume *Systems of Organization* (1967). While many of the elements of this perspective were already present in the pioneering work of the Tavistock Institute of Human Relations (now the Tavistock Institute), it was not until this volume was published that they were put into a systematic framework that could rightly be called an interdisciplinary field which attempted to integrate the emerging insights of groups relations theory, psychoanalysis, and open systems theory. It is also fair to say that this is still an emerging field of social science, the boundaries of which are continually being refined and redefined. [*ibid.*, p. 2]

What, then, is the connection between a systems-psychodynamic perspective in relation to the work with organizations and its application to the field of executive coaching? Here I need to make explicit the assumption that *all coaching is primarily a psychological endeavour*. This leads me to quote a definition by Grant and Palmer (2002) of "coaching psychology" that is seen as "enhancing well-being and performance in personal and work domains underpinned by models of coaching grounded in established adult learning or psychological approaches". Given this view, the present volume is about the integration of a psychodynamic, psychological approach, as it pertains to the individual, with an open systems approach, as it pertains to the organizational, by working on the seams of these overlapping boundaries in the practice of executive coaching.

Specifically, the psychodynamic element refers to

> psychoanalytic perspective on individual experiences and mental processes (e.g. the transference, resistance, object relations, fantasy, etc.) as well as on the experiences of unconscious group and social processes, which are simultaneously both a source and a consequence of unresolved or unrecognised organisational difficulties. [Gould, Stapley, & Stein, 2001, p. 3]

In relation to the systemic element, this refers to:

> the open systems concepts that provide the dominant framing perspective for understanding the structural aspects of an organizational system. These include its design, division of labour, levels of authority, and reporting relationships: the nature of work tasks, processes, and activities: its missions and primary task; and, in particular, the nature and patterning of the organisation's tasks and sentient boundaries and the transactions across them. [*ibid.*, p. 2]

Furthermore, as Armstrong (1995) suggests

> it is precisely the conjunction itself that creates the emergent, but not yet fully articulated field of systems psychodynamics. In this vein it may be argued that a systems psychodynamic perspective implies working simultaneously from "the inside out and the outside in", with neither perspective being privileged. [Quoted in Gould, Stapley, & Stein, 2001, p. 4]

Given the basic parameters of the system, i.e., the dynamics of the psychological work undertaken with individuals in their professional work roles, approaching this simultaneously from "inside out" and "outside in" is, in essence, what I would define as the uniquely characteristic feature of executive coaching practised from a systems-psychodynamic perspective.

In this book, therefore, I hope to demonstrate that systems-psychodynamic coaching is a multi-factorial, multi-layered process that primarily addresses itself to *the person-in-role* and the *multiple organizational and social fields* that comprise the context in which work with the client takes place.

In this sense, the contributors to the present volume, attempt to demonstrate how, by virtue of working with and making links across *person–role–system* boundaries, this is a powerful, robust approach to the practice of executive coaching.

The book is divided into four sections:

● Towards an ecology of systems-psychodynamic coaching;
● The anatomy of systems-psychodynamic coaching;
● Applications of systems-psychodynamic coaching;
● A directory of resources.

The twelve authors invited to contribute to this book share membership of the International Society for Psychoanalytic Study of Organizations, or some professional association with ISPSO. This, combined with a psychoanalytic/psychotherapeutic background shared by most of the contributors, gives this book its particular flavour. It will be apparent, in reading these chapters, that the authors hold the individual client firmly in focus, while being able to appreciate and work with the systemic, organizational context, which plays a significant role in how their clients function. Further, their psychotherapeutic background does not lead these contributors to "conduct psychotherapy in the workplace" at the expense of the employing organization. It needs to be emphasized in this context that executive coaching *is* a psychologically informed developmental process, not a treatment for emotional disturbance (see chapters by Brunning, Spero, and Alcock in this volume). Put somewhat differently, each coaching intervention described in this book is conceptualized and firmly positioned within the organizational system of the client. In this sense the overarching hypothesis of this book could be stated as: *the particular positioning of coaching, simultaneously as both psychodynamic and systemic endeavour, differentiates it from other approaches to coaching.*

The book opens with a comparative study between psychodynamic and non-psychodynamic approaches to coaching. Vega Z. Roberts and Michael Jarrett examine the differences between various approaches based on in-depth interviews with experienced coaches representing some of the major "schools" of executive coaching. They also propose a robust typology of different approaches and place systems-psychodynamic coaching as one approach within that frame.

In her chapter about a contextualized approach to coaching, Clare Huffington argues for an "embedded" perspective that sets the work with an individual client against much wider societal and organizational contexts. Her work also demonstrates how an appropriately chosen coaching intervention with an individual client could result in positive and far-reaching organizational implications and become an organizational intervention. Further, she attempts to conceptualize what is an appropriate ethical frame for this approach to executive coaching.

Angela Eden, in her chapter on coaching women in executive roles, focuses on the resistance and blockages experienced by women in attaining senior roles within their organizations. These blockages are examined within contemporary organizations themselves and the wider societal frame in which the exercise of power and the dynamics of exclusion operate.

The second section of the book, "The anatomy of systems-psychodynamic coaching", looks into the constituent elements and the building blocks that characterize this approach to coaching.

There are four chapters in this section. The first, by Gordon Lawrence, is an invitation to broaden the discourse by arguing for the inclusion of elements of unconscious thinking and reverie as both legitimate and necessary aspects of the executive coaching process.

Jane Pooley's chapter is about a longitudinal and an in-depth framing of the coaching process. She offers a systemic approach to coaching, not only as a developmental process, but also as a unique opportunity for the client to examine new meanings that may emerge during the coaching process. Her chapter clearly demonstrates how this process can contribute to the effectiveness of both the coaching client and the larger organization.

In my chapter I have taken this theme further, and propose a multi-layered model of coaching where the examination of meaning is a central tenet. The six domains of coaching refer to different aspects of the person, the role, and the organization, and these are examined in one in-depth case study and a number of shorter vignettes. In the summary, I have contrasted coaching with other person-centred activities such as counselling, psychotherapy, personal development, etc., and define the field of coaching as a distinct field of activity that is none the less enriched by many other endeavours.

The fourth chapter in this section identifies further building blocks of the coaching repertoire. Richard Kwiatkowski's chapter addresses the theme of inside out and outside in, as noted by Gould, Stapley, and Stein (2001), and illustrates the role that psychometrics, and, especially, personality testing, plays within the coaching enterprise. His extensive case study also examines the application and implication of 360 Degree feedback, both in theory and in practice.

The third section of the book is about the application of a systems-psychodynamic approach to executive coaching. To this end I have invited in-depth case studies from senior theorists and practitioners. Four case studies by Gould, Stapley, Spero, and Alcock, respectively, illustrate in detail how they think about and work with their clients.

Laurence Gould's chapter describes his coaching work with a newly qualified manager who was caught up in a complex systemic labyrinth of contradictory organizational meanings and messages. With this material, Gould illustrates that, while engaging clients in coaching, it is important to enlarge the scope of work by integrating, as a major factor, their developmental life stage.

Lionel F. Stapley's chapter is about the application of role consultancy to the field of sports psychology. Interestingly, he does not call it "coaching" here, because this word has a very prescriptive and specific meaning in sport. Stapley's case study illustrates the importance of working with biographical data elicited from the client. He demonstrates the importance of making sensitive and appropriate links between the here and now of the work-related problems and the attachments and object-relations patterns prevalent in the client's early life.

In her case study of a lawyer in transition, Marlene Spero proposes that coaching is really a transitional space and, as such, is particularly suited to helping clients manage work and life-related changes. Spero also defines her work as simultaneously paying attention to the multiple contexts within which her client must function, once again evoking the person, the role, and the system frame.

Finally, in her work with a senior civil servant, Miranda Alcock shows how early problematic attachments and unresolved psychic pain can unexpectedly resurface later on in life in a different context, e.g., within a work situation. In describing her intervention, Alcock also clarifies the difference between psychotherapy and coaching.

All contributors were invited to share the sources that influenced their thinking and current practice of coaching. They have also attempted to articulate their generalized conclusions about the practice of executive coaching. It is my hope that in so doing, these endeavours, taken collectively, will not only contribute to the development of the field, but will also, as a by-product, contribute to laying the foundations of a competency-based framework of a systems-psychodynamic approach to coaching.

In addition, and specifically in relation to the case studies, the authors also needed to ensure that a respectful negotiation with their original clients took place about the use of confidential material in preparation for publication. All contributors have concealed and/or changed their clients' identifying details, so as to render the individuals and their organizations unrecognizable. In some cases, the authors decided to describe a composite case study in order to heighten the heuristic value of examples given. Many authors also addressed the issue of ethics and ethical practice, either directly or indirectly in their chapters.

The last section of the book, "A directory of resources", provides a list of the organizations, private firms, and consultancies of the contributors that utilize and/or provide training in the systems-psychodynamic approach to coaching.

As a concluding note, I wish to make some links between who I am and my motivations and aspirations for creating this volume. Throughout my life, I have learned to recognize the importance of meaning that was either immediately obvious or obfuscated, to seek and to unlock its presence in unfolding events and experiences. I have always been fascinated by the fusion of ideas, collages, and juxtapositions between several already existing, but now differently repositioned, objects, by the integration of various contexts, by unification of principles, concepts, and different layers of meaning. This has been the driving force behind my interest in systems psychodynamics, and its major influence in shaping the fundamental underpinnings of my therapeutic, consultative, and artistic endeavours.

I believe that the space created by these multiple overlapping contexts brings many new, rich, colourful, and creative possibilities. I tried to capture this with my chosen image on the book cover, based on the Max Daches' original 1972 tapestry entitled "The possibility of connectedness".

This book is an expression of my deep belief that the powerful fusion of systemic and psychodynamic approaches to executive coaching creates a humane and empowering learning environment that has the capacity to profoundly benefit both individuals and their organizations.

Who is this book for?

This book will be of interest to experienced practitioners of coaching, those wishing to train as coaches, and those interested in expanding their coaching perspectives—psychotherapists, counsellors, psychologists, educators, and organizational consultants. It can also be profitably read by managers, executives, researchers in this and related fields, and last, but hardly least, by those in organizations who may be considering executive coaching as a potentially useful activity for their ongoing effectiveness and development.

References

Armstrong. D. (1995). The analytic object in organizational work. Paper presented at the annual meeting of the International Society for the Psychoanalytic Study of Organizations, London.

Gould, L., Stapley, L. F., Stein, M. (2001). *The Systems Psychodynamics of Organizations*. London: Karnac.

Grant, A. M., & Palmer, S. (2002). Coaching psychology. Workshop and meeting held at the Annual Conference of Division of Counselling Psychology. The British Psychological Society.

Loh, M., & Kay, P. (2003). The coaching menace. *The Business Times* online edition, published 25 February.

Editor's note

In this volume I attempted to define and demonstrate how a systems-psychodynamic approach to executive coaching can be utilized for the benefit of the individual and the organization.

I am glad to note that another book addressing similar issues is shortly to be published by Karnac (*Coaching In-depth: The Organizational Role Analysis Approach*, by Susan Long, John Newton, and Burkard Sievers (Eds.): Karnac, in press).

I hope that our endeavours and research into this field will help to define and illuminate the systems-psychodynamic approach to coaching as an example of professional practice grounded in theory and supported by a wealth of in-depth experience. This is being offered to the clients as a safe, expert, and ethical endeavour.

PART I
TOWARDS AN ECOLOGY OF SYSTEMS-PSYCHODYNAMIC COACHING

What is the difference and what makes the difference? A comparative study of psychodynamic and non-psychodynamic approaches to executive coaching

Vega Zagier Roberts and Michael Jarrett

E xecutive coaching is a burgeoning industry. A recent survey undertaken by the Chartered Institute of Personnel and Development of its thousands of members revealed that up to 95% of firms were using some kind of coaching or mentoring, at a cost of at least £15 million per year. The growth rate is staggering. According to a report in *The Economist*, the Hay Group HR consultancy reported that executive coaching is growing at about 40% a year (*Economist*, 2002). In the corporate world, executives are using coaching to manage the pressures and loneliness at the top, increased competitive stress, and greater expectations from external bodies such as regulators and analysts. Hogan, Curphy, and Hogan (1994) found that over 60% of CEOs were failing in terms of not meeting their objectives. The average length of CEO tenure has halved and shareholders expect more. The situation in the public sector is similar. Thus, it is not surprising that the drive for workplace development has increased as executives seek ways to enhance performance, make the transition across roles, and manage their own sense of dis-ease and potential derailment.

A quick tap of the words "executive coaching" into a typical search engine will yield about a million sites. Coaching and consulting practices make a variety of claims and attempt to distinguish themselves from one another in a very competitive market. Each has a method or process that offers "new" opportunities for executive development. The purpose of this chapter is to look a little deeper into these claims of distinctiveness: what are the differences among the various approaches, and what makes the difference for the clients? It is based on in-depth interviews with very experienced coaches[1] representing some of the major "schools" of executive coaching, all working in or trained by organizations regarded as leaders in the field, as well as interviews of clients, both direct clients of coaches we had interviewed and corporate purchasers of coaching. (See Acknowledgements.)

One interesting finding was how little practitioners knew about others' practices, even within their own "school", let alone outside it. What little they thought they knew about each other was often grossly inaccurate. For example, many psychodynamically orientated practitioners believed that coaches of other persuasions provided mainly advice, training, and "quick fixes", with little long-term impact on development. Coaches from other perspectives thought that coaches using a psychodynamic approach were "touchy-feely", engaging in an endless pursuit of insight at the expense of tangible results. The authors have each had formal training in both systems psychodynamics (role consultancy) and non-psychodynamic approaches to coaching: this chapter was prompted by a mixture of curiosity about the real differences between these, and by a wish to dispel some popular misperceptions.

Why do people seek a coach?

Clients undertake coaching for a variety of reasons. Box 1 lists the most prevalent "presenting requests" as reported by our sample of both clients and coaches. We have grouped these into three categories: perceived problems at work, specific developmental goals, and broader developmental aims.

Sometimes the reason for seeking a coach does not quite fit in any of these three categories, while including elements of each. The client may well have particular issues to work on, but above all feels the need for "space to think", which they find difficult to

---

Box 1.   Examples of clients' presenting issues

Problems

- Difficult relationships—most often with one's boss, but also with peers, hard-to-manage subordinates, stakeholders; conflict in teams.
- General unhappiness at work, stress, impaired job satisfaction.
- A perceived deficit, often identified in 360 degree feedback or appraisal;[2]
- implementing a change process to which there is resistance.

Specific goals

- To increase outputs—land bigger contracts, sell more.
- To improve personal skills—listening, emotional intelligence,[3] making presentations.
- To improve organization skills—political, partnership working, strategy, tendering.
- To position oneself for promotion.

Broader developmental aims

- Following promotion—"to grow into my role, own it, feel good in it and good at it".
- "Raising one's game" (corporate language)—for people who are performing well but feel they have capacities they are not fully mobilizing.
- To understand self and/or others better.
- To increase one's repertoire—new ways of thinking about and tackling work challenges.

---

safeguard within their pressured everyday routine. The coach is seen as someone objective, outside the workplace, who will both challenge and support them in thinking about aspects of their situation which the constant pressures for action have pushed out of view.

One might speculate that one driving factor in the increased uptake of coaching is the decrease of one-to-one support and containment in the workplace. As managers are increasingly driven to achieve bottom-line results, the containment function of leadership gives way to task and target-focused line management/supervision. Space to think—to listen to oneself and to be listened to by another—and support for individual development are sought elsewhere.

The origins of executive coaching

From sports

The 1980s saw the introduction of the term "executive coaching" in the UK through a small band of people including John Whitmore, Graham Alexander, and their associates, who started as sports coaches using the Inner Game approach invented by Timothy Gallwey in the USA. Traditionally, sports coaches had observed athletes and then instructed them, for example, in how to move more efficiently. However, Gallwey, drawing on his experience of Zen and meditation, found it was far more effective to enable people to become more aware of their internal state. In his best-selling book *The Inner Game of Tennis* (1986) he proposed that the opponent in one's head, the internal critic, is far more formidable than the opponent on the tennis court. By silencing this internal critic and thus reducing the internal obstacles to their performance, the player releases their natural ability and their performance can increase enormously without technical instruction from the coach. Gallwey subsequently extended this approach to other sports, including some he was not expert at, and then—at the invitation of his corporate tennis-playing clients—into the world of work. His work gave rise to the GROW model, described later in this chapter, which became a cornerstone of executive coaching.

From systems-psychodynamics consultancy and group relations training

One-to-one consultation to managers and executives was already taking place, however, before the Inner Game coaches appeared on the scene, although it was not yet called executive coaching. From the late 1950s The Christian Teamwork Trust, which evolved into The Grubb Institute in 1969, was providing consultancy to organizations as well as group relations training and other kinds of training events to develop participants' understanding of organizational behaviour and dynamics. From this emerged Organizational Role Analysis (ORA), a method for working with individual managers and leaders to enable them to take up their roles more effectively (Reed, 1976; Reed & Bazalgette, 2006). Interestingly, the Grubb Institute did use the word "coaching" in the 1980s, not for their work with executives but in a project undertaken with school-leavers. These young people were matched with older people who "coached" them about working life, "on the model of a football coach who helps others develop skills" (Bazalgette, 2003). ORA has been adapted by many practitioners of systems-psychodynamics-based organizational consultancy, who variously refer to their work with individuals as "organizational role consultancy" or simply "role consultancy", and more lately—largely for marketing purposes—as executive coaching.

From individual therapy

A more recent development has been the movement of psycho-therapists from working with patients to consulting to individual organizational clients. In the health service, clinical psychologists and psychotherapists are often invited to provide occasional internal consultancy, applying their understanding of individual and interpersonal difficulties to problems in teams, or to contribute to service development. They also provide external consultancy to institutions such as schools, social care agencies, residential units, and the like. In many cases, this consultancy role has come to include coaching. Therapists in private practice are also increasingly interested in providing coaching, in part driven by the need to find alternative ways of deploying their skills as long-term therapy wanes in popularity. As Peltier puts it, "The 'talking cure' . . . is too slow, too personal, it provides no guarantees, and it lacks the punch and focus demanded by those in the fast lane" (Peltier, 2001, p. xvi). These coaches may or may not continue to practise as therapists, and come from a wide range of backgrounds, including psychoanalytic, behavioural and cognitive–behavioural, Rogerian, and Gestalt therapy among others.

Definitions and aims of executive coaching, and underlying values

This chapter, and indeed this book, is about "executive coaching". While this term is often used to refer to the coaching of the "top" people in an organization, we are using it in the broader sense of consulting to individuals on their executive functions, that is, the requirement on them to plan and take actions to fulfil the aims of their organizations. This said, however, it is worth noting that much of the financial investment into coaching is made by and for top executives, where enhancing performance is likely to have most impact. Marshall Goldsmith, a leading American executive coach points out that

> the marginal gain for helping a highly successful person move from the top five percent to the top one percent may be greater (to the organization) than the gain from helping the average performer move from the top 50 percent to the top 20 percent. This is especially true with high-potential leaders who represent one of the greatest sources of value for the organization of the future. [Goldsmith, 2003, p. 16]

Coaches of corporate leaders are typically paid between 10 and 15% of the client's annual salary, further evidence of the high level of expectation that coaching will yield high leverage.

The discussion of definitions and aims that follows is confined to coaching focused on workplace issues. We have not included life coaching that claims to work more "in the round" and addresses any aspect of life that clients wish to bring. Neither have we included mentoring, a term often used interchangeably with coaching, but which has its origin in Greek mythology[4] to refer to "a guide, a wise and faithful counsellor" (*Brewer's Dictionary*, 1952). Mentoring in the workplace generally involves pairing people with someone "older and wiser", further along their own career path, who passes down their knowledge and experience.

Gallwey defined coaching as unlocking a person's potential to maximize their own performance, helping them to learn rather than teaching them. Other leading writers on coaching (Downey, 2003; Landsberg, 1996; Whitmore, 2002) use similar definitions, although the emphasis on the different components varies. This was also true of the coaches we interviewed, as the quotes in Box 2 illustrate.

Thus, there is broad agreement that coaching is a two-way developmental process that enhances performance, and in which the coach's role is primarily facilitative, enabling clients to find their own solutions rather than providing answers. The main variations in defining the aims of coaching are to be found in where individual

---

Box 2.   Aims of coaching—what the coaches said

- "A means for clients to access more of their own resources."
- "Increasing awareness of oppressive patterns so the client is enabled to change these."
- "Reconnecting clients to their own aspirations, meanings and authority so they feel less 'done to' and more positive."
- "Overcoming internal obstacles to success."
- "Looking at issues from new perspectives, reframing them, so as to discover new options for action."
- "Enhancing achievement and developing capacities."
- "Delivering results—development follows in the wake of results, it is not the primary aim."
- "Giving space to think about client's role and actions—can be very practical, like goals and work-plans for the year, or broader, like preparing for the future."
- "Surfacing the client's mental picture of the organization in which they work, how they influence it and how it influences them, so they realize there is much more they can influence than they previously thought."
- "Transforming desire into purpose and then into action."
- "Providing a sounding-board which enables people to make more use of their talents."
- "Insights which increase personal and role effectiveness."
- "Increasing awareness of the internal and external forces that are shaping clients' behaviour, decisions and actions."
- "Bringing about individual change that meets the needs of the individual and the organization."
- "Facilitating the learning and development of another through raising awareness, clarifying and focusing."
- "Provides a safe place for thinking, learning, facing difficult things."

coaches put the emphasis and in their use of language. For example, for some coaches in our sample "enhancing performance" was primarily about identifying and achieving specific goals, while for others improved performance flowed from clients learning to construe their situations in new ways. Many, but not all, coaches referred to "learning", while others used terms like "insight" and "increasing self-awareness".

Inherent in these definitions is a set of values and beliefs about the innate capacities people have: that the client rather than the coach is the expert in their own business and is responsible for the choices they make, and that coaching is a meaningful process which can make a difference. With few exceptions, these were held in common by our interviewees, as shown by their answers to the question "why do you do it ?" (See Box 3.)

The value of coaching

The aims of coaching, as described in Box 2, above, suggest a modesty among coaches belied by the claims made for it, not only in the publicity produced by providers, but also by some of the research. For example:

- Hall, Otazo, and Hollenbeck (1999) identify from their study of seventy-five executives in Fortune 100 companies the elements of what makes coaching work and some of the qualitative benefits of coaching. The report concludes that executive coaching leads to improvement in task performance, personal change in attitudes such as more patience and adaptability, leading to developing a wider repertoire of behaviours, increased self-awareness and personal confidence.
- A survey conducted by Manchester Consulting (McGovern et al., 2001) suggested that on average the return on investment was 5.7 times the cost of coaching.
- Bolch (2001) also reveals findings that

  53% of executives report a company increase in productivity, while 48% report an increase in both quality and organizational strength. Among personal benefits of coaching, executives report improvements in working relationships with direct reports (77%),

Box 3. Values and beliefs—how coaches answered the question "Why do you do it?"

- "My own experience of developing in my various roles, and what supported me—helping build people's confidence and competence."
- "Enabling people to take up their own authority."
- "I get very close to clients, the coaching is very important to them."
- "It fits my values, that so much is possible for individuals, so it's rewarding."
- "I am fascinated with the dynamics of experiences in organizational life, so it's a research interest and also makes a real contribution to how organizations function."
- "We believe it is possible to make a difference—systems psychodynamics gives people leverage, they discover they are empowered."
- "I believe people are natural learners and self-motivated, the work is about creating an environment that increases motivation and learning, releases energy—it's win–win, both the organization and the individual benefit."
- "Clients access more of their own resources, it's wonderful to be part of that process."
- "Can benefit people very quickly, help them integrate different elements of their lives—a conviction that this is possible and that it matters."
- "It's often the quickest and most effective way to make a difference in the organization or team as well as the individual."
- "I have become increasingly concerned with the huge stress managers are under, often at unacceptable cost to themselves."
- "Coaching supports their capacity to think, be effective, be less damaged (and therefore also less damaging), to bring more of the best of themselves to their jobs, therefore greater work satisfaction—also I enjoy it, find it interesting."
- "Working really closely and collaboratively with clients, it's a privilege."

relationships with immediate supervisors (71%), teamwork (67%), relationships with peers (63%), and job satisfaction (61%). [Bolch, 2001]

- A study by Personnel Decisions International (Withers, 2001) showed that executive coaching programmes were twice as effective as behaviour modelling, which had been the previous winner.

It seems, then, that coaching is perceived to have value and to produce results.[5] Some of these results are explicit, others less so. For example, one of the authors worked with a global pharmaceutical company that brought executive coaching into the firm in the early 1990s, before its use became widespread in the UK, in order to accelerate the development of leadership capabilities in its senior managers. In a subsequent review carried out by the company, participants were glowing about the results. "I had no faith in this sort of thing at first but now I think it's great," said one executive. But perhaps more telling was the next comment: "No executive should be without a coach. It's part of the deal, like having keys to the executive loo." At one level, there was a perception that being offered coaching was a reward, a confirmation of status, or a perk of a high-level job. At another, that coaching is a sort of cleansing and unburdening process—getting rid of the stresses, toxicity and mess of life at the top.

Different approaches to achieving these aims

Both a review of the literature and our own study suggest that executive coaches are working to broadly similar aims. So what are the differences among the different schools of coaching? We initially hypothesized that we would be able to identify a continuum of approaches from those focusing primarily on tangible and measurable outputs at one end to those focusing on insight and self-reflective learning at the other, as shown below:

Outputs <————————————————————> Insight

We anticipated that variations in practice, types of issues, or clients worked with, and so on, could be plotted along this continuum in such a way as to distinguish these schools of coaching from one another. To our surprise, this was not borne out by our initial interviews of coaches, as shown in Table 1. Rather than clustering, these potentially distinguishing aspects of coaching turned out to be virtually independent variables.

On re-examination, it struck us that the continuum we had in our minds at the outset of our study was conflating ends and means, and that we might make better sense of our data by considering these as two separate dimensions.

Table 1.   Interview responses regarding potentially distinguishing characteristics of different approaches to coaching.

	GROW	Therapy informed	Behavioural– cognitive	Role consultancy
Directive	L	L	H	L
Structured sessions	H	L	H	L
Duration	Average of 6–12 months[1]			
Length & frequency of sessions	Average of 1.5–2 hour sessions at 3–4 week intervals[2]			
Attention to personal (non-work) issues	M	H	M	L
Coach from psychology or therapy background	Mixed with a majority from psychology/ therapy across all schools[3]			
Contracting	Mixed—two-way or three-way[4]			
Presenting issues	Any of the issues from Box 1			
Intended outcomes	See Box 2			
Type of clients (sector)	Private and public			
Type of clients (level in organization)	Middle to senior management			

H = high   M = medium   L = low

[1]Shortest was three months, longest was ten years, but variations did not correspond to any particular school of coaching.
[2]The main exception is that some sessions in a behaviourally-orientated coaching programme might be longer if involving a role-play or other more formal training. Classic ORA comprised eight fortnightly sessions, but realities of executive life have tended to lead to longer gaps.
[3]Slightly less the case for GROW.
[4]Some coaches had formal contracts with the organization, most contracted directly with the coachee who discussed the contract with their line manager, and a few met with the coachee and their line manager together to agree goals.

Dimension 1: aims

This is based on whether the chief or primary purpose of the coaching is to bring about external changes, such as measurable outputs or changes in behaviour, or internal ones. Clearly, these are not mutually exclusive—most coaches would say they aim for both—but there seemed to us to be a useful distinction between that which is primary and that which is secondary.

PRIMARY AIM

Internal change <————————————————> External change

Dimension 2: methods used to achieve the primary aim

This second dimension is concerned with whether the process of coaching is focused on the individual (internal world) or on the organization (external world). Again, this is not an "either/or" distinction but a question of where the primary emphasis of the coaching process lies.

PRIMARY FOCUS OF ATTENTION

Individual <————————————————> Organization

In any one session, a coach may be working on any or all points of either continuum. However, by using these two dimensions as the axes of a grid, as in Figure 1, we were able to identify four relatively distinct models or "stables" of coaching. We have drawn these as clouds to acknowledge that experienced coaches work flexibly in response to the different clients and different situations, and that it would be doing them an injustice to attempt to place them in rigid boxes.

For readers who may be unfamiliar with one or more of these models, we have given a brief description of each in the four sections that follow.

The GROW model

This approach to coaching came out of Gallwey's Inner Game, and remains one of the most widely used models in the coaching industry. Gallwey proposed that that we each have a Self 1 and Self 2. Self 1 gives negative commands ("don't mess it up this time"), makes

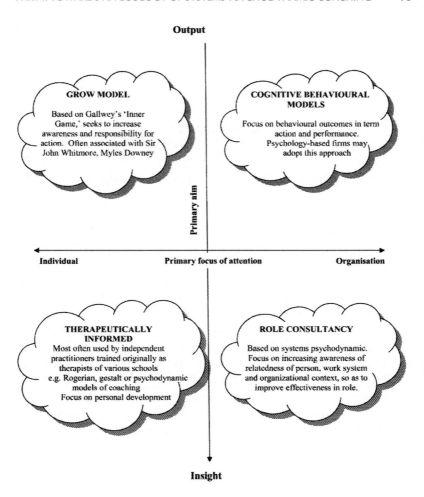

Output

GROW MODEL

Based on Gallwey's 'Inner Game,' seeks to increase awareness and responsibility for action. Often associated with Sir John Whitmore, Myles Downey

COGNITIVE BEHAVIOURAL MODELS

Focus on behavioural outcomes in term action and performance. Psychology-based firms may adopt this approach

Primary aim

Individual ◀——— **Primary focus of attention** ———▶ Organisation

THERAPEUTICALLY INFORMED
Most often used by independent practitioners trained originally as therapists of various schools e.g. Rogerian, gestalt or psychodynamic models of coaching Focus on personal development

ROLE CONSULTANCY

Based on systems psychodynamic. Focus on increasing awareness of relatedness of person, work system and organizational context, so as to improve effectiveness in role.

Insight

Figure 1.   Four models of coaching

judgements ("we can't afford the time"), and acts as an internal saboteur ("you'll never get them to agree"). Self 2 is the human being him or herself. "It embodies all the inherent potential we are born with, including all capacities not yet realised" (Gallwey, 2000, p. 7). The Inner Game refers to the internal dialogue between Self 1 and Self 2 that undermines confidence and interferes with mobilizing one's innate capabilities. The object of coaching is to reduce this interference, so as to reduce the gap between the client's potential and their performance. Practitioners often express this idea as an equation:

POTENTIAL minus INTERFERENCE is equal to PERFORMANCE

GROW is an acronym for the four key steps in the coaching process:

1. G *(Goal)*: The client sets goals for the coaching programme, and also for each session. Whitmore (2002) distinguishes "end goals", such as becoming a market leader or being appointed to the executive board, which are often not entirely within the individual's control, from "performance goals"—identifying the performance level that will give one the best chance of achieving the end goal. The client is encouraged to define goals positively as precisely as possible: the coach will help by asking questions such as "how much", "how many", "by when?".

2. R *(Reality)*: Client and coach explore the current situation, seeking to reduce assumptions, prejudgements, and other "interference". For example, for the client who wants to develop better presentation skills, anxiety about the audience acts as interference. GROW coaches believe that focusing on the detail of reality shifts the client's attention away from their anxiety and therefore enhances performance. The coach will help to increase the client's awareness of reality, including the internal and external obstacles to achieving their goal(s), how much control they have over their current situation, why any previous actions were unsuccessful, and so on, often encouraging them to quantify their answers. An important component of R is self-awareness, notably about one's own contribution to the issues at hand.

3. O *(Options)*: Here the client is invited to consider as many ways forward as possible so as to maximize choices and to reduce negative assumptions such as "it can't be done". The coach nudges the client to think beyond current roadblocks, perhaps asking questions such as "what would you do if you had more time, a larger budget, or could start all over with a new team?" These can open up new possibilities that the client had previously ruled out without seriously considering them. The options are then examined in terms of the advantages and disadvantages of each.

4.   *W (Will)*: Finally, clients choose which actions they will take by
     when, and make a firm commitment to their action plan. Often
     the coach will ask them to score on a scale of 1–10 the likelihood
     they will actually carry it out; experience suggests that a score
     of less than eight means the action is unlikely to be imple-
     mented, in which case the coach might pursue the matter by
     asking the client what prevents the score being ten, and what
     might raise their commitment to the action(s) they have chosen.

These four steps are followed in each session. The core guiding
principles for coaches include:

●   Being positive, because one believes in human potential.
    Initially, clients often state their goals negatively, and are
    helped to convert these into the positive. For example, goal
    definition might shift from "I want my team to feel less depen-
    dent on me" to "I want team members to take more initiative".
    This is sometimes called moving "from problem to project".
●   The focus is always on learning, particularly though increasing
    clients' awareness.
●   Responsibility remains firmly with the client. GROW aims to
    foster the client's sense of personal choice, control, and owner-
    ship of the process and its outcomes. The coach "follows client
    interest" rather than directing their attention and actions.

Therapeutically informed approaches

Coaches in this quadrant of Figure 1 are likely to have trained originally as therapists, and may come from a number of different theoretical and clinical perspectives including:

●   *Psychodynamic psychotherapy.* The focus is making links
    between past and present to enable the client to recognize,
    understand, and change repetitive and oppressive patterns
    that have evolved as defences against unconscious internal
    conflicts. The coach seeks to understand the client's inner
    world, especially through attending to their own countertrans-
    ference, that is, the feelings evoked in them by the client's
    material, as information about what may be going on outside
    the client's conscious awareness.

- *Gestalt therapy*. The coach seeks to change the client's ways of perceiving themselves and the world around them. "Gestalt" is a German word meaning "shape" or "form", and is used to refer to the patterned whole formed by one's perceptions, including awareness of the body itself. Disturbances in the client's ways of dealing with the phenomenological world are attributed to interference with the mechanisms of attention (what is "figure" or central, and what is "ground" or peripheral), inadequate perception, or the blocking of the expression of need. The emphasis is on current experience rather than on understanding the past.
- *Person-centred therapy* (also called humanistic or Rogerian after its founder, Carl Rogers). The focus is to enhance the client's capacity to be open to experience, to be self-trusting and willing to grow. The attitude of the coach is considered paramount, notably being authentic, having unconditional positive regard for the client, and demonstrating accurate empathic understanding of the client's experience. The direction of coaching is determined by the client, involving an active partnership and personal relationship between them and the coach.
- *Family systems therapy*. The coaching brings into view the "interactional force field" (O'Neill, 2000), recognizing that the system within which the client works influences their thinking and behaviour. A shift in one part of a system (in family therapy, one member of the family) affects other parts of the system, which then also changes. (McCaughan & Palmer, 1994). Conversely, there may be "investment" in the wider system in maintaining the status quo; the problem or symptom serves a purpose for others that need to be understood in order to bring about change (Campbell, Draper, & Huffington, 1989).
- *Cognitive therapy*. Coaching seeks to change specific thinking patterns and even particular thoughts. The focus therefore is on conscious thinking rather than unconscious processes, based on the idea that changing one's habitual ways of thinking has a powerful effect on both feelings and behaviour. For example, the thought "if you want it done right, do it yourself" can interfere with appropriate delegation. The coach actively challenges the client's current ways of thinking and helps them develop and sustain new ones (Peltier, 2001).

Coaches may also come from a background in other modalities such as neuro-linguistic programming (NLP), existential, or rational–emotive therapy, among others.

While some therapeutically informed coaches describe their model as eclectic because they use perspectives and techniques originating in a number of different therapeutic models, others may use only one of these.[6] Coaches from other "stables" also use elements of some of these therapeutic approaches, particularly as they develop their practice and seek to expand their repertoire of interventions.

Behavioural approaches

Generally speaking, coaching based in any of the therapy-based perspectives above will focus on personal development, although how this is defined, and the kinds of interventions involved, vary greatly. While behavioural approaches to coaching also come from a therapeutic or clinical base, we have separated them from the others because the primary focus is on the client's external rather than their internal world, that is, on observable behaviours rather than on emotional or mental states.

A core theoretical concept is that behaviour is reinforced by its consequences: positive consequences strengthen and amplify the behaviour, while negative consequences tend to diminish or extinguish it. Attention is also paid to aspects of the environment, which are likely to increase or decrease the desired behaviour. Techniques include modelling, desensitization (working through worst scenarios), role-plays, and developing reward systems to support incremental changes towards the desired behaviour.

Behavioural and cognitive perspectives are often combined, since thinking and behaviour are so closely, even causally, related. Practitioners believe that changes in both cognitive and behavioural patterns can be taught and learned: coaching is likely to involve significant amounts of direct teaching and training input. Changes are then practised until they become transferable into the workplace without further reinforcement by the coaching process.

Role-consultancy

The focus here is the client's organizational role, role being where person and organization intersect (see Figure 2).

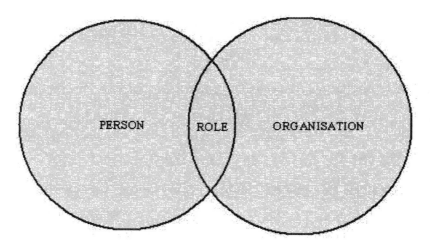

Figure 2.   Role.

Role is defined as "an idea or conception in the mind through which one manages oneself and one's behaviour in relation to the system in which one has a position, so as to further its aims" (Grubb Institute, 1991). Thus, a role is not merely *given* by the employing organization; it is also *taken*—that is, the person in the role makes of it something personal, based on individual's skills, ideals, beliefs, and their understanding of what is required. However, what one makes of a role is also influenced by the system, not only by tangible factors such as job descriptions, hierarchical position, and the resources one has access to, but also by others' expectations of the role and by the culture of the system (Krantz & Maltz, 1997).

Role consultancy draws on theoretical concepts from a number of different sources including:

- systems-psychodynamics, in particular the concept of social defence systems, splitting, projection, and projective identification;
- group relations training with its focus on the exercise of authority and leadership;
- the psychic meaning of the work of an organization and how far this informs how one thinks, feels, and acts.

Particular attention is paid to "organization-in-the-mind", that is:

what the individual perceives in his or her head of how activities
and relations are organized, structured and connected internally. It
is a model internal to oneself, part of one's inner world, relying
upon the inner experiences of my interactions, relations and the
activities I engage in, which give rise to images, emotions, values
and responses in me, which may consequently be influencing my
own management and leadership, positively or adversely. [Hutton,
Bazalgette, & Reed, 1997, p. 114][7]

Thus, core to the practice of role consultancy is surfacing
and articulating the client's internal model of the organization:
the client learns to become aware of and reflect on their emotional
experience as crucial data. The consultant[8] is always alert to the
organizationally-determined dynamic in the client's material,
whether the conversation is about a critical incident at work, a new
strategy or project, or an anecdote apparently unrelated to the
client's work preoccupations. The assumption is that whatever
the client brings is at some level an echo or reflection of the organization, and therefore relevant as a diagnostic tool. The consultant
also works constantly with their own countertransference, the
emotional resonances in themselves that provide further clues about
the client's experience that may not necessarily be communicated in
what they say (Armstrong, 2003).

As organization-in-the-mind comes ever more sharply into
view, the client gains deeper understanding of their organization
as a system, and an enhanced capacity for using the full range of
their experience as a resource for understanding their own and
others' behaviour. Consultant and client together develop working
hypotheses about what is going on, which the client then tests out
in the workplace. There is thus an iterative process as the client
moves back and forth between the organization and the consultancy sessions: the learning in each setting informs and feeds into
learning in the other. Over several such cycles, the client also
"learns how to learn" in this new way—the process becomes
internalized.[9]

Summary of differences in interventions used

In our initial interviews of coaches, we asked relatively broad
questions about technique and interventions. We found that the

meaning of some terms varied considerably for different coaches. For example, essentially everyone claimed they were non-directive, perhaps because non-directiveness is regarded as a professional ideal. For some coaches, particularly those using GROW or a person-centred approach, non-directiveness was absolute ("follow client interest"). Others, who described themselves as non-directive because they did not provide clients with solutions, did in fact regularly direct the client's attention to what the coach considered significant. In subsequent interviews, therefore, we asked more specific questions regarding particular "tools" and interventions coaches from the four schools used. Answers to these are shown in Table 2.

Defining success

Having identified some of the differences between the different approaches of coaching, we turned our attention to exploring the second part of our title question: "what makes the difference?" To do this, we first asked coaches how they defined "success". Their responses are shown in Box 4.

What makes the difference?—the client's viewpoint

A study of multi-national and Fortune 250 companies (Peterson, Uranowitz, & Hicks, 1997) asked clients what were the most useful factors in the coaching that they received. They replied:

- clear, constructive feedback (30%);
- supportive, trusting relationships (25%);
- information on developing specific skills (16%);
- information on organizational strategy (13%);
- specific actionable advice (13%);
- other (2%).

Another, more focused study, undertaken jointly by Personnel Decisions International (PDI) with a large corporate client, looked at the impact of executive coaching on performance, salary, and

Table 2. Use of specific tools and interventions across the four schools of coaching.

Interventions	GROW	Therapy informed	Behavioural/ cognitive	Role consultancy
Advice	L	L	M	L
Suggestions	L	M	M	L
Teaching/conceptual input	L	L	M	M
Role play/other structured exercises	L	L	H	L
Assigning "homework"	L	M	H	L
Drawings	L	L[1]	L	H
Hypotheses	L	variable[2]	L	H
Feedback	M			
to client	M	H	M	
Shadowing/observing client at work	L	L	H	L
Involving others in coaching sessions	Some coaches from all four schools regularly had 3-way meetings with the line manager at intervals; others from all four schools never did so.			
Use of subjectivity (coach using own feelings as data)	L	H	L	H

L = low frequency of use, M = medium/moderate frequency, H = high frequency of use.

[1]A minority used drawings very frequently. Variations here seemed based on personal preferences of the coach rather than on the particular therapeutic base they were using.

[2]Variation linked to which therapeutic approach the coach was drawing on: psychodynamically-informed coaches used hypotheses as a core tool, while coaches from other therapeutic bases did so rarely, if at all.

advancement potential. Data collected from seventy executives who had participated in coaching programmes with PDI, and also from their immediate supervisors, indicated significant impact. For those individuals who were regarded at the outset as high performers with high potential, 70% reported moderate to substantial development, and their average salary increase was 145% of the company

---

Box 4.   Coaches' indicators of success

- "Where the individual and the organization are broadly aligned, and explicit tangible aims have been achieved."
- "Presenting symptoms have diminished and the client is aware of related issues."
- "Greater effectiveness at work—client feels more effective and produces better results."
- "A healthy happy worker."
- "Neither under-estimating nor over-estimating what is possible in their role."
- "Tangible business achievements, sales target met or banks built, but also where people enjoy work and are more fulfilled."
- "Client repeatedly has new insights that lead to functioning differently, making greater use of the opportunities revealed by the process."
- "Meeting client's personal and business objectives."
- "When the boss says 'I've seen a big difference' and the individual also says they see a big difference."
- "Rapid movement from exploration to action."
- "Increase in client's energy level."
- "When there is organizational impact as well as role and personal development."
- "I become redundant."

---

average at their level. For "solid performers", moderate to substantial development was reported for 41%, with salary increases at approximately the predicted level for the company (102%), while for candidates seen as "derailment risks", 80% reported little or no development and salary increases were lower than the average for their positions (78%). There appeared to be substantial correlation between the degree of reported benefit from coaching, and the impact on salary. When asked to describe specifically how coaching had enabled participants to impact positively on the company's bottom line, the most common responses related to the impact of improved communication skills, closely followed by improved influencing and negotiating skills.[10]

Our own research, based on interviews of clients of the coaches in our sample, is summarized in Box 5a.

Box 5a.   What makes the difference?—what the clients said

General features of coaching

- "Committed time set aside to reflect and work on things."
- "Having another person to think with."
- "The structure—knowing I have another session coming up keeps me focused on what I want to achieve."
- "Thinking in advance and at the beginning of each session what I wanted out of it, and being disciplined (both me and the coach) about how we used the time."
- "a different kind of conversation than I can have with my wife, friends or colleagues—about what I really want, not what someone else thinks I want or should do."[11]
- "Being challenged, but in a supportive affirming way."
- "It provided a safe environment, you can discuss things that won't go any further, a feeling of trust."
- "Coach didn't give answers but explored and gave options."
- "We would go round and round on an issue until we achieved a solution together; he wouldn't just tell me what to do, asked me lots of questions, so in the end I felt I had ownership of the solutions and was able to implement them."
- "Giving seriousness and a name to meaningful vague thoughts, and turning them into tangible things."
- "I still 'talk' to my coach in my head, think 'what questions would she ask about this', that leads me to thinking about things from new angles."

Self-awareness/awareness of organizational dynamics and context

- "Seeing my part in the difficulties with X, so I felt less of a victim, less resentful."
- "Revisiting my priorities, not just assuming they were the same as they used to be."
- "Realizing I have to take risks in order to have the impact and influence I want to have, and how I avoid taking risks."
- "Discovering it makes me anxious when others have the good ideas, as if it should always be me."
- "The coach's questions pushing me to be more precise in describing my situation"
- "The coach's hypotheses about what might be going on led to my thinking in new ways, which opened up new options for action."

- "The coach's really attentive listening to what is under the surface and reflecting this back so I became aware of more than the content of what I was saying, but also of the feelings and assumptions I had."
- "We thought about so many different things in a profound, deeper, more unusual way than I could ever imagine doing internally without a coach."
- "Learning to separate out what is about me (personally), and what is about my role or my organization—makes it easier to accept the negative effects without taking it all so personally."

New skills, strategies and achievements

- "Working together on how I would facilitate a two-day team retreat with my team to plan the restructuring of our department—finding a balance between providing direction and giving them space to work out their own roles in the new structure; on my own, I would have probably done too much of one or the other."
- "We were bringing two business together so there were integration issues, people and strategy issues; now we have better relationships and are better at decision-making."
- "I am now a company director, I have matured and feel able to make bigger and better decisions; my team had a big backlog to catch up when I first came; this was achieved, also there is now shared clarity about the task and priorities of the department—the coaching sessions went between."
- "I now have a strong voice in the Cabinet [of an international charity], can influence more effectively."
- "I was able to confront underperforming individuals who had been left to drift for years, and manage them without having to sack anyone—courage to address the hard things."

It is worth noting that some clients responded to the question primarily in terms of the process of coaching, while others focused on content or specific outcomes. What clients identify as "making the difference" of course depends not only on what kind of coaching they have had, but also on their own "mind-set". For example, the same coach worked with two women in senior executive roles, each with the presenting issue of how to deal with a new male boss whom they experienced as restricting their former autonomy and creativity. Both felt the coaching had enabled them to shift the relationship very positively. One, a director in a large mental health trust, attributed the change to insights into her own behaviour and needs. The other, an executive in a multi-national corporation, attributed the change to the specific strategies and action plans evolved during coaching sessions. In fact, the coaching sessions in both cases involved a combination of increasing insight/self-awareness and planning actions, but each client came into coaching—and left it—with different assumptions about what enables people to tackle the challenges of working life most effectively.

What makes the difference?—the coaches' point of view

When we asked coaches to think of specific examples of "successful" work with clients and to identify what had made the difference, they very rarely cited particular interventions but focused almost entirely on process, as shown in Box 5b.

Thus, we see that coaches attribute success in significant measure to the client's motivation and ability to learn. This links to the findings cited above, that high performers tend to benefit most from coaching, while low performers benefit least, possibly because they are "sent" and therefore engage less in the process. Executive coaching is not for everyone, nor is it a substitute for management within the organization. This links with the last quote in Box 5b about organizational investment, and points to a major area for further exploration on the potential misuses, and even abuses, of coaching by the commissioning organization. This is, however, beyond the scope of this chapter.

Choosing a coach

Looking again at the presenting issues listed in Box 1 (p. 5), and the descriptions of the four models of coaching, one might imagine trying to match the two. For example, role consultancy might be deemed the best choice for the client seeking to develop into a new role, GROW for specific performance-related aims, therapy-based

---

Box 5b. What makes the difference?—What the coaches said

- "Crystal-clear contracting so coach, individual client, and the organization are all aligned; if partway through the original aims are achieved and we get into deeper more important stuff, we need to re-contract."
- "A client willing to engage really values the coaching and really works with it."
- "When the client develops a clearer understanding of the state of mind of their organization and can use this to develop more creative solutions to conflict and strategy."
- "Understanding the presenting symptom so it can be resolved or dissolved."
- "Being truly *with* the client, forgetting oneself, getting into their world."
- "Clients tell me it's the way we listen, give value to their story so the client gives new value to aspects of the story, especially their feelings as indicators of what is going on."
- "Asking tough questions in a playful way."
- "Tapping into client's motivation, so she could make big level changes."
- "Client who is able and willing to learn."
- "Client who can be surprised and use this."
- "Client who can work with metaphor and meaning."
- "Organizational investment in the coaching and supporting it, not just paying for it."

---

approaches for low job satisfaction, or behavioural approaches for skills deficits.

However, this kind of matching is premised only on the narrowest view of each of the four "stables" of coaching. In practice, the coaches we interviewed had worked with clients on virtually all the kinds of issues on the list. The main exception was that coaches using role consultancy did not think their approach would be suitable for clients with highly specific performance goal. However, this had rarely been put to the test, as clients of this type usually find their way to other sorts of coaches. While it was common practice to refer clients elsewhere if they appeared to need therapy rather than coaching, there were no examples of referring to coaches from another stable.

This may be at least partly due to the nature of our sample that was confined to very experienced coaches; only 20% had been coaching for less than ten years, and none for fewer than six. With experience, coaches learn to adapt their "tool-kit" to a range of issues and client learning-styles rather than adhering rigidly to their original orientation. Many coaches also seek out new tools to add to their repertoire as they encounter the limitations of their existing skills. For example, several coaches in our sample who had started as GROW practitioners had, over years of practice, found that in some situations they needed a deeper understanding of human development, and had subsequently undertaken a psychotherapy or counselling training. Their current practice now lies predominantly in the therapy-based quadrant of Figure 1, although they may still use elements of the GROW model. Conversely, several of those who had originally come into coaching from a clinical background had sought further training in organizational theory and role consultancy.

Clients very rarely choose a coach by considering which stable is most appropriate to their particular aims: the choice is nearly always based on personal recommendation. This might appear to leave matters almost entirely to chance. However, the importance of personal networks is forcefully made by Gladwell (2001). The potential client is likely to make their enquiries among people they know and who are therefore from their own world, often facing similar issues. This makes for a degree of matching, albeit not a formal one.

Furthermore, what people hear when given information about a potential coach is filtered through a complex set of desires, fears, and prejudices, some conscious and others unconscious, which vary over time. Clients may make a choice based on what they believe to be rational criteria, whereas in fact they may be influenced by the unconscious desire to find a coach who will not take them too far out of their "comfort zone". The final choice is usually made after an initial meeting between coach and client to explore whether they both feel they can work well together. Here, too, unconscious factors can play a part: a mutual sense of "good fit" may indicate potential for effective collaboration, but it may also indicate that coach and client are at risk of colluding in avoiding some of the most difficult issues.

So what should people look for when looking for a coach? We asked this question of the clients in our sample; their answers are given in Box 6.

As we can see from Box 6, some of the answers contradict others. The question of how best to match client and coach is far from simple. One complicating factor is that what clients think they want may not be what they are actually looking for. They may, for example, seek help in developing particular skills while inwardly troubled with doubts about the direction their career is taking. Do they then select a coach who "hears" the underlying issue, or one who joins them in addressing the stated goal?

Box 6.   What should people look for in choosing a coach?—what the clients said[12]

- "A coach who forgets themselves, really listens to the clients, has time to get into their world, is grounded and confident. The essential qualities are hard to train."
- "Important to have psychological understanding, some training in this."
- "Needs to understand the business world, which is the client's world."
- "No idea, which is a weakness of the coaching industry, there is no accreditation, it needs a more professional presence."
- "There is so little information to go on, things are done based on stereotypes and prejudice. You tend to rely on reputation and recommendation."
- "Someone who will see the process through. Sometimes there is more emphasis on learning particular skills than on implementation—look out for that."
- "Previous experience of working on the particular kind of issue the client wants to address."
- "Reputation and experience are what count, qualifications are irrelevant. I would not want to see a situation where not having a formal qualification is bad."
- "At the end of the day, it's a very personal thing, how well two people can work together on the issues."
- "Courage and wisdom—someone who won't avoid the hard things."

A second factor is the desire for a special relationship—again, a desire often split off and disowned by high-achieving pragmatic executives. Any one-to-one relationship can stir up such a desire; coaching, with its total focus on the needs and aspirations of the client, perhaps more so than many others. As one coach put it: "While we are actually together, the client is the most special person to me, and I am the most special person to them." While many coaches (as well as clients) might recoil in righteous denial of such feelings, they play a part, consciously and unconsciously, both in starting and maintaining a coaching relationship.

What matters most?

We initially asked this as part of exploring the question "what makes the difference?", but coaches' answers were almost universally about standards of good practice, perhaps because good practice is instinctively regarded as providing the framework within which positive change is most likely to occur. We have therefore collated these results in Box 7 under the heading "elements of good practice".

These views of the principles of good practice were shared across all the schools of coaching in our study, although specific interpretations varied, particularly with regard to defining appropriate boundaries. For example, coaches had different views about the terrain of executive coaching, particularly how far they would go (if at all) in discussing personal life issues. They also differed with regard to the level of reporting back to the organization that they would agree to: some refused to give any form of feedback, while others would agree to report on the use the client was making of the coaching and to provide other general information. In all cases, they insisted that the level of reporting back was agreed in advance with the person undertaking the coaching.

The level of agreement we found regarding the principles of good practice was in contrast to the impression one can get from the literature and from anecdotal accounts by coaches of one orientation regarding shortfalls in other approaches. Misperceptions often arise because good practice in one is compared to bad practice in another. For example, Berglas (2002) tells some hair-raising stories

---

Box 7.   Elements of good practice

- Genuine commitment to the client and their success.
- Clear contracting so coach, client, and organization have shared expectations and objectives; includes shared explicit agreement about confidentiality.
- Honesty: no secret agendas between coach and organization, such as assessing the client; address possible conflicts of interest between coachee and their organization.
- Know and work within one's own limitations, in particular "not unpacking what you don't have time or skill to pack up again".
- Appropriate task boundaries—clarity about what kinds of issues are "legitimate".
- Appropriate role boundaries—clarity whether one is in the role of facilitator, teacher, expert, friend, and aware when there is conflict or confusion about the coach's role.
- Awareness of the potential for creating dependency, vigilance not to exploit this.
- Having a broad flexible repertoire of interventions and ways of thinking about people and organizations.
- Regular review of one's work in formal or informal supervision with colleagues.

---

to illustrate the necessity for coaches to have psychological training, but in effect illustrates instead the dangers of unethical and incompetent practice. Since many coaches' "knowledge" about other approaches to coaching comes mainly from clients who have had unsatisfactory experiences of coaching in the past, they may draw some unfounded conclusions about others' standards of practice.

According to conventional wisdom, marketing strategy requires the identification of what is distinctive about the product. Might market forces push practitioners—at least those not famous enough to be bought as a brand name—to claim unwarranted distinctiveness (or worse, unproven superiority) over other approaches? Alternatively, might conviction about one's distinctiveness be used to bolster a sense of expertise and professionalism?

Many readers of this book will be familiar with the fierce debates that have long raged among psychoanalysts and therapists of different persuasions about the validity of their theories and the success of their interventions. Yet large numbers of studies comparing outcomes have failed to support these claims. A study published under the ironic title "Everyone has won and all must have prizes" (Luborsky, Singer, & Luborsky, 1975, updated recently by Luborsky, Diguer, Luborsky, & Schmidt, 1999) known as the Dodo verdict (from Lewis Carroll's *Alice in Wonderland*), found that patients benefited more or less to the same extent regardless of which particular therapy they had. Numerous other studies have produced similar results (Andrews & Harvey, 1981; Smith, Glass, & Miller, 1980), some even going so far as to propose that professional therapists produced no better results than empathic but untrained lay people (Russell, 1981; Strupp & Hadley, 1979).

A more recent, large-scale study of outcome and quality of psychoanalytic treatments, using both quantitative and qualitative measures, similarly found no significant correlation between "good enough" therapy outcomes and the particular theoretical school to which the analyst belonged (Leuzinger-Bohleber, Struhr, Rüger, & Beutel, 2003). They did, however, identify a number of characteristics that correlated with good outcome, in particular empathy and flexibility, where "technique was orientated towards the patient's needs, not primarily towards their own convictions or beliefs". In contrast, in treatments with poor outcome,

> both treatment technique and the underlying dynamic and adaptive processes of perception and insights seemed restricted and narrow. Some of the analysts described their painful memory that they were not able to enter into an "inner, resonant" dialogue with the patient over a long period of time. Some of [their] former patients complained about an analogous perception. Some of them mentioned their assumption that the analyst had forced his/her own concepts and ways of understanding on them. [*ibid.*, p. 282]

Significantly, most of the 207 analysts in the study had had this kind of experience with some of their patients, occasionally to the point that they could see no way out of the impasse other than referring the patient on to a colleague. The authors note that this might have proved beneficial in a larger number of poor outcome cases, and pose the question whether a change of therapist constitutes a taboo in the professions. We might well ask the same about coaching, where referral to a "competitor" is a rare event indeed.

While one must be careful about drawing analogies between therapy or psychoanalysis and executive coaching, as these are two very different enterprises, we feel that some of the conclusions of the Leuzinger-Bohleber study are relevant to coaching. In particular, that what makes the difference to clients has less to do with the specific theoretical school or methods of the practitioner than with other factors, notably:

- the quality of the relationship with the client—how understood and safe the client feels;
- the degree to which the practitioner can draw on a wide range of perceptions and interventions rather than adhering rigidly to a narrow framework;
- interventions offered cautiously, creatively, and within a continual process of reflections and exchange.

Together, these factors can help clients to internalize new ways of thinking about their situation and to "talk to themselves" in a different way from before, one which can endure long after the coaching process itself has ended.

Conclusion

In the absence of any large-scale studies of quality and outcome across different schools of coaching, we can draw only very tentative and provisional conclusions. Our own small-scale qualitative research—while it revealed interesting differences in technique, language and emphasis—suggests there is less difference in broad aims, values, client satisfaction, or standards of practice than many practitioners believe. However, the finding that equally good outcomes are achieved by coaches from all the main stables we have studied by no means implies that their background and training does not matter.

As previously noted, we deliberately restricted this first exploration to very experienced, soundly trained and highly regarded coaches and clients nominated by them. Comparing our findings with some of the reports in the literature, we believe that what makes the difference—what matters most—is not which school the coach comes from, but whether they are good, bad, or indifferent. Good practice, in our view—a view shared by all the coaches in our study—requires training in a discipline. Or, to put it another way, coaching at its best is disciplined work, not merely empathic support. This requires supervised practice over a period of time and cannot be achieved in the kind of brief workshops that are increasingly marketed as routes to quick transitions from the boardroom or sports-field (or life more generally) into coaching.

Furthermore, coaches from all four stables agree that it is crucial to be alert to the shortcomings in one's approach. Our own bias is that one needs in particular to be alert to the potential for unconscious collusion with the client—to shared "blind-spots"—and that this is a particular strength of the systems-psychodynamics approach described in this book. While we suspect that the popularity of some of the less rigorous approaches in the market may well be linked to their reliance on providing a large dose of the "feel-good factor", involving collusion and mutual idealization, this falls outside the scope of this study.

Coaching is still a relatively new activity, and so far not recognized as a formal profession—hence unregulated and without an agreed code of ethics. Anyone can call themselves a coach without any specific qualifications or experience, laying the field wide open to sweeping criticism, some of it justified, but much of it not (Parsloe & Wray, 2000; Williams & Irving, 2001). It is, then, hardly surprising that reputable practitioners are often very anxious to publicize the soundness of their own approach. Through lack of knowledge, or a patchy acquaintance with other schools of coaching (often through having clients whom other coaches have failed), they may well imply that other approaches are unsound. Although we have sought in this chapter to dispel some of their unwarranted assumptions and criticisms, we share their concerns about quality.

The coaching industry could perhaps usefully learn from the field of psychotherapy and take the first steps to self-regulation, the development of accredited training, and recognized professional standards. There is some evidence that this is starting to happen: for example, the International Federation of Coaching is an attempt to professionalize practice in the United States. It is still very early days. In the meantime, greater awareness that all the major approaches to coaching espouse high standards and are in broad agreement about what constitutes good practice, may pave the way for the various schools to join together to agree basic standards, and thus to decrease the risks of maverick and dangerous practice.

Acknowledgements

We would like to thank all those who gave so generously of their time to participate in our research. Participating organizations and individuals include: Terry Bates; Halina Brunning; The Change Partnership; Deborah Davidson; Rose Mersky Associates; Myles Downey, The School of Coaching, Downey Associates; The Grubb Institute; KPMG; Rose Mersky Associates; Meyer-Campbell; Personnel Decisions International; Jon Stokes, Director, Stokes & Jolly Limited; Tavistock Consultancy Service; The Tavistock Institute of Human Relations.

Coaching and consultancy firms and other organizations where interviewees trained or have had professional affiliations include, in addition to those cited above: Alexander, Coutts, GHN, London Business School, Penna, William Alanson White Institute.

Material concerning the impact of coaching came from both coaches and from individual clients who agreed to be interviewed. While names are not given in order to preserve confidentiality, we append a list of the kinds of organizations the coaches in our sample were working with and from which our client sample was drawn. These included: insurance, pharmaceuticals, financial services, legal firms, manufacturing, education, health service, probation, prison service, religious organizations, the arts, professional partnerships, voluntary sector organizations, and international charities, among others.

Notes

1. Minimum length of working as a coach was six years; average across the sample was fourteen years.
2. Where the deficit is identified by others, the client may be "sent" for "remedial" coaching. However, this was true for only a small minority of clients seen by the coaches in our sample.

3. A term first used by Goleman (1996) to denote the capacity to know, control, and use one's emotions; for example, to "read" others' feelings and therefore handle relationships effectively.

4. Mentor was the form taken by Athena, goddess of wisdom, to accompany Telemachus, the son of Odysseus, in his search for his father (symbolically, the adolescent journey towards maturity).

5. Even where these results are more equivocal there is an expectation that even relatively small changes in senior level executives can have a significant effect on productivity (Lidbetter, 2003).

6. See case studies by Alcock, Pooley, Brunning, and Spero in this book for illustrations and discussions of some of these issues.

7. See the chapter in this book by Huffington, where this idea is illustrated.

8. Since we are referring to this model as "role consultancy", we are using the term "consultant" here rather than coach. However, the organizations in the UK that have been most prominently associated with this method, such as the Grubb Institute, The Tavistock Institute of Human Relations and the Tavistock Clinic, are now also referring to this work as "executive coaching".

9. See the chapter in this book by Stapley, where this process is described.

10. No reference is provided for this study in order to protect the identity of the client organization within which it was carried out.

11. Many people think that the burgeoning of coaching is because it is a substitute for personal support networks. We believe this is a misperception. The client quoted here had a sound marriage, many friends, and good relationships at work, as did most of the others in our sample, and highlights a qualitative difference between coaching and other kinds of relationships clients have.

12. "Clients" here includes corporate purchasers of coaching we interviewed, as well as individual clients.

References

Andrews, G., & Harvey, R. (1981). Does psychotherapy benefit neurotic patients? *Archives of General Psychiatry, 38*: 1203–1208.

Armstrong, D. (2003). Interview with the authors. 3 November.

Bazalgette, J. (2003). Interview with the authors. 29 October.

Berglas, S. (2002). The very real dangers of executive coaching. *Harvard Business Review*, June: 84–92.

Brewer's Dictionary of Phrase and Fable (1970)[1870]. London: Cassell.

Bolch, M. (2001). Proactive coaching. *Training*, *38*(5): 58–63.

Campbell, D., Draper, R., & Huffington, C. (1989). *A Systemic* Approach *to Consultation*. London: D. C. Publishing.

Downey, M. (2003). *Effective Coaching*. London: Texere.

Economist (2002). Executive coaching. *364*(8284): 51 (8 March).

Gallwey, T. (1986). *The Inner Game of Tennis*. London, Pan.

Goldsmith, M. (2003). Helping successful people get even better. *Business Strategy Review*, *14*(1): 9–16.

Goleman, D. (1996). *Emotional Intelligence: Why It Can Matter More Than IQ*. London: Bloomsbury.

Gladwell, M. (2001). *The Tipping Point*. London: Little Brown.

Grubb Institute (1991). Professional management. Notes prepared by the Grubb Institute on concepts relating to professional management.

Hall, D. T., Otazo, K. L., & Hollenbeck, G. P. (1999). Behind closed doors: what really happens in executive coaching. *Organizational Dynamics*, Winter: 39–53.

Hogan, R., Curphy, G. J., & Hogan, J. (1994). What we know about leadership effectiveness and personality. *American Psychologist*, 49(6): 493–503.

Hutton, J., Bazalgette, J., & Reed, B. (1997). Organization-in-the-mind. In: J. Neumann, K. Kellner, & A. Dawson-Sheperd (Eds.), *Developing Organizational Consultancy*. London: Routledge.

Krantz, J., & Maltz, M. (1997). A framework for consulting to organizational role. *Consulting Psychology Journal*, *49*(2): 137–151.

Landsberg, M. (1996). *The Tao of Coaching*, London: HarperCollins.

Leuzinger-Bohleber, M., Struhr, U., Rüger, B., & Beutel, M. (2003). How to study the "quality of psychoanalytic treatments" and their long-term effects on patients' well-being: a representative, multi-purpose follow-up study. *International Journal of Psychoanalysis*, 84: 262–290.

Lidbetter, K. (2003). For good measure. *People Management*, 9 January: 46.

Luborsky, L., Singer, B., & Luborsky, E. (1975). Comparative studies of psychotherapies: is it true that "Everyone has won and all must have prizes"? *Archives of General Psychiatry*, 32: 995–1008.

Luborsky, L., Diguer, L., Luborsky, E., & Schmidt, K. A. (1999). The efficacy of dynamic versus other psychotherapies: is it true that "Everyone has won and all must have prizes"?—an update. In: D. S. Janowsky (Ed.), *Psychotherapy Indications and Outcomes*. Washington, DC: American Psychiatric Press.

McCaughan, N., & Palmer, B. (1994). *Systems Thinking for Harassed Managers*. London: Karnac.

McGovern, J., Lindmann, M., Vergara, M., Murphy, S., Barker, L., & Warrenfeltz, R. (2001). Maximizing the impact of executive coaching: behavioral change, organizational outcomes and return on investment. *Manchester Review 6*(1): 4–25.

O'Neill, M. B. (2000). *Coaching With Backbone and Heart: A Systems Approach to Engaging Leaders With Their Challenges*. San Francisco: Jossey-Bass.

Parsloe, E., & Wray, M. (2000). *Coaching and Mentoring*. London: Kogan Page.

Peltier, B. (2001). *The Psychology of Executive Coaching: Theory and Application*. London: Brunner-Routledge.

Peterson, D., Uranowitz, S. W., & Hicks, M. D. (1997). Management coaching at work: current practice in multinational and Fortune 250 companies. Personnel Decisions International.

Reed, B. (1976). Organizational role analysis. In: C. L. Cooper (Ed.), *Developing Social Skills in Managers*. London: MacMillan.

Reed, B., & Bazalgette, J. (2006). Organizational role analysis at the Grubb Institute of Behavioural Studies' Origins and Development in Coaching in Depth. In: S. Long, J. Newton, & B. Sievers (Eds.), *The Organizational Role Analysis Approach*. London: Karnac.

Russell, R. (1981). *Report on Effective Psychotherapy: Legislative Testimony*. New York: R. R. Latin Associates.

Smith, M. L., Glass, G. V., & Miller, T. I. (1980). *Benefits of Psychotherapy*. Baltimore: Johns Hopkins Press.

Strupp, H. H., & Hadley, S. W. (1979). Specific and non-specific factors in psychotherapy: controlled study outcome. *Archives of General Psychiatry, 36*: 1125–1136.

Whitmore, J. (2002). *Coaching for Performance: GROWing People, Performance and Purpose* (3rd edn). London: Nicholas Brealey.

Williams, D. I., & Irving, J. A. (2001). Coaching: an unregulated, unstructured and (potentially) unethical process. *The Occupational Psychologist*, April.

Withers, P. (2001). Bigger and better. *B.C. Business, 29*(4): 50–56.

CHAPTER TWO

A contextualized approach to coaching

Clare Huffington

Setting the scene

Executive coaching involves a one-to-one relationship between a consultant or coach and a client, usually a senior executive leader or manager, which aims to further the effectiveness of the client in his or her role in the organization.

Therefore it is a dyadic task relationship, but with an important difference from, for example, psychotherapy, in that it is a relationship in which there is always an implicit external context in view. This is the organization in which the client comes, in which he or she works, and which pays for the coaching. In other words, in all the exchanges that take place between the client and the coach, there is always a third party in the wings. This "third party in the wings" is present in at least two ways:

- as an internal reality in the mind of the client and the coach;
- as an external reality out there, to be engaged with or not.

Therefore, what the client says or does and what this elicits in the coach, as he or she listens and observes, needs to have reference to this omnipresent, sometimes hidden, third. What I am referring to here is the client and coach's shared experience of the organization through the client–coach relationship.

In referring to the coach as a consultant, I am deliberately framing coaching as organizational consultancy delivered through an individual. This is relevant even if one never engages directly with the organization, apart from contractually. It could also be argued that this is the type of consultancy currently acceptable to organizations, or, as one client put it, "coaching is the new organizational consultancy". Indeed, working with individuals in organizations was once termed by consultants trained in the Tavistock tradition as "role consultation" or "organizational role consultation" or "organizational role analysis" (Reed & Bazalgette, 2003). This work quite explicitly addresses the client's exploration of the interplay between himself or herself as an individual, in role in relation to the whole system or organization, and seeks to help the client in a leadership role to develop the capacity to think systemically. According to Miller and Rice (1967), the interplay between the individual in their role in the organization or system can be represented as in Figure 1.

When "executive coaching" began to gather pace as a mode of intervention in organizations, I and colleagues at the Tavistock Consultancy Service,[1] partly for marketing reasons, began to redescribe role consultation using this label. Indeed, there are close parallels between how we work or worked as role consultants and how we currently work as coaches. There are, however, various respects in which this change of labels has led us to redesign what we do and how; also to bring into view and emphasize certain

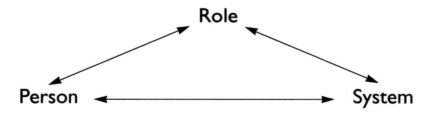

Figure 1. The relationship between person, role, and system (Source: Miller & Rice, 1967).

elements more than others. For example, in role consultation, the emphasis tends to be more on reflection and understanding as ends in themselves rather than on action and outcome; whereas the reverse might be said to be true for coaching, at least as practised by some in the field (e.g., Whitmore, 1994). Previously we might have worked with a client on helping them to develop a vision for their organization or area of work. Now we might also be inclined to work with them on implementing this vision, setting goals, and checking progress towards them.

In this respect, it is possible to see coaching as a variety or sub-set of process consultancy (Schein, 1988, 1990) focused on work with the individual or a number of individuals in an organization. It may be possible to engage directly with the organization in order both to help the individual and to feed back broader organizational themes that may assist the organization in its development, as well as engage in wider consultancy activities delivered from the launch pad of coaching. Doing so raises a number of dilemmas, which need careful consideration; for example, how to hold individual client confidentiality if one is engaging more widely with the organization.

In this chapter, I will explore some of the conceptual, practical, and ethical consequences for coaching of keeping the context in mind in this way. This is what is meant by a contextualized approach to coaching.

The chapter begins with a description of the conceptual framework behind a contextualized approach to executive coaching and how it can work in practice. Then there is a deeper exploration of the conceptual territory covered by the approach from the springboard of the concept of "the organization-in-the-mind" (Armstrong, 1997).

Next, a particular take on the current context in and around organizations is offered as an explanation for the growth in the demand for coaching. This aims to clarify some of the needs coaching seems to be addressing in individuals and organizations and the nature of the coaching response that therefore appears to be required.

Last, there are examples of way in which the coach can engage directly with the organization and some of the opportunities and dilemmas this can present.

The contextual perspective: the conceptual framework in practice

In listening to the client's story, the coach uses himself or herself "rather like a tuning fork—a place of resonance against which data takes on meaning that can be tested or refined and applied to the problem at hand" (Pogue-White, 2001). The coach is not only listening, associating to, or tuning in to the "person" of the client in his or her context, but also to the organization conveyed in and through his or her words, silences, and feelings. It is this kind of "dual listening" (a) to the individual in the organization and (b) to the organization in the individual that one tries always to keep in mind. It is through this dual listening that the nature and implications of the dilemmas, difficulties, and challenges the individual is facing in his or her role come more clearly into view and can be tested in behaviour.[2]

If we consider executive coaching to be a variety or sub-set of organizational consultancy, and bearing in mind the organization as the "third party in the wings" or even in the meeting room, what might this look like in practice? Clients bring concerns and issues that look, sound, and feel highly personal as well as those that are more clearly connected to their role in the organization or, more widely, general organizational issues. There could be, in addition, issues that sound more obviously personal or "private"—work–life balance, marital difficulties, or personal distress of various kinds. While these "personal issues" can be worked with as individual concerns separate from the organizational context, they can and should also be read—at least initially—organizationally, against an organizational boundary as well as an individual one. Doing so can reveal insights for the client as both an individual and a member of an organization and, potentially, for the organization as a whole. An example of working in this way is described later in order to make this clear. However, before presenting this, I would like to expand the idea of organizational context from the person–role–system model mentioned earlier into a series of concentric circles around the individual client, as in Figure 2.

It is useful to consider the client in relation to a series of interlocking boundaries or hierarchically organized "layers of meaning" (Cronen, Pearce, & Tomm, 1985) against which his or her issues can be understood. For example, in helping to consider a job change,

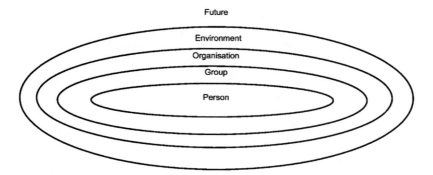

Figure 2. The contextual perspective (Copyright: The Tavistock Consultancy Service, 1998).

one might explore this in the context of the marketplace and competitive environment around their current organization; or opportunity, or lack of it, in the organization itself; or one might think with the client about whether the desire to leave their current organization is connected to relationships in the immediate work group; or in other more personal ways, for example, connected to the stage of professional development reached by the client. Each of these lines of enquiry would create a complex set of meanings for the client to consider, expanding their understanding and future options for changing jobs. The important theme here is not to "fall in love with and marry" a particular hypothesis or way of explaining a client's issue, thus getting stuck in one circle of context, particularly the personal (Campbell, Draper, & Huffington, 1988, 1989). It is important for the coach to keep alive in his or her mind a range of possibilities and ways of understanding the "presenting symptom", often and increasingly felt as personal, especially in the individualized and survivalist culture of organizations today (Kilburg, 2002). A good piece of advice is to start thinking as widely as possible, being reluctant to see an issue or concern solely owned by the individual when he or she is coming from an organization to be coached.[3]

Another, more developed way of thinking about this contextual framework is shown in Figure 3 (Blom, 2004). This shows a framework that can be used by the coach in working with a client to ensure all relevant potential issues affecting the client's work performance can be explored. Blom separates personal from

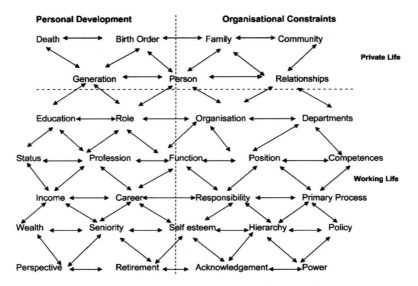

Figure 3.   A contextual framework for executive coaching (source: Blom, 2004).

organizational issues and "private life" from "work life" issues, but shows how the personal–private–work context can be connected. A further conceptualization would be the Six Domains Model presented by Halina Brunning in Chapter Six of this book.

Case example 1[4]

Nicola, a Vice President in the Operations side of an investment bank, was meeting me for a series of executive coaching sessions. These were built into a leadership development programme for people entering senior management roles for the first time. Soon after we began meeting she brought for discussion a difficulty that had been pointed out to her by her line manager and about which she was quite distressed; that she was very poor at making presentations and getting her point across in meetings with senior colleagues. It had been suggested to her that she sought presentation skills training to solve her problem, which was seen as personal, but she felt that this was not the whole story and wanted to explore it further with me.

It turned out that Nicola thought she was very good at making presentations and asserting herself with her team of sixty people, and she also felt she had no difficulties with senior colleagues in the Operations side of the bank. The situations that were difficult were meetings that involved senior colleagues in the Trading part of the bank; and this is where she thought the feedback about poor presentation skills had originated.

Trading is the exciting, risk-taking, deal-making part of the bank, whereas Operations is the "boring", back-room part of the bank that processes the deals and takes care of risk management, audit, and record keeping. Traders serving a particular financial sector were organized into business units, and traders and operations' staff serving that business unit would meet regularly as a team to review business progress. Traders historically tended to see themselves in a lead role in these meetings with operations' staff present to react to their requests.

Nicola experienced difficulty in the meetings because she and others at her level in Operations were being encouraged to take a strategic and more proactive approach to the business, especially on issues like risk management and cost reduction. The bank was worried about crises in the financial world following various dramatic business collapses and lack of confidence in professional dealing with audit and investment. So, there were pressures coming from the environment on the bank, which was, as a result, changing the way it conducted its business. It was important for Nicola to be able to use the meetings with traders to point out the risks of taking one particular course of action or another, so that steps could be built in from the start of a venture to counteract any problems. She found it stressful to operate in this new way because traders were used to being in control and having their own head, and resented what she felt they experienced as let and hindrance from her.

So, in addition to information about environmental pressures on the organization, there was also evidence to suggest that Nicola's individual difficulty represented something about inter-group issues in the bank; the resistance of traders to operations' staff asserting themselves, instead of taking up a traditional passive role. Nicola was stepping into the middle of tensions associated with the way in which investment banks manage the anxiety associated with "gambling" with other people's money. They make an organizational split[5] between those taking risks and those managing them. In being reminded about the risks, the traders might feel infected with anxiety that would make it impossible to act with the usual daring, so they might wish to resist and push the anxiety back to Nicola and to Operations. This might contribute to her "poor performance".

A further dimension was that Nicola was one of the few women at her level in the bank. There were no women at her level among the traders, so they had little experience in dealing with senior women as well as a lack of experience of women in Operations acting assertively. Their expectation that Operations should act passively might have been strengthened by the expectation that women should or do act more passively than men in the bank or in life generally. Unfortunately, Nicola felt she could not explore this with people directly because gender issues were not talked about openly in the bank. This was because of the fear of saying something discriminatory, following some high profile court cases involving sexism in investment banking. Political correctness in the bank, due to fear of more litigation, made any reference to gender a taboo subject.[6] The last point is about the personal relevance for Nicola of the issue of asserting herself with authority figures. She had a difficult upbringing with strict parents who would often punish her for mistakes she made. She described herself as afraid to assert herself with authority figures for fear of the consequences if she got it wrong. She thought she definitely took these feelings from childhood into meetings at work with senior people. Usually she was able to manage her anxiety in these situations but, in meetings with traders, I would suggest because of the organizational dimension with its special ingredient of inter-group tension, Nicola was pushed into incoherence and poor self- presentation.

Once we had explored Nicola's issue in these ways,[7] she saw that there were actions she could take to help herself, both individually and organizationally. Individually, she could prepare herself differently for the meetings now she understood that she made the traders anxious with her attempts to assert herself; this was quite a new perspective for her. She would need to think about how she could present her ideas in a more collaborative and less challenging way. Organizationally, she checked with other vice presidents about their experience in similar meetings. She discovered that they too, and especially women, had parallel problems. In fact, colleagues thought the traders did not know about the policy of a change of approach in Operations. The vice presidents in Operations decided to meet formally as a group, which had not happened before, to plan how to tackle their shared problem, with a view to an approach to the Head of Operations. The aim was to promote discussion across the bank as a whole about whether the new approach was working and how it should continue with effective support from traders.

As a result of the changes Nicola made in her approach to the meetings, her performance improved greatly. The vice presidents' group was also able to stimulate a wider discussion across the bank and to inform traders about the policy change, with the result that business unit meetings became much longer, at times more conflictual, but also more collaborative. Since promotion crucially depended on recommendations from traders in the business unit, this was important for Nicola's future. She was promoted to Director later that year. Subsequently, traders began to ask for coaching for the first time, which I tend to see as the result of their experience of greater personal anxiety. This could have been because the management of task anxiety was now more shared across the organization, rather than being split and only managed by Operations, where Nicola worked.

This example illustrates how it is possible to help the client read individual experience organizationally and help him or her to arrive at solutions that not only deal with their own "problem" but also impact on the organization in positive ways. Nicola was able to use the meetings with the coach as a "third party" to negotiate a different relationship between herself and the organization. It was also possible to help the organization become aware of the need for change in the way it operated: Nicola was able to engage with the organization via her meetings with her peers and this resulted in wider organizational changes. This raises the question, which will be dealt with later in this chapter, of whether and how the coach could directly intervene to bring about change in the organization.

Now I would like to turn to explore in more depth the concept of "the organization-in-the-mind".

The "organization-in-the-mind"

In "Setting the scene", I referred to two ways in which the organization is present in the discourse between the client and the coach; as an internal reality, or an internal object in the mind of the client and as an external reality independent of the coach and client. In this section, I shall turn to the first of these two ways in which the organization is present in coaching as the "third party in the wings".

The concept of "the organization-in-the mind", or organization as an internal object, was originated by Pierre Turquet and developed by David Armstrong and colleagues at the Grubb Institute (Hutton, Bazalgette, & Reed, 1997) and by David when he joined the Tavistock Consultancy Service (Armstrong, 1995). He defines it as not the client's mental construct of the organization, but rather the emotional reality of the organization that is registered in him or her, that is infecting him or her, that can be owned or disowned, displaced or projected, denied, that can also be known or unthought.

This experience becomes the material of coaching as it is discussed by the client with the coach and the layers of meaning, conscious and unconscious, become apparent.

In this definition, emotional experience is seen not as the property of the individual or individuals but "emotional experience that is contained within the inner psychic space of the organization and the interactions of its members—the space between" (Armstrong, 1997). This is akin to the notion of countertransference from psychoanalytic work, but needs to be reconstrued in that what is evoked in the consultant or coach is some element of his or her own "organization-in-the-mind" in terms of the organizational setting in which the coach works or has worked over time. Other layers of this complex picture that may become important include the coach's "organization-in-the-mind" of the client; and the client's "organization-in-the-mind" of the coach.

One way of reading the emotional experience of the client in the organization (from, for example, Jaques, 1989) would be that this represents an enactment of the stresses and strains of organizational life and is "extraneous noise" connected to individual or group pathology, a side effect of defective structures or processes in the organization. And that to understand and work with these better, the coach needs to learn about the patterning of individual and group behaviour under stress; also perhaps that the work of the consultant should be focused on recommending different structures and processes which do away with "dysfunctional" emotions and behaviour. There would, for example, be various structural solutions to the need to pay more attention to risk management in the investment bank, of which the creation of business unit teams was one example, with its consequences for Nicola and her colleagues. This is perhaps the explanation for the restructuring fever that afflicts organizations from time to time.

No doubt some organizational problems that create concomitant negative emotional experience and dysfunctional behaviour in its members can be helped by changing structures and processes, but the argument here is that there is something more pervasive or constitutive of organizations that explains the emotional experience we feel and see in our clients. This could be thought of as its primary process, "not its aim, but rather something without which none of its stated aims was likely to be achieved" (Armstrong, 1995). In the example of the investment bank, one take on the "heart of the transformation process of the organization" (Armstrong, 1995) might be the risky business of gambling with other people's money. The emotions of fear, greed, and excitement tied up in this, and registered in Nicola and in me as she told me her story, is the primary process or daily stuff of organizational life in investment banks, however this is structured or processed by traders or Operations. At that point in time, the issue seemed to be Nicola's self-confidence, just as, in investment banking world-wide, there was also a larger scale crisis of confidence. It was as if the lack of confidence in the system had got into Nicola because of her personal valency for feeling this way (Bion, 1961). This is something to be understood, acknowledged, and managed, and, where possible, its creative potential exploited; rather than something to be avoided, denied, and structured out, which I am suggesting is a useless pursuit. Over the years, and influenced by pressures from society, the marketplace, and other factors, the primary process finds various means of expression that impact on individuals and groups in various ways mediated by their own constraints, opportunities, and valencies. In the case of Nicola, her "personal problem" was simultaneously an expression of individual, group, inter-group, wider organizational and societal turbulence, only some of which she and I could work on, either directly or indirectly. It had its own distinctive flavour imparted by the "organization-in-the-mind", or our minds as we tried to read together the primary process of the organization, starting with her individual experience.

It is not always possible to capture the "organization-in-the-mind" of clients as clearly as with Nicola; in others, it emerges fleetingly or haltingly or not very much at all. One might wonder why this is the case; what is it about these organizations that means they register so patchily in the minds of their leaders? What might this mean about the organization, or its environment, or the work group, or the individual in question? In other cases, it is quite a clear and distinctive flavour. In order to illustrate this, I will describe three examples of the "organization-in-the-mind" of clients in very different organizational settings and how this was used in my work with them.

Case example 2[4]

Ian is a senior manager in a food manufacturing company and the issue he brought was about developing a greater capacity for strategic thinking. He needed this to progress to the next level in the company. He was highly intelligent and competent at his job, which was as a country manager in this global company. He had previously worked for another company in a different industry sector, where he had also been very successful. Great things were expected of him in terms of progressing up the hierarchy. His company was, however, struggling in the marketplace and a number of ways of reorganizing its work were in play at the time.

Over a series of meetings Ian arrived each time looking stressed and complaining of overload and not being able to think. At the same time, he seemed excited about his relatively new job. He described panic and initiative fatigue in the company, and having 500 e-mails in his in-box that he was never able to clear. He was becoming increasingly focused on detail and operational issues as things became more and more chaotic in his work environment. I found myself feeling confused and not able to identify what issue to help him to focus on, as well as anxious that there might be something I was missing in all the detail. I found myself wanting to provide solutions for each of his many operational problems. Yet this was not why he wanted my help. Then I found myself asking, "Why does the organization need to operate in crisis mode and appear not to take any time to think things through?" It was important to be able to reflect on my experience in the room with Ian, since my feelings appeared to mirror his experience. This is often the first clue to the organization-in-the-mind of the client.

In the meantime I had visited his organization to run a team day for another client, and had seen bowls of company products, sweets, on meeting tables in their offices, and noticed how people grazed on them throughout meetings. When I commented on this, one staff member said, jokingly, "It's mother's milk!" He seemed to be suggesting that they were feeding themselves with the products and perhaps values of the company as a kind of instant gratification or, perhaps, reassurance.

At the beginning of the next meeting Ian talked about the scrapping of the latest strategic plan developed by outside consultants and of the teleconferences with his boss, who was delivering a bewildering onslaught of instructions, each either duplicating those he had been given before or countermanding some previous initiative. He described the organization as having a "hand-to-mouth" existence and, at the same time, how good everyone was in a crisis. This was interesting because it echoed the "hand-to-mouth" behaviour observed in the team meeting. I shared my observations with my client. This led into a discussion of how the organizational task of meeting the basic need of hunger, or even greed, the *raison d'être* of a food company, had perhaps got into the way the organization worked. This was reflected in the tendency to be in crisis intervention mode, rather than in reflective or planning mode. We then discussed the difficulty the organization as a whole apparently had with strategic thinking. We concluded that it was not just Ian's problem. In reaching this point, Ian realized it would be very difficult for him to develop strategic thinking, as he had originally construed it, in this organization.

We then discussed how strategy did, in fact, get decided upon in the company, as it undoubtedly did, however chaotic it appeared, and Ian went away with the resolve to find out about how it was done so that we could work on a reframed notion of what he needed to do to progress in this company.

This example illustrates a number of things; first, that the data one is drawing upon to develop one's thinking and that of the client comes from a variety of sources—what the client says and does not say; how they look and seem to feel; how you feel and what you find yourself saying or doing; observations outside coaching sessions, especially if you can visit the organization; and so on. Metaphors, images, dreams, drawings—all help to reveal the "organization-in-the mind". Some clues arrive as gifts—like the sweet bowls or metaphors such as "hand-to-mouth", and others can be engineered; for example, by asking the client to make picture of themselves in their organization in their role; or by asking the client to describe a dream or day-dream. There is a feeling of evidence mounting until the right moment to engage with the client emerges.

Case example 3[4]

This next example concerns a comprehensive school in a deprived part of the UK and the coaching was with Peter, the head teacher, and his deputy head teachers.

> This school was very challenging in that it had many students with difficult behaviour and great learning needs.
>
> Working as a teacher at the school was demanding, but the staff group was loyal and many had been there a very long time. The leadership of the school was effective and standards were improving, but the school was constantly under external pressure to achieve higher targets.
>
> The topic about which I heard the most from all three clients was about conflict in the leadership team, which they led and of which they were also members. This conflict was of a particularly nasty personal kind and the original point of conflict usually concerned different ideas about how to lead particular projects within the school. Sometimes it involved talking about members of the team behind their backs; sometimes there were rows in the corridors. There were often threats to walk out or resign. Most of the rows were partly secret in that others were not supposed to know about them and could apparently not be discussed in the team as a whole. I would hear about them from various perspectives, including victim and perpetrator, when the rows involved my clients. I felt uncomfortable, worried about my capacity to hold the material confidential and of the possibility of a destructive breakdown in relationships at the top of the school.
>
> When I first heard about these rows I was also surprised, as these professionals seemed thin-skinned and the arguments so like the arguments of the adolescents they were teaching. I also heard about rows between teachers elsewhere in the school. The conflict seemed to be both rife and normal. At the same time, in visiting the school where the coaching took place, I could see that relationships between staff and students seemed excellent and mostly of a very friendly nature. I would often meet one of my clients just as they finished a supportive conversation with a student, to be followed by the beginning of our meeting, the first few minutes of which would consist of a tirade about another member of the leadership team. It seemed as if the good relationships with students came at the price of difficult relationships with adults in the school.
>
> Then it became clear that Peter and his deputies' identification with the students needed to be strong in order to effectively take up their

leadership roles in the organization. In other words, in order to be followed by students and staff in a challenging environment, the leadership team needed to get close to their followers. This included displaying personal vulnerability, rather than distance. This was a learning institution, so all involved had to show a need to learn that was a vulnerability in itself. This seemed to be the key feature of the primary process of the organization—managing the vulnerability involved in learning. Vulnerability, together with the aggression and sexuality the students were learning to control, proved an unstable cocktail that the head, deputies, and leadership team dealt with on a daily basis. The rows among members of the leadership team appeared to represent an expression of vulnerability, identification, and stress relief all at the same time.

I took a risk in feeding back my thoughts on the "organization-in-the-mind" to Peter, with the result that he felt it would be useful if I shared them with the leadership team as a whole and helped them to think about how they could use team meetings to share and work at some of the feelings that otherwise spilled over into rows. These team meetings facilitated by me became a regular event in the school calendar and, while the rows still occasionally take place, the team as a whole is taking a much more active collaborative role in sharing the leadership task of managing vulnerability, including the difficult emotional work that goes with it.

This example is interesting in that it shows that data about the "organization-in-the mind" can come from a variety of sources in the organization if one is working with more than one coaching client in that organization. This does raise issues of confidentiality which need careful consideration (see below under "Engaging with the organization") but the overall advantages to the organization of the coach being able to feed back themes from the coaching to assist organizational development were the reasons for the school choosing to use one coach to work with all three clients. It again emphasizes how important it can be to have direct experience of the client's organization, as in my observation of the relationships between staff and students at the school because the coaching took place there.

In all three case examples I have described so far, what might be described as the "emotional life of the organization" (Huffington, Armstrong, Halton, Hoyle, & Pooley, 2004) had considerable impact on the individuals concerned, giving a frame and meaning to the issues they brought. These were not emotions that could be "structured out" but needed to be properly understood and managed, making the most of their creative potential. It was possible to tap into this via the "organization-in-the-mind" of the client alone, in the case of Nicola, as well as via direct contact in their organizations, in the case of Ian and Peter, respectively.

I will now turn to a consideration of the layer of meaning around the organization itself, the current context of organizations in general in the first decade of the twenty-first century, and how this impacts on the coaching process.

The current context in organizations

The growth in the popularity of coaching for those in leadership roles in organizations in the last ten years has been remarkable. This can be explained in part by the dramatic changes in organizations in this period in all sectors of the economy. There has been extreme turbulence created by

- the revolution in information technologies and the transmission of knowledge;
- globalization of markets and hence competitive pressures;
- increasing levels of risk created by these changes;
- changing social and cultural patterns—in families and between generations; in attitudes towards gender and race; and in the concern about work–life balance;
- ecological awareness and sensitivity;
- wider issues of social responsibility;
- economic and political restructuring; for example, in Europe;
- customerization and an increasing emphasis on consumer or client sovereignty;
- the emergence of a contract culture, especially in the public sector, tied to rigorous and imposed criteria of accountability (Huffington, Armstrong, Halton, Hoyle, & Pooley, 2004).

Associated with these changes are corresponding shifts in the structuring and patterning of organizations. Organizational boundaries, both internal and external, are increasingly fluid, internal structures and roles less clearly defined, and conventional hierarchies less evidently relevant. Mergers, strategic alliances, and partnerships have become commonplace. There has been a growing preoccupation with the language of vision, mission and corporate values, ownership, and "empowerment", alongside the harder edge of "outsourcing", "downsizing", and "target-setting". Within the business world and elsewhere, stable work groups are being replaced by project, sometimes virtual, teams on short-term assignments cutting across traditional professional and positional boundaries. An emphasis on innovation and creativity rubs up against the pressures on delivery and results (Cooper & Dartington, 2004).

The impact on those in decision-making roles has been to stress the leadership, as opposed to management, component of their roles. The changes in organizations appear to have fundamentally ruptured the relationship of the individual to the organization and one of the leader's new tasks is to focus on negotiating the psychological contract with followers, as this can no longer be assumed (Obholzer, 2004). A more personal and laterally distributed version of leadership has emerged that can be felt to be more personally demanding (Huffington, James, & Armstrong, 2004). At the same time, the emphasis on performance and targets can lead to a persecutory environment in which creativity struggles to flourish. It could once be said that the organization contained the individuals within it through the management of boundaries, systems, and processes (Miller & Rice, 1967). However, despite the drive towards better performance, there is now a sense of a lack, or abdication, of management and, hence, a lack of containment, safety, and support for people in organizations. Individuals can thus be said to contain the organization within themselves, rather than the other way around. Employees have to manage their own careers, decide their own development plans, organize personal support for themselves via coaching, mentoring, and other leadership development; yet they may still look to the leader of the organization to provide this sense of both containment and inspiration (or what has been called "pro-tainment" by Huffington, James, & Armstrong, 2004).

The person element of leadership thus appears more important than role or system (in the person–role–system model mentioned earlier) and there is a relative absence of the mediating concept of role in the individual's experience of his or her encounter with the organization, if my coaching clients are representative. This perhaps accounts for the popularity of the idea of "emotional intelligence" (Goleman, 1998), as leaders need to capture the hearts and minds of the individuals in the organization rather than being able to rely on loyalty, deference, or hierarchy to get things done. There tends to be a relative avoidance of the team or group dynamic, despite the need to work in groups, especially because of the reduction of face-to-face contact between people working together across the globe, often virtually. Therefore, there is a sense of no organization or system that can be relied upon. There is then a danger that leadership becomes fragmented.

Coaching itself could paradoxically compound the problem if each director is getting his or her support from an external coach as a substitute for genuine connectedness across the team or organization. Organizations seem to be struggling to find the kind of relatedness they need to do business and that can foster growth and innovation. The issue of life–work balance seems not to be so much about the volume of work or the need for flexible work patterns but about the psychological intrusiveness of the organization upon the individual and the need to limit it. The leader has to decide where to draw the boundary between the person he or she is at home and the person he or she brings to work, as this is now no longer clear.

In fact, one could almost get to the position that leadership is so difficult as to be impossible because of the high expectations, personal exposure, and the likelihood, or perhaps inevitability, of failure, judging by the fate, for example, of football managers. The average longevity of Chief Executives is now only two or three years, which is barely long enough to implement a change programme. There is a great deal of questioning, challenging, and criticism of leaders in the media and in organizations. It appears almost impossible for leaders to lead and many are deposed and replaced by new ones who are soon criticized and challenged. There appears literally to be an intolerance of leadership. At the same time, there is a great deal of rhetoric about leadership and a plethora of leadership development initiatives in all sectors of the economy. It is as if there is a longing for leadership that no one can fulfil.

It seems that the leader is now being thought of as an individual taking power to him or herself in a hierarchical way, rather than acting on behalf of the organization or system in taking up the leadership role, or function, or state of mind. It is possible to see that people in organizations are tending to operate more as individuals, or perhaps pairs, in survivalist mode, rather than being able to connect in a wider way to achieve things as a system, where necessary trusting others to act on their behalf. The concept of the organization as a system of interconnected parts in fact appears absent from the way people think about getting things done. This tends to lead to a state of affairs in which the collaboration needed for creativity and development is missing. People seem to be living in the present and depending on themselves; a kind of feral existence in which leadership means very little. It is what one client called "a post leadership situation".

The popularity of coaching suggests that leaders are looking for a creative partnership in their relationship with a coach to help release them from the isolation and frustration they experience in their leadership roles. Among other issues, the challenge appears to be to help these clients develop the kind of relatedness in their organizations that will allow creativity to flourish, rather than encouraging a split-off outsourcing of support. A pairing with a coach seems to create a transitional space, in the absence of a clear concept of role, which can allow the client to negotiate a new relationship with the organization, dealing with their feelings of dependency, wish for a fight, or to avoid conflict or leave. In this sense, the coach is a transitional object for the client.[8] The relationship can be represented as shown in Figure 4.

Figure 4, in an interesting counterpoint to the Miller and Rice diagram (Figure 1), shows how the "coach" can replace "role" as a

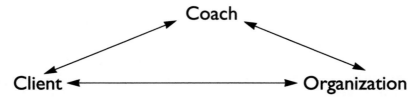

Figure 4.   The relationship between coach, client, and organization (copyright: The Tavistock Consultancy Service, 2004).

mediating variable between the "individual" and the "organization".

This means helping the client to turn back to the organization
rather than away from it by working with the client on improving
relationships with bosses, colleagues, and direct reports in service
of the client's leadership and management tasks. This provides
another reason why keeping the organization in mind is so important. A concern about coaches working as individual freelancers is
that they may be disenfranchised or disillusioned members of organizations and may be seeking to regain influence in organizations
from the outside via coaching its leaders. Therefore, they may not
be able to assist their clients to genuinely engage with the organization in a collaborative way.

Characteristics of coaching clients and coaching responses

Coaching clients

It is clear from the perspective outlined above on the external
context around organizations, that clients come into coaching with
issues connected with this turbulence around them. The organizations in their minds are fragile and fragmented places. Put another
way, what they bring seems to centre around the development of
confidence in an environment where there is little confidence in the
organization. An appreciation that an experience of vulnerability at
a personal level could be seen as normal and based on the reality of
organizations today can be a huge relief for the client, who may
come feeling that they are just not up to the job. In fact, over time,
this experience of vulnerability, possibly easier for female leaders to
own up to (Coffey, Huffington, & Thomson, 1999), can become a
valuable indicator of the current state of the organization if the
leader can learn to "read" it as emotional intelligence (Armstrong,
2004). Paradoxically, an important role for a coach, then, is to be
able to help the client to value and learn from their experience of
vulnerability; and to help leaders to change their behaviour while
not feeling confident, entering their "risk zone", but feeling confident as a result; or perhaps helping leaders to learn to behave like
a confident person in order to inspire others to have confidence in
them (Sandler, 2003).

Broadly, clients seem to be bringing the following groups of issues into coaching.

- Anxiety connected to an experience of vulnerability, as above, as well as ambivalence about having a leadership role, partly reflecting the ambivalence people seem to have about leadership—longing for it but hating it too. Clients may need help in dealing with others' idealization of them in the leadership role as well as denigration, its inevitable bedfellow.
- Difficulties with the public performance element of a leadership role, such as making presentations, motivating teams, and unstructured social interaction with clients, stakeholders, or colleagues.
- Getting things done using directive styles of leadership that are so unpopular in these days of inclusivity and empowerment; and due to the increasing fear of litigation from disgruntled employees. Many coaching clients want help in dealing with managing poor performance in their staff.
- Dealing with overwork and being bombarded with tasks and information. Clients want help with time management and filtering what might be called "toxic waste" coming over the organizational boundary. They may need support with developing a critical and reflective approach to things they are asked to do, instead of being over-reactive (Obholzer, 2004).
- The tendency to avoid relatedness and delay in dealing with uncomfortable relationship problems, especially conflict; also the wish to avoid tackling organizational politics.
- Leaders often seem to have difficulty letting go of the operational and technical parts of their role that got them the job in favour of a more strategic approach. They may need help with delegation and sharing or distributing leadership as well as dealing with the differently patterned organizational dynamics that result from this. (Huffington, Armstrong, Halton, Hoyle, & Pooley, 2004).
- Risk-taking is often difficult for leaders who are feeling fragile; yet it is essential to move the organization from survivalist mode to creative development.
- Leaders new in role often need help to think more broadly than the specific function they may have had previously, so they can

think about the whole organization and the systemic ripples between its constituent parts and with the environment around it. The coach is, in a way, helping the leader to develop the ability to consult to his or her own organization by improving his or her systemic thinking.

Listed below are some specific case examples of the general areas described above.

1. A senior manager in the public sector, who is intellectually brilliant and completely devoted to his job, is unable to confront poor performance and deliver bad news, leaving it too late or relying on others to do this for him. As a result, several staff have taken out grievances against him. He comes into coaching for help with the stress this is causing him.[9]

2. A senior partner in a professional services firm is not being admitted to the elite partner group, because he tends to get into conflicts with his peers and will not share work with them. He also can't see the need to understand and manage organizational politics. He comes into coaching for help with how to get the promotion he is being denied.

3. A high-flying young woman leader in a manufacturing company spends no time on networking in the organization and is not well known to the level above her. She is seen as too competitive and territorial about her own division. She comes into coaching having been told she will not progress in the firm, as she wishes to do, unless she can become more "corporate" in her behaviour.

These three examples illustrate three broad areas in which coaches are often asked to help:

- "fixing problem people";
- helping a client to make a transition from one career step to another;
- learning skills of leadership (Peltier, 2001).

Coaching responses

The overall framework around coaching that allows the coach to keep the organization in mind is a process consultancy approach

(Schein, 1988) or "combining coaching with consulting" (Kilburg, 2002; O'Neill, 2000; Peltier, 2001). This means that the coach begins with the issue that the client has brought but attempts to work with the client to understand and resolve it within the broad systems framework described above. The aim is for the client to be able to develop a contextual perspective on an issue that may feel very personal, so that eventually they can appreciate the relative contributions of the organization in them as well as them in the organization. Specific techniques borrowed from family therapy can help the client to develop this wider or systemic perspective; for example, the use of reflexive questions (Campbell, Draper, & Huffington, 1988, 1989; Hieker, 2003). The use of these kinds of questions can bring about change in themselves and is known as "interventive interviewing" (Tomm, 1987, 1988).

The coach and client would then carefully work through the stages of the consultancy process based on an action research model as in Figure 5. (Huffington, Cole, & Brunning, 1997). This perspective is a good example of the fusion contained in the title of this book *Coaching from a Systems-Psychodynamic Perspective.*

This is what we at the Tavistock Consultancy Service (TCS) have called a "process coaching" approach. For different clients, there would be varying emphasis on the three main elements of the coaching response described by Sandler (2003) of extending insight,

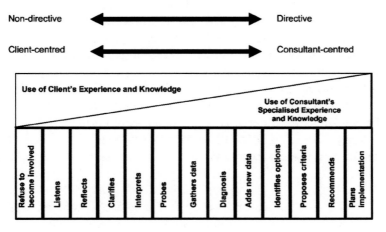

Figure 5. A continuum of consultancy styles (source: Schmidt & Johnston, 1970).

managing emotions, and developing behavioural strategies. This could involve giving advice and being directive at times if that is what the client needed to help them move on in their development. It is, however, a subtle and complex process that is different from both organizational consultancy and psychotherapy and counselling, from which professional fields executive coaches are often drawn. It requires a blend of skills from both fields and a mind-set that is different again. TCS provides in-depth training in this approach that requires careful development and ongoing supervision.

The emphasis on achieving behaviour change and outcome in terms of better individual performance in role, or better overall organizational performance, provides an obvious practical link between coaching and the organization via the results of coaching. Organizations that use coaching to develop their leaders are concerned to show that coaching is a worthwhile investment for the organization as well as for the individual (e.g., Rolph, 2004). Clients enter the process, be it organizational role consultation or executive coaching, not primarily to gain more or a deeper understanding, but to improve something, change something, become more effective themselves, and/or enable the organization and those who work in it to become more effective. Understanding, for most clients, is valued as a prelude to action, or perhaps no action. Moreover, there is a real sense in this work, as against, say individual psychotherapy, in which, just as understanding may be the prelude to action, action is the test of understanding. In other words, it is through an iterative process of gaining understanding, testing understanding in practice, and using the results to test one's understanding that the process really takes off. Coaching could thus be seen as a kind of guided or facilitated action research. One of my clients described it as "guided self-exploration".

Mary Beth O'Neill (2000), emphasizing the need to clearly link coaching to the organization, describes the essentials of the task to be

- bringing a results orientation to the leader's problem, staying focused on how the leaders can make the organization successful;
- partnering the client to greater effectiveness;

- helping the leader to face, not avoid, his or her specific leadership challenges;
- turning the leader towards his or her team (*ibid.*, pp. 7–8).

Depending on the circumstances, the coach may work solely with the individual client and his or her organization-in-the-mind, or may have the opportunity to engage directly with the organization in various ways. I shall now turn to some of the issues connected with doing so.

Engaging with the organization

In this section, I turn to the second of the two ways in which the organization is present in coaching as "the third party in the wings"; that is, as an external reality with which the coach can engage directly. It is another demonstration of helping the client develop their relatedness to the organization rather than engage in coaching as a split-off or privatized development activity.

While working directly with the client's organization provides many opportunities to enhance the coaching outcome, there are a number of issues the coach needs to consider carefully.

Contracting issues

The framing of the initial contract with the organization and with the client is crucial to being able to keep open the possibility of working directly with the organization. Even if the coaching does not involve explicit contact with the organization thereafter, many organizations, especially large corporates, set up the contract for coaching via a meeting between the client, the client's line manager, and the potential coach. This is often so that the line manager can set out the aims he or she has for the coaching based on the client's development needs, sometimes identified by 360 Degree Feedback assessment processes in the organization or a personal development plan. This line manager then legitimizes payment for the coaching. Sometimes, this contracting and legitimizing process may additionally involve a representative from the human resources, training, or development arm of the organization. A similar meeting between client, line manager, and coach can sometimes be required at review points and at the conclusion of the coaching contract. The important issues here are as follows.

- The coach needs to be able to take up his or her authority as a coach to work on the client's agenda while staying close to the needs of the organization. There is a kind of double contracting needed—once with the organization, and again with the client, in the light of the organization's needs. Clearly, in the triangular relationship between the client, coach, and organization there is potential for divergence and splitting. This might, for example, happen if the organization is using coaching as a means of controlling a problematic individual and attempting to use the coach to collude in this process. There is a danger of the coach being "set up" by the organization and failing either the organization or the client. For example, I was once asked by the trading arm of an investment bank to work with a male client who had been accused of bullying. It was made clear to me that if he did not improve his behaviour through a set number of coaching sessions, he would be sacked and so would I! The issue I then began working on with the angry client, who did not want to be coached, was whether it was possible for us to contract for work together in this coercive, even bullying, organization. Fortunately, using this frame in my negotiations with the client allowed us to work at the reasons for his anger and that of the organization. The outcome was that he decided to leave the organization of his own accord. While always holding open to myself the possibility of refusing to agree a contract if I felt my authority as a coach was compromised, I have never actually needed to do so.
- The second issue is about confidentiality, as the line manager can feel legitimized, by virtue of a contract with the coach, to ask the coach for progress reports on the client without his or her knowledge. It is important in the contracting stage to attempt to rule this out as a possibility further down the track by telling the client and manager together that any progress reports for the manager will be created by the coach and client together, not by the coach alone. Even if the manager does contact the coach for a report, he or she would need to be

reminded of the original agreement, as this is essential to the integrity of work with the client. I have, however, found it useful in these circumstances to ask the manager what has happened in the organization that has made him or her want feedback about coaching progress now, as the response to this question can yield valuable information both about the client and about the organization. It can often be tricky for the coach at this point to make a judgement about what is in the best interests of the client and organization, and this needs to be decided on a case-by-case basis with the help of the external supervision that all coaches need.

• Last, there is the issue of evaluation, which is becoming increasingly important as part of the professionalization of the field of coaching (Berglas, 2002; Rolph, 2004). Organizations are increasingly asking coaches to give evidence of the effectiveness of their methods and will often ask how the success of coaching an individual client will be assessed. A coach working within a process consultancy framework should not have too much difficulty with this, in that negotiation of methods of evaluation would usually be inbuilt at the contracting stage as expectations of the outcome of coaching are discussed with the client and their manager, if involved. During the first few sessions the coach would work carefully with the client to articulate their goals from coaching and, where possible, specify these in behavioural terms, even though goals will shift and change over time. For example, if the client says they want to become more confident, the coach would ask "How would this show?"; "In which situations?"; "What difference would this make to your leadership?"; "Who would notice?"; and "How would they show that they had noticed?" And, at review points, the coach would remind the client of the last goals set and the expected behavioural indices of change in order to evaluate success and set new goals and new indices.

Interventions in the organization

If one has a background as an organizational consultant and is extending this into executive coaching, the idea of engaging directly with the organization is not an unusual thing to do. However, if one has a background as a psychotherapist who has previously focused on the inner world of the patient or client, this can feel like breaking a taboo. My experience is that it can be enormously liberating and illuminating to have direct experience of the "third party in the wings".

I have used three kinds of intervention:

- Additional services to support coaching to the individual. At The Tavistock Consultancy Service, we call this "Coaching Plus" as depicted in Figure 6. These additional services include 360 Degree Feedback interviews with direct reports, peers, bosses, and other stakeholders the client works with; observation of the client in the workplace; team coaching.
- Feedback to the organization about themes from coaching, where more than one client is involved.
- Working with the whole organization from the platform of coaching.

I would like to take you through a practical account of using these modes of intervention, some of the opportunities and dilemmas they present and illustrate how I have managed them.

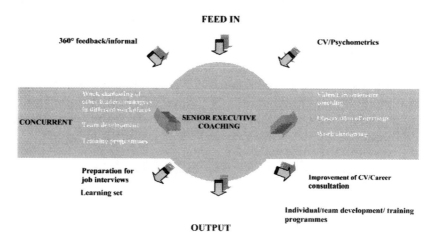

Figure 6. "Coaching plus" – senior executive coaching (copyright Tavistock Consultancy Service 2002).

Additional services to support coaching

While this does not happen with every client, for some who are feeling particularly stuck or who seem lacking in feedback about their impact, progress, or potential in the organization, it can be very helpful to gather additional data about them. The added benefit is of the active involvement of a neutral third party, the coach, through which members of the organization can communicate about the individual and about the organization. Then the coach is no longer the "third party in the wings" or hidden, from the perspective of the organization.

360 Degree Feedback interviews[10]

These are so called because they offer the client the possibility of feedback from multiple or all-round perspectives. They can be conducted by the coach face to face or by telephone and set out to gather feedback about the client in specific areas chosen by him or her. The responses are confidential and the feedback given to the client anonymously. In carrying out the interviews the coach can test out a variety of hypotheses about the organization and the relationship between the client, the organization, and the issues brought. If it is possible to pose systemic questions, for example, "Why do you think your organization fails to give praise and appreciation?", the interviews can shift thinking in those being interviewed and so have the potential for greater mileage. The impact of doing these interviews can be powerful in that members of the organization are alerted to the client's need and wish for personal development and become subtly co-opted into the process, becoming monitors or evaluators of progress. They can be interviewed again at a later stage to tap into this. It can also create an opportunity for the client to relate to the respondents differently following the interviews, when new conversations have taken place via the third party involvement.

Observation of the client in the workplace

I have found this useful when a client is having difficulties in specific settings or in particular relationships; for example, chairing meetings. While others present can feel initially self-conscious about the presence of the coach in the room, this quickly disappears. It is important to clearly contract with all those present and explain about the purpose of the observation, which is primarily to assist the client, not to observe others or consult to the team or meeting. It can be helpful to invite them to privately feed back their ideas on the client to you as coach during or after the meeting. Also, one can offer to give general feedback about the meeting if requested. A variation on this pattern is "real time feedback", or coaching during the meeting. This entails setting up twenty-minute breaks at regular intervals throughout the meeting to share feedback on specific behaviours.

For example, I was once asked to help a client be less directive in the team meetings he led as he was trying to be more open, inclusive, and to say less, but his team still found him overbearing. My feedback throughout the day-long meeting was to what extent he was managing to achieve his aims and how and in what ways he could do more, taking account of the team dynamic of which he was not fully aware. In well-entrenched behaviour patterns like those of my client and his team, the disruption of my presence and frequent breaks were needed to create some capacity for them all to reflect on the stimuli that led him to be so controlling and for others to let him. The relief of all was apparent at the end of the day and I was subsequently invited to get involved in team coaching.

Team coaching

Clients often ask a coach to work with their team, but this request should be viewed with caution. The reason is that working with the client's team challenges the paired relationship the coach has with the client in various ways.

- It will be difficult for other members of the team to trust the coach; they will tend to believe that the coach will see the world and them through the client's eyes.
- It can be difficult for the coach to challenge the client in front of the team.

- The client often has an agenda which is about "licking the team into shape" his or her way, rather than offering a consultation or coaching to the team as a whole. This might be valuable to the team but it might not be experienced that way and a fight/flight dynamic (Bion, 1961) can emerge.
- A different skill set and personal valency (Bion, 1961) is involved in team coaching, which involves an understanding of group dynamics and group facilitation; it is not simply a matter of scaled-up one-to-one coaching.

Thus, a very effective coach can be rendered "incompetent" working with the client's team. I usually ask a colleague in my team to take up team coaching for my client and we then work together on the issues involved. I have found that this releases feedback about the client and the organization that is valuable in the coaching; and often the colleague continues to act as a resource to the team and more widely in the organization.

Giving feedback to the organization

If one is working with more than one senior client but not the boss in an organization, or if the coach is working with colleagues coaching other clients, it can be very useful to feed back some of the themes from this work in the organization, without breaching individual confidentiality and with the permission of the clients concerned. Some organizations do not ask for or welcome this, whereas for others it can be part of the coaching contract. I would see the lack of interest in some organizations as connected to the way coaching can be seen as an "executive perk" and a cut-off or privatized form of personal development. Even in these circumstances, I would make a big effort to find opportunities to feed back on organizational themes. The reasons would be two-fold:

- so as to understand the organization better in order to enhance the coaching of individuals;
- to give feedback to the organization that they might not otherwise have and that might enhance organizational development.

For example, I was working with five clients in an investment bank and became aware of shared themes in the work with the individuals that did not seem to be taken up by the organization. The Human Resources department sponsored the coaching but did not have a way of tapping into general feedback on themes from coaching. I asked for quarterly appointments with the HR director. I discovered that, even though he had not sought it out, he was interested in hearing feedback from me as it might help the bank hold on to its high performers who were being coached. I offered feedback about their problems in developing strategic thinking, dilemmas experienced by women in senior leadership roles, and difficulties in managing poor performance. This led to the development of specific training modules for senior staff as well as thinking about flexible work packages for men and women. In return, I heard about various aspects of organizational strategy that I had not picked up on from individual clients. It continues to be a valuable interchange that the clients themselves see as a useful channel of communication to the organization through me.

In other situations, where I have been working at CEO and Board director level, I have been able to feed back themes that potentially impact organizational strategy as a whole.

Working with the whole organization from the platform of coaching

My experience of doing this is that it is usually difficult. First, one ideally needs to be working at CEO or Board level to have any impact on the organization as a whole, but, even then, the pairing relationship can get in the way as I have already suggested above (under team coaching). The clients tend to be reluctant to extend or share the one-to-one relationship more widely, except perhaps with their immediate team. This appears partly due to the need they have for exclusive support, given the isolation, vulnerability, and frustration of the leadership role. My experience is that more extended work is likely to grow from an initial contract—which includes coaching amongst other activities—and then coaching itself facilitates the development of other forms of intervention. The role can then be seen more clearly as organizational consultant, or resource to the organization as a whole, rather than just to an individual leader.

For example, I had an initial contact from a head teacher about help for an under-performing senior management team, following a negative inspection result. When I met the head teacher, he seemed lacking in confidence in his own ability to lead the school's recovery and he said the senior management team morale was low. The first phase of my work was a development needs analysis of the team. I made several recommendations about team develop-ment, including coaching for the head teacher. From this, and over time, a range of other interventions developed; coaching for other members of the team; team coaching; assistance with selection of new team members, including ideas for the interview process; design of and participation in a conference for students; input to business planning . During the next two years, the school improved its performance greatly and was assessed positively when it was inspected again. The head teacher and his team were praised for demonstrating good leadership and management. In all this, and despite the organizational consultancy frame, my primary relation-ship was with the head teacher, the person in the ultimate leader-ship role. All the interventions needed to have reference to his vision for the school. This did not mean that it went unchallenged but this was done in one-to-one coaching. Other staff often sought opportunities to give me feedback on the head's vision, strategy, and behaviour, and it was then important to reflect on the meaning of this and ensure that I was not being used inappropriately as substitute management in the organization. At points like these, it was useful to involve other colleagues in the work where my paired relationship with the head teacher would have got in the way; for example, coaching one of the deputy heads on his future develop-ment into headship; coaching for a very junior member of staff; team coaching for a member of the management team.

Conclusions: the confident organization

In this chapter I have described executive coaching as a variety of organizational consultancy from a conceptual, practical, and ethical point of view. My tendency is to think of executive coaching as the form of organizational consultancy that is currently acceptable to organizations, given the current climate of fragility in and around them. It appears that the pairing relationship of client and coach is the kind of relationship that has the most potential for promoting creativity and growth of leaders in organizations. I would say that, in order to help the leader to develop his or her confidence and effectiveness, coaching needs to take account of the "third party in the wings", or organization where the client works. This is so that the client does not use coaching to turn away from the organization to the privatized pairing of coach and client and thus avoid his or her relatedness to the organization. The coach needs to help the client face into it and manage the uncertainties. Then there is some possibility that, in developing the leader's personal confidence, this will also help to develop a sense of confidence in the organization as a whole. The confident organization is more likely to be able to be creative, take risks, survive, and grow in the future.

Notes

1. The Tavistock Consultancy Service (TCS) is a unique organizational consultancy unit within a National Health Service Trust in the UK. It works to develop organizational health using a systems-psychodynamic framework. Its clients are from the public, private, and voluntary sectors. Services include senior executive coaching, top team development, organizational interventions, research, and training. Clare Huffington is the current Director of TCS.
2. See also the chapter in this book by Gordon Lawrence.
3. This should equally apply to clients coming from an organization but paid for by themselves, perhaps without the knowledge of the organization; and one might wonder as a first hypothesis what it is about their organization that means that executives privatize their own learning and development. This does not mean that one would not attend to personal distress if it really did seem to be personal, but one would then perhaps be assisting the client to find psychotherapeutic support. This could take place alongside coaching, which fulfils a different function. Indeed, one might say that the coach has, as a goal of coaching, the improvement of the client's ability to think and act systemically about issues that are initially personal; and indeed part of the coaching task is to help the client to read their emotions in this way, as intelligence about the organization (Armstrong, 2004).

4. All case examples used in this chapter do not concern real clients but are an amalgam of material from a number of clients. Names, details, and organizations have been changed to protect client confidentiality.
5. They make this split for perfectly sensible governance reasons but I am suggesting here that it also serves a psychological function in the organization.
6. See also the chapter in this book by Angela Eden.
7. Of course, it would have been possible to have explored it in many other equally valid ways.
8. See also the chapter in this book by Marlene Spero.
9. See also the chapter in this book by Miranda Alcock that concerns a case of this kind.
10. See also the chapter in this book by Richard Kwiatkowski on the use of psychometrics in coaching.

References

Armstrong, D. (1995). The analytic object in organizational work: Occasional Paper, The Tavistock Consultancy Service.

Armstrong, D. (1997). The "institution in the mind": reflections on the relation of psychoanalysis to work with organizations. *Free Associations*, 7(41): 1–14.

Armstrong, D. (2004). Emotions in organizations: disturbance or intelligence? In: C. Huffington, D. Armstrong, W. Halton, L. Hoyle, & J. Pooley (Eds.), *Working Below the Surface: The Emotional Life of Contemporary Organizations* (pp. 11–27). London: Karnac.

Berglas, S. (2002). The very real dangers of executive coaching. *Harvard Business Review*, June: 87–92.

Bion, W. R. (1961). *Experiences in Groups and Other Papers*. London: Tavistock.

Blom, H. (2004). Personal communication.

Campbell, D., Draper, R., & Huffington, C. (1988). *Teaching Systemic Thinking*. London: Karnac

Campbell, D., Draper, R., & Huffington, C. (1989). *A Systemic Approach to Consultation*. London: Karnac.

Coffey, E., Huffington, C., & Thomson, P. (1999). *The Changing Culture of Leadership: Women Leaders' Voices*. London: The Change Partnership.

Cooper, A., & Dartington, T. (2004). The vanishing organization: organizational containment in a networked world. In: C. Huffington,

D. Armstrong, W. Halton, L. Hoyle, & J. Pooley (Eds.), *Working Below the Surface: The Emotional Life of Contemporary Organizations* (pp. 127–150). London: Karnac.

Cronen, V., Pearce, W., & Tomm, K. (1985). A dialectical view of personal change. In: K. Gergen & K. Davis (Eds.), *The Social Construction of the Person* (pp. 203–224). New York: Springer-Verlag.

Goleman, D. (1998). *Working with Emotional Intelligence.* London: Bloomsbury.

Hieker, C. (2003). Reflexive questions in a coaching context. Unpublished paper.

Huffington, C., Cole, C., & Brunning, H. (1997). *A Manual of Organizational Development: The Psychology of Change.* London: Karnac.

Huffington, C., James, K., & Armstrong, D. (2004.) What is the emotional cost of distributed leadership? In: C. Huffington, D. Armstrong, W. Halton, L. Hoyle, & J. Pooley (Eds.), *Working Below the Surface: The Emotional Life of Contemporary Organizations* (pp. 67–82). London: Karnac.

Huffington, C., Armstrong, D., Halton, W., Hoyle, L., & Pooley, J. (Eds.) (2004). *Working Below the Surface: The Emotional Life of Contemporary Organizations.* London: Karnac.

Hutton, J., Bazalgette, J., & Reed, B. (1997). Organization-in-the-mind. In: J. E. Neumann, K. Kellner, & A. Dawson-Shepherd (Eds.), *Developing Organizational Consultancy* (pp. 113–126). London: Routledge.

Jaques, E. (1989). *Requisite Organization: The CEO's Guide to Creative Structure and Leadership.* Arlington, VA: Cason Hall.

Kilburg, R. (2002). *Executive Coaching: Developing Managerial Wisdom in a World of Chaos.* Washington, DC: American Psychological Association.

Miller, E. J., & Rice, A. K. (1967). *Systems of Organization: Task and Sentient Systems and Their Boundary Control.* London: Tavistock.

Obholzer, A. (with Sarah Miller) (2004). Leadership, followership, and facilitating the creative workplace. In: C. Huffington, D. Armstrong, W. Halton, L. Hoyle, & J. Pooley (Eds.), *Working Below the Surface: The Emotional Life of Contemporary Organizations* (pp. 33–48). London: Karnac.

O'Neill, M. B. (2000). *Executive Coaching with Backbone and Heart.* San Francisco, CA: Jossey-Bass.

Peltier, B. (2001). *The Psychology of Executive Coaching: Theory and Application.* New York: Brunner-Routledge.

Pogue-White, K. (2001). Applying learning from experience. The intersection of psychoanalysis and organizational role consultation. In: L. Gould, L. Stapley, & M. Stein (Eds.), *The Systems-Psychodynamics of Organizations* (pp. 17–43). London: Karnac.

Reed, B., & Bazalgette, J. (2003). *Organizational Role Analysis*. London: Grubb Institute.

Rolph, J. (2004). Standard issue. *People Management*, 11 March.

Sandler, C. (2003). Executive coaching. Unpublished presentation given at Reflection Day held by The Tavistock Consultancy Service.

Schein, E. (1988). *Process Consultation, Volume I: Its Role in Organizational Development*. Reading, MA: Addison-Wesley.

Schein, E. (1990). A general philosophy of helping: process consultation. *Sloan Management Review Reprint Series*, 31(Spring 3): 57–64.

Schmidt, W. H., & Johnston, A. V. (1970). A continuum of consultancy styles. Unpublished paper.

Tomm, K. (1987). Interventive interviewing: Part II. Reflexive questioning as a means to enable self-healing. *Family Process*, 26: 167–183.

Tomm, K. (1988). Interventive interviewing: Part III. Intending to ask lineal, circular, strategic or reflexive questions. *Family Process*, 27: 1–15.

Whitmore, J. (1994). *Coaching for Performance*. San Diego, CA: Pfeiffer.

CHAPTER THREE

Coaching women for senior executive roles: a societal perspective on power and exclusion

Angela Eden

> "A state of being neither in the boundary of one's own culture, nor fully a member of other, but always on the boundary"
>
> Sitaram & Prosser, 1998

I choose to open with this quotation as it encapsulates the dilemma that women have in achieving recognition at senior levels in organizations. I want to reflect on matters that affect the inclusion or exclusion of women in senior executive roles. I would like to examine what aspirations women might have, any barriers that might limit their success and explore this in the context of institutional sexism. These issues have to be raised as part of the landscape when working with women in a coaching role. In thinking about the organizational environment I am writing this chapter not as a guide to coaching, but taking a reflective stance and asking "why", and "what" does that mean for a coaching relationship, given the current societal pressures on women's performance and careers.

Current issues related to seniority, promotion, and board profiles

I hold two parallel images of the culture in organizations. In a traditional model, as people rise through the ranks, they are recognized for their skills and achievements. They are rewarded through promotion and increased status. However, there is also the shadow-side in organizations, where promotion is based on "corridor politics" and informal communication systems. Somewhere between these two polarities lies the reality for many people. However, there is increasing evidence that access to promotion is still not equally available to women, or to people from different backgrounds than the white, middle class, educated elite. This is a remarkable statement to make in the twenty-first century, but the evidence is there.

The Centre for Developing Women has researched the progress of women in FTSE 100 companies. By 2002, a milestone had been achieved. In a recent article they state that:

> The number of female directorships has reached 101, which is up by 20% on last year (101 women out of 1172 board places = 8.6% women). Passing this milestone is significant. However, whilst these results are better than before, there is still much to do. Girls are achieving the best results in schools and universities, but that is not reflected in their careers. Excellent women have been in the pipeline for long enough. Chairmen and CEOs are accountable for developing women in their companies and using their talent not just for the advantage of the companies but for the country. We urge companies to develop women.

> But progress is being made mostly in companies, which already had women directors. A third of women directors have titles (Baroness, Dame, Prof, Dr) compared to only a fifth of male directors. Do women still have to prove themselves with a title, whilst men are appointed on promise? [Singh & Vinnicombe, 2004]

The message is so clear that changes have to be made and UK government departments are charged with influencing that change to diverse representation at senior levels. The Civil Service focused on their own recruitment practice, and announced that within their sector women take up 26% of senior roles, compared to only 2% in the private sector. However, they recognize the need to encourage diversity in the boardrooms of private companies.

Harriet Harman wrote on the DTI website: "British boardrooms are one of the last remaining 'no-go' areas for women. We lag far behind the US, where business recognises the value of diversity and reflects on their boards the importance of employees and woman consumers".

Yet, in 2002, 60% of the top 100 companies had no women on their boards. Patricia Hewitt, Secretary of State for Trade and Industry and Minister for Women, followed this in 2003:

> It's obvious that far too many directors are still recruited by word of mouth, with the result that less than one percent of chairs are women and only six per cent of non-executive posts are held by women. Having more women and people from diverse backgrounds means that companies represent—and better understand—the customers they want to attract, leading to improved competitiveness and productivity. They also bring different skills and opinions to the board.

In this chapter I begin by asking why, with all the evidence, the market imperative, and a strong steer from the government, women are still not seen as natural leaders. This inevitably affects women's sense of their own potential, their ambition, achievement, and self-esteem. I would argue that working with a coach might help to decrease this drain of skills and increase the representation of women at senior levels in organizations, institutions and the government.

Understanding societal pressures

If the wider social system seems to exclude women so easily, then perhaps we need to ask whether there is a deeper, social unconscious at work that needs to be examined as a factor. I hold the premise that the existing power structure in organizations has a vested interest in being exclusive. This is visible in the way a system creates a power elite, then reinforces the barriers and thus creates exclusion. The concept of a "power elite" is used by Richard Zweigenhaft (1998), who proposes that thinking about access and exclusion is the essence of the issue. How can the power elite hold their power and why is it so difficult to share it, or include others?

I have considered a number of possible hypotheses that might shed some light on the phenomenon of institutional-level exclusion of women from holding senior positions.

First, there seems to be a myth that power is a limited resource and therefore it can be depleted. This belief system has a built-in self-centredness. It offers a rationale for senior people to acquire power in order to maintain their own position. It is as if they could not open the door to others in case their own elite position would be depleted. Inevitably, there is a vested interest in maintaining the exclusivity of their power base and a vested interest in excluding others, especially people who are, or appear to be, different.

Swingle (1974) suggests another exclusion hypothesis. He talks of a power addiction and describes the need for acceptance in an elite club. He argues that this craving for acceptance is deeply embedded into the Judeo-Christian culture of dependency and deference to authority. People learn that being accepted is being part of the hierarchy of power. It is possible to imagine how much satisfaction this could bring: to want success and then to achieve it by being included within the power elite. The additional expectation is to use this hard-won power to exclude others and to keep the walls of the bastion intact. Exclusion is therefore built into the system.

These ideas resonate with theories of early infant development, notably those of Klein (1957) and Winnicott (1958). This hypothesized desire for acceptance could be seen as part of an earlier, infantile hunger and be traced back within the unconscious drives. If the reward is difficult to achieve and if there is a struggle to get fed, or if the reward is withheld, then this only feeds the cyclical hunger–feeding–hunger pattern and makes the attainment of *the reward* even more valuable. This links to an addiction pattern of wanting, withholding, being rewarded, and thus could create a dependency. Having a long-term initiation before becoming accepted makes the achieved status even more desirable: this in itself feeds the desire (and the addiction) for even more acceptance. Evidence shows that this is not exclusively a male or a female response, as women in power also exclude others. Margaret Thatcher, as the first female prime minister in the UK, surrounded herself with a cabinet of male colleagues and failed to open the power base to other women.

Manfred Kets de Vries (1993) suggests that people seek power as a way of minimizing an unresolved sense of self and an unrealistic idea of potency. To relinquish power, or even to share it, may lead to a loss of identity, influence, affirmation, and can undermine sense of self, suggesting that holding on to power is a way of minimizing that potential loss.

Golembiewski (1995) points to the "simplicity of homogeneity" versus the "complexity of diversity", which confirms the argument that people with power want to stay with *the sameness*. If this were true, trying to shift the current power elite is a bigger task than we had imagined: for sharing a power base with women or people from differing backgrounds is a threat to that homogeneity. The data from the US is salutary, as it shows that the power base is still firmly conservative, despite forty years of civil rights' consciousness.

Zweigenhaft and Domhoff (1998) note that

> The fact is more than an irony, it is a dilemma. It combines with the dilemma of race to create a nation that celebrates equality of opportunity, but is, in reality, a bastion of class privilege and conservatism. Diversification, yes, but no change in class structure, no effect on the way power elite functions or on class structure itself, American individualism prevails. [p. 194]

They amalgamated surprising evidence about diversity and race, and gender. They conclude that women are reaching the Boardroom and are more likely to do so if they have an Ivy League education, have a middle class professional family background and a light skin tone, and share the prevailing ideology (Zweigenhaft & Domhoff, 1998, pp. 41–77).

Women's experience

Given this socio-political framework, we are better prepared to look at the profile of women at senior and board level in UK organizations. Cranfield's research (Singh & Vinnicombe, 2004) has found that certain industries (retail, pharmaceuticals, financial) have better female representation at senior levels and others (media, tobacco, energy) have fewer. It would be interesting to do a culture audit in those industries to develop a hypothesis about the reasons for these differences. It may be that some sectors are built on male models and that the "smart" industries realized they needed to represent their customer base.

In their book *The Changing Culture of Leadership*, Coffey, Huffington, and Thomson (1999) found that

> There are downstream reasons why having so few women exercising power and influence at the top of organizations is important. (. . .) One result of this lop-sidedness is that organizational cultures are being largely shaped by men. (. . .) This may actually be inhospitable to women, which in turn may mean that women do not thrive and may choose to leave. [p. 84]

Cranfield's research (Singh & Vinnicombe, 2004) quotes the following:

● "Women are proving their ability in education, as entrepreneurs and in the workplace. Against their success in these areas, the inability of boardrooms to include women among their number begins to look like sheer resistance."
Angela Ishmael, Diversity Consultant

● "There are a lot of extremely able women lawyers, but there aren't that many in the top management positions at law firms. To get to the top you really have to cut out of your life anything that's not important."
Lesley McDonagh, Lawyer

● "It is difficult for women juggling all sorts of priorities from families to careers. I have been very lucky in that I have been presented with opportunities and have gone for them—but I acknowledge there are problems for other women."
Denise Lewis, Group Director in the Telecommunications Industry

These issues are illustrated in the following vignette of a coaching relationship.[1]

Natalie was a contract manager in a large international finance firm. She decided to work with a coach because she was not passing promotion panels, though she was eminently qualified for her job. She wondered if her image or style was holding her back and wanted to address this in a coaching relationship outside the company. She noticed at client meetings, where she was client liaison for a critical contract, that she was well respected, gave good advice, was listened to, and felt valued. But, whenever she attended meetings with male colleagues, her role shifted and she felt sidelined. She discussed this with her manager, who thought she might be too sensitive, as there had been only praise from the client. She was encouraged to go for a promotion board, which was appropriate in the context of her work and her own peer group promotions.

She did not pass the promotion board, because the panel felt that she lacked gravitas. This prompted her to obtain some presentation skills training. She was referred to me as I had commercial experience, an interview and recruitment background, and a theatre-based training.

When we met I was struck by two contrasting images. She presented herself as a softly spoken young woman, well dressed in a "corporate uniform" of a dark suit and a pale shirt. Yet, her slight build and youthful look contrasted with a firm handshake and a sense of confidence when she spoke. As she described her work and her obvious pleasure in meeting the demands of her clients, I was confident that she had the skills and experience to move to a higher level in the company. In fact, she was already doing the work at the higher level, but that was not formally acknowledged.

At this stage, a difficult ethical dilemma emerged, which, as her coach, I had to address with my client. She needed to decide whether to challenge the male hegemony by standing on principle, or compromise in order to get the promotion by playing with the masquerade (Riviere, 1986).

In this case, as the job was important to her, she decided to change her image and prove something to herself without being too challenging of the company. We agreed that we would work on her interviewing skills as well as on the presentational image expected of a senior woman manager. My hypothesis was that her ability and image, although clothed in corporate-wear, were not really appreciated within her company. She looked young and lightweight, *as if* she could not carry the heaviness and gravitas of a senior role. This was compounded by her own inability to describe and celebrate her own achievements in an interview. Even though she worked well with the clients, she was not able, or willing, to find appropriate words to demonstrate this to the promotion panels.

As our work progressed, she learnt to rephrase her responses, lower her voice through practised exercises and changed the way she walked; she even bought new clothes.

I heard later, after our work had finished, that she had achieved the senior position. The feedback from the promotion board was that the panel were able to see past their own initial perception and hear a mature, talented, and able person, somebody who was in effect a high-achieving asset for the company.

As a coach, my response to this was ambivalent: initially, it is helpful to recognize organizational and cultural barriers. It is always gratifying when a client takes to the work and understands the rationale for change. However, it is also exasperating to be forced into changes that are made only in order to pacify other people's expectations. My client was already capable of doing her job: the coaching only helped her to be *seen as capable*. We were both willing to work with the constructs of the hegemony, because it made sense for that client at that point of her career. The work of the coach is to address this dilemma and to help the client decide whether they wish to stay with the organization.

In a 2004 exhibition ("Iron Ladies: Women in Thatcher's Britain") at the Women's Library in London, Dr Harriet Jones, the Curator, wrote:

Margaret Thatcher's rise to power was a reflection of the fact that many women of her generation were beginning to break through in the professions. Thatcher's papers reveal that like many women she had to overcome considerable prejudice and that she was at times deeply frustrated by "anti women" attitudes. In the 1980s the proportion of women in senior positions remained small. The more subtle barriers to promotion became better understood after the publication in 1990 of the report by the Hansard Society on *Women at the Top*, chaired by Lady Howe, which concluded that "for many women there is a glass ceiling blocking their aspirations, allowing them to see where they might go, but stopping them from arriving".

Visiting the exhibition and writing these amalgamated stories re-affirmed that sense of frustration, dealing with the barriers that inhibit women's advancement are not solely in the hands of women with ambition for senior roles, nor their coaches or mentors. The new data in *The Changing Culture of Leadership* (Coffey, Huffington, & Thomson, 1999) identifies a range of barriers that still operate. These are both systemic (e.g., recruitment practices) and attitudinal (e.g., myths about women's skills and abilities). Although coaching can be a helpful intervention in developing confidence, clarity, and focus, it is unlikely to have a direct influence on inherent sexism.

Coaching for what and how

I have indicated that women have to make choices about achieving senior posts. Even though the western industrialized world has had thirty years of political awareness about both conscious and unconscious sexism, there is still a power group that remains predominately male. This hegemony reinforces a conservative culture in which people prefer to work with their own familiar connections. This is epitomized by the male network of school–university–social lives and family connections. The women struggle against traditional perceptions, against the benchmark of the accepted male model of success. Some women try to be "male", some try to be "female", but the middle path of trying only to be *authentically oneself* can often lead to invisibility. Unconscious projections by other women, linked back to their own experience of their mothers, sisters, and friends, can exacerbate this struggle, as identified by Josefowitz:

> Women have different expectations of other women in high places than men have. They expect women to be their sisters, mothers and supporters, and the women who are hanging on by their fingernails are not always prepared to do that. We must change our expectations of women; we should show compassion for their loneliness. They may need support from us. [1980, p. 202]

In a recent article, Michael Maccoby (2004) has written about transference to a leader and the symbolic role that women might hold, which can have an impact on how women are being seen.

> Maternal transference: Usually draws on an earlier childhood relationship. The mother is often seen as both an authority figure and

as a giver of unconditional love. She is a protective figure who gives life and showers us with support, but she also is the first person to say no. [*ibid.*, pp. 77–85]

Maccoby describes a series of complex relationships about women in senior positions. Given the impact that unconscious perception and projection can have upon a relationship, it is no surprise that women hoping for senior roles may be distorted and damaged by these projections. If relationships with senior women are being filtered through a lens of memory of their mothers, grandmothers, or sisters, how can they develop a serious professional relationship in a workplace?

In the earlier part of this chapter I looked at the context, the influences, and the motivation for excluding or including women in the boardroom. Finally, we can return to the central theme of this book, which is the role and task of the coach. Women who want to progress have to consider many complex issues. If they expect a coach to help them with this, then the partnership needs to question a number of important assumptions. I use a series of questions, a sample of which is given below, that may help the client to consider the implications of taking up a senior role. Each question may take the coach and client towards enquiry and each answer may bring some clarity about issues such as ambition, personal values, identity, or self-awareness.

- What is your experience of being a woman in this organization?
- Is there a value system in the organizations that makes you uncomfortable?
- What would you have to do to fit in to a male hegemony?
- What would you have to do to fight and change the existing culture?
- How much are you prepared to compromise?
- What might be the consequences of being a woman with a higher profile?
- Are you prepared to be under stronger scrutiny?
- Can you find your own authenticity in the role?
- Do you want to stay in this organization?

- If nothing changed, are you willing to leave?
- If you left this job, would you want to be employed or self employed?
- Could you start your own company based on your own value system?
- How many allies (both men and women) do you have inside and outside this organization?

These may be probing questions, and infer that the relationship between coach and client is robust enough to explore possible answers together as this work needs to be done within a boundary of mutual trust, honesty, and respect. The work should also acknowledge the reality of the social system and the unconscious influences within us, as these relate to our identity and our need for recognition.

Strategies for inclusion

This last section loops back to a socio-technical perspective of change. When coaching women it is an important task to help them project their skills and to take authority for their own performance. The shadow side of being a confident and assertive woman is that her acceptance into seniority has to be supported by a change in the wider system.

Here we look at organizational changes that might influence a shift towards a more open culture of inclusion. Assuming that organizations are truly committed to having women work more productively at senior levels, a new set of principles, policies, and practice could be considered and adopted.

- *Look at language and unconscious communications*
  Because of employment legislation, formal policies are written to be inclusive; however, in reality, it is the informal communication and behaviour that needs attention. If organizations look at the way they communicate, it becomes obvious that they tend to exclude, rather than include, diversity at the senior levels of hierarchies. Unwritten rules are powerful and help to exclude people, as they tend to create double standards

and inconsistencies that are illusive by nature and therefore difficult to challenge.

- *Consider prejudice*
  As prejudice is based either on a lack of knowledge or on a set of beliefs based on incorrect knowledge, it is important to disentangle the belief systems that may bias judgement in relation to recruitment and promotion.
- *Limit the stress*
  Women at senior levels often find themselves as the "lone voice" within their organization and "in the spotlight" at the same time, and this increases the level of stress. Boards and senior teams need to be aware of that stress and build supporting systems, e.g., mentoring, networks, external development, and to recognize the role of work–life balance.
- *Coaching senior men*
  Coaching senior men might be a useful intervention in introducing change within organizational culture. If a male-defined hegemony is part of the problem, then teaching men to think in a broader terms might be part of the answer. Fairholm (1994) suggests that in order to challenge the old models and culture of control, prejudice, and exclusion leaders should also learn about emotional intelligence, co-operation, power sharing, and ethics.
- *Horizontal allocation of resources*
  Build egalitarian decision teams based on linear, horizontal rather than vertical, allocation of resources. If vertical lines of management are reduced, then the distance to power holders is also reduced. Senior managers can become more inclusive, both in relation to their peer group and towards people who report to them.
  Coffey, Huffington, and Thomson (1999) recommend that companies "ensure that bright young people are chosen to work in the 'cabinet office' of the executive team, include young women as well as young men".

Strategies for women in senior executive roles

This section addresses some of the isolation that women experience in senior roles. Most women appreciate the support and sponsorship of a more senior mentor; this should be somebody who can open up access, give visibility, and share knowledge in the organization. Opening the door to give others a power base is an important step.

If the mentor comes from a different cultural group, this could be helpful to both parties as it can address the inherent power dynamics between men and women, age and youth, black and white. The mentor can also learn from the relationship and it might help to shift prejudice and ignorance.

Women who move up into senior positions need to make use of different networks: above, below, and with their own peers. Building these alliances is invaluable for obtaining support and feedback. Additionally, it is important to acquire the expertise, requisite skills, and knowledge essential for the senior role, and this is the traditional way to achieve personal authority and status. There is also a new trend, based on an alternative set of skills: creativity and co-operative learning. This is increasingly seen and acknowledged as the "new" way for organizations to succeed. The irony of this "new" leadership model is that these very skills tend to be naturally within the repertoire of women's set of skills.

Concluding with the paradigm shift

This chapter took a wide perspective in discussing coaching women for senior roles. My argument is that women can fulfil leadership roles, but have to do so within a culture that is unconsciously disabling them. Coaching may be one way of contributing to improved self-esteem and increased confidence as part of realizing one's potential. In looking for strategies, I have explored some of the wider socio-psychological and cultural arenas that we need to work in.

Adler (1974) leads us to think about the necessary steps for breaking down the barriers of exclusion. In his chapter on "Beyond Cultural Identity" he describes the transitional place, standing between old and new, a boundary position. He constructs an image of the "new" leader, not defined as either male or female, who is always ready to learn, is responsive to change, and tolerant of different cultural forms. These characteristics can be developed in a coaching relationship.

We need to work towards a new, diverse power base, made up equally of men and women, different cultural and educational backgrounds, and diverse experiences, which will set the criteria for success from a position of equality and inclusion.

Should this shift occur in the leadership of organizations, it might benefit not only that specific place of work, but also their customer base and the wider society, and we would see a diversity of styles, a variety of cultural expectations, and a better representation of the international aspects in our world.

Note

1. The identifying details have been altered to maintain anonymity of the organization and the individual. The coaching contract ran for six sessions over three months.

References

Adler, P. S. (1974). Beyond cultural identity: Reflections upon cultural and multicultural man. In: R. W. Brislon (Ed.), *Topics in Culture Learnings, 2* (pp. 23–40). Honolulu, HI: East–West Centre.

Coffey, D., Huffington, C., & Thomson, P. (1999). *The Changing Culture of Leadership: Women Leaders' Voices*. London: Change Partnership.

Department of Trade and Industry (DTI). Women and Equality Unit. www.dti.gov.uk

Fairholm, G. W. (1994). *Leadership and the Culture of Trust*. London: Praeger.

Golembiewski, R. T. (1999). *Managing Diversity in Organizations*. Tuscaloosa, CA: University of Alabama Press.

"Iron Ladies: Women in Thatcher's Britain" (October 2004–April 2005). Exhibition at The Women's Library. Curator: Harriet Jones. www.thewomenslibrary.ac.uk

Josefowitz, N. (1980). *Paths to Power: A Woman's Guide from First Job to Top Executive*. London: Columbus.

Kets de Vries, M. F. R. (1993). *Leaders, Fools and Impostors: Essays on the Psychology of Leadership*. San Francisco, CA: Jossey-Bass.

Maccoby, M. (2004). Why people follow the leader: The power of transference. *Harvard Business Review, Autumn*: 77–85.

Riviere, J. (1986). Womanliness as a masquerade. In: V. Burgin, J. Donald, & C. Caplan (Eds.), *Formations of Fantasy* (pp. 35–44). London: Methuen.

Singh, V., & Vinnicombe, S. (2004). Why so few women directors in the top UK boardrooms? Evidence and theoretical explanations. *Journal of Corporate Governance: An International Review*, 12(4): 479–488. Centre for Developing Women Cranfield School of Management. Business Leaders, Cranfield School of Management.

Sitaram, K. S., & Prosser, M. H. (Eds.) (1998). *Civic Discourse: Multiculturalism, Cultural Diversity, and Global Communications*, Vol. 1. London: Ablex.

Swingle, P. G (1974). The management of power

Winnicott, D. W. (1958). *Collected Papers*. London: Tavistock.

Zweigenhaft, R., & Domhoff, G. (1998). *Diversity in the Power Elite: Have Women and Minorities Reached the Top?* New Haven, CT: Yale University Press.

PART II
THE ANATOMY OF SYSTEMS-PSYCHODYNAMIC COACHING

CHAPTER FOUR

Executive coaching, unconscious thinking, and infinity

W. Gordon Lawrence

Frames for thinking within the role of the executive coach

T he purpose of this chapter is to affirm the importance and to situate unconscious and infinite thinking in the context of executive coaching.

In her clear exposition of executive coaching, Halina Brunning shows the multi-factorial holistic process whereby individual clients identify the resources to pursue their goals and enhance their potential for attaining them. The areas of counselling, qualification, professional development, business context, organizational dynamics, psychotherapy, and personal development are identified and elaborated in her seminal article (Brunning, 2001). These domains are systemically inter-related and, while they are not addressed directly, like a checklist, they form the background to the actual conversational field that the coach and client evoke in the course of the coaching sessions. These domains constitute the basis for the *explicate* conversation that evolves between client and coach. At the same time, there will be an *implicate*—below the surface of consciousness—conversation that, one hopes, will also be attended to and addressed. Indeed, one could go as far as to say this exploration *must* be addressed as well if the coaching process is to have a lasting effect on the inner conceptions of the client.

The task of coaching will be examining how the client is managing herself[1] in her role by exercising her authority and her ability to follow a task leader in the work system. This *ficelle* of exploration can always be returned to when explorations of unconscious and infinite material proves too daunting.

The psychological basis on which the role of an executive coach is entered and made moment-by-moment in the coaching session is critical. In this chapter the focus is on the coach, as opposed to the client. This reverse perspective is to highlight the personal, psychological requirements that allow individuals to develop and mature in the role of an executive coach.

The working hypothesis is that the executive coach must pay attention to how they are developing and growing themselves in their role if they are to act as competent practitioners of executive coaching.

The development of a frame of values, beliefs, and knowledge, and learning when to go beyond them, is a life-long task for any professional worker. The frame is rarely fixed or absolute, for it tends to expand as more is experienced and learned. The frame depends on how much the coach is able to address reality as it is being presented by other people, and the coach testing how much of that reality she can bear, judging how much it is based in psychotic thinking or not. So, the frame that develops is a result of an oscillation between *"what we think we know"*, based on our experience and reflection, and *"what we guess we cannot bear to think"*. It is on how to begin to bear to think the unthinkable that is the essence of this chapter.

This oscillation between knowing and not-knowing is the personal drama that is mirroring the perennial, human struggle involved in acquiring finite knowledge through accessing the infinite. "Accessing" is being used here in the sense of being available for no-thinking and thinking. To get into this position requires the cultivation of a *mental disposition*, or a frame of mind, that is curious, has the capacity for wonderment, and is alive to the possibilities of thinking through mystery. It also depends on our ability to attain the limits of comprehension. Is this attainment the beginnings of wisdom? It is only when these limits are attained, when the unknown comes into sight, that we begin to think of the significance of our emotional experience, to explore its complexity, to put into thinking, thought, and words the embryonic meaning, which has been intuited and understood, so that what has been found can be communicated to others with truthful conviction.

The assumption is that there will be a body of knowledge that each executive coach will have acquired in the course of their own personal and professional development. They will be familiar with management, will know something of counselling skills and all the other domains that Brunning (2001) has detailed. However, the knowledge is valueless unless it has been internalized in the sense of knowing *of* rather than knowing *about*. Until the coach has developed an internal world in which to receive and make that knowledge intimately his own, any knowledge will be inert and lifeless. The mental disposition is to continue the process of coming to know that which has hitherto belonged to the unconscious and the infinite.

Another working hypothesis offered here is that the executive coach must feel that they deserve to be in the role. They have to give themselves inner sanction to carry out the role of coach. If they do not, a whole train of falsehoods inevitably gets established for the particular coach to justify their holding on to the role. The point is that the simple lie gives rise to more complex lies, until a point is reached where the coach can no longer distinguish between truth and lie. More particularly, the authority to carry out a coaching role comes from (i) the "client", who is the subject of the coaching; (ii) from any peers of the coach, professional colleagues and the like; and (iii), as has been indicated from the coaches themselves. When the client is sent by the organizational system (iv), not a totally free choice, these issues (i–iv) will have to be addressed directly until the coach feels the client has given himself authority to be in the role of client.

Irrespective of the legal arrangements for providing coaching, it is the authority of the client and the coach to take up their respective roles that is most important. The client's sanction has to be continually earned by the coach. However, the basis on which executive coach came into the role will have an effect on the nature of the client sanction and on how the coaching role is fulfilled.

Perhaps the most important aspect of role and authority is the mental disposition already alluded to. The mental disposition is orientated towards truth and the avoidance of lie because phenomena—

the thing in itself -it can never be known absolutely. At best, we can have approximations of the truth. Nevertheless, it is possible to hold on to a mental posture orientated towards truth seeking.

The mental disposition of truth seeking is posited on the way reality is viewed and construed. Truth seeking means to question the cultural assumptions of our society and its related institutions. This means disentangling the cobweb of myths and mysteries in order to differentiate between what is conventionally agreed to be reality and what constitutes reality for the scrutinizing individual.

Scientific objectivity conventionally requires that individual subjectivity be suppressed and controlled. Alternatively, it is being proposed that objectivity is essentially the clarification of individual subjectivity in relation to others (Lawrence, 1979, p. 235). Objectivity, which civilization values as an ideal, is, in fact, consensually agreed subjectivity.

In this process, however, as the individual tries to regulate the boundary between his inner world and the outer world of conventionally agreed reality, she is confronting those very cultural forms that provide the defensive structures that satisfy her primitive needs. Therefore, in working out her own definition of reality, by questioning others' definitions, the individual gives up certainty and security by substituting uncertainty and insecurity. This is, inevitably, a lonely position to occupy.

To hold on to this rigorous idea is the way that the coach manages herself in her role *vis à vis* the client. This means being vigilant about how one conducts the coaching session, for the chances are that the client will be imbued with the conventional reality of their own culture. It is the coach's questioning and curious attitude that can cause the clients, in turn, to question their carefully maintained structures of belief. More accurately, it is the ruminative, speculative, wondering, non-confrontational qualities of the coach that can provide a safe, containing climate for the exploration of conventional reality.

Empathy

Essential to this mental disposition is the cultivation of empathy. This is the ability to see the other as one would see oneself by imagining what it might be to be the other. The truth of the other will always be a conjecture and can never be known absolutely, but despite this constraint an attempt has to be made to attain it.

Clearly, empathy relies on the ability to have the compassion to be able to identify with the other's suffering. That means being alert to whatever comedies and tragedies may have befallen them and to understand the fateful absurdity of human existence. It means, it can be hypothesized, that the coach has to have attained what Symington (1986, p. 242) calls the "tragic position". This, crudely, is to situate one's private troubles in their historical context; to see that one's depression and paranoia, etc., is not just because of mother, or whoever, but because of the social situation that mother was in. If the coach has had similar experiences and had undertaken the inner reparative work of attaining the "tragic position", she will be receptive to the catastrophe of such events and intuit the meaning from the client's perspective. Coaches cannot have experienced everything, but they can imagine, and, therefore, identify with the other's experience; they can enter into their client's world.[2]

Bion (1992, p. 125) pointed out that compassion and truth are both senses that mankind wants to express. Each human being wants the other to be aware of their own compassion while dealing with each other. Similarly, truth is something wanted to be communicated and wanted to be received from others.

Since a coaching process is about the development of the mind in relation to the work (and life) situation, it is critical for the coach to develop empathy and understanding, so that she can accommodate the social *milieu* of the client in her psychic world.

A *leitmotif* of the coaching process is the client developing an empathic relationship for himself in his role. Clients have the evolving task of learning to love themselves in their role, while recognizing their personal flaws of character. This self-compassion can be difficult to achieve, even to conceptualize. Once it is achieved, the client can take up a more objective stance to himself by identifying the more unpleasant and hateful aspects of his own role performance. A leader, for example, who finds himself holding a totalitarian state-of-mind, comes to recognize his being driven into this invidious position by others seeking satisfaction of their certainty and security needs in a turbulent business world (Lawrence, 1995a,b, 1997). This position of distance, or look of distance, is how individuals stand outside their psychic skins and look at themselves (cf. Turquet, 1975).[3] But this hinges on the client's ability to be attentive to the others in his surroundings, relying on his ability to see and his ability to feel-into and feel-with the others in his social milieu.

Thinking in the role of coach

The authority of the role of an executive coach, the fashion in which it is taken up and carried out, together with the linked mental disposition of empathy, etc., come together in the orientation to the practice of coaching in the actual session.

This mental disposition is connected with the function of thinking in the coaching session. Armstrong (1998) has made a useful distinction between what he calls "Thinking 1" and "Thinking 2". The former is when thought or thoughts require a thinker and owe their existence to a thinker. They are capable of being "owned", can be manipulated, and require exegesis to explain and justify them. Such thought might be called accepted or culturally enshrined thought.

The latter, Thinking 2, is the opposite in that thought or thoughts are not the product of thinking. Rather, thinking is an apparatus that evolves for the communication of thoughts. They, therefore, do not require a thinker for their existence. But a thinker is needed to "receive" them and "publish" them like a wireless receiver, which does the same with radio waves. The former is prior to thought, the latter to thinking. The difference between these two verbs is critical, for it is to concentrate more on the wave function of thinking and less on thoughts as particles, to borrow from quantum physics.

Armstrong offers a tentative answer to his question: what kind of entity is thoughts? In Thinking 2, thoughts are objects of emotional experience that make themselves felt as a presence initially, as something absent, not there, or a no-thought. They emerge from the not-known and are felt as a limitation or a frustration, a terror, or a mystery. When this not-known begins to take shape it is as if it communicates with oneself. This speaking to oneself is in relation to the context one finds oneself in, be it group, organization, the social world, or the universe. Thought, in Thinking 2, is always contextual and belongs to the system one finds oneself in. It is not a "private" thought, but belongs to the shared environment of others. A dream, for example, is conventionally seen to be a private possession but, in fact, is rooted in the environment of the dreamer and is a public possession.

A distinction has to be drawn between change and transformation. Change comes from the outside, from some other source or impact, but transformation relies on thinking from the individual for himself. In the coaching process the emphasis should be on transformation, rather than change. If the client owns this thinking for herself, it will have a lasting consequence, whereas ideas of change can only be transitory. Transformation requires that the client exercise authority for herself, whereas change just requires competent followership.

Transformation of thinking brought about by empathy—and compassion and truth seeking—is consistent with Thinking 2, not only because it has a systemic context, but also because it is thinking that is authored in the moment by the thinker and not the thought of others in the past.

Politics of revelation

The orientation to executive coaching can be of two kinds: either the politics of salvation or the politics of revelation (Lawrence, 1994). The politics of the coaching process can be interpersonal between coach and client, and so there is a pressure to make it egocentric. The politics of thinking takes the protagonists beyond their psychic skins. Who is to hold influence and power, client or coach? Or can the two stand outside the thinking generated in the coaching session, as if it were a cultural object in the space between them, assess and weigh it, to come to an evaluation of its quality?

The concept of the politics[4] of salvation is taken from the "rescue phantasy" (Dubbane & Lee, 1980), where the client, in their case the psychoanalytic patient, is seen as in a position of wanting to be cured. This is a distortion of the psychoanalytic process, because it is an avoidance, and collusion between patient and analyst, of the analysis of unconscious material.

In the coaching session this can be seen most clearly when the coach enters the teaching mode where, on the basis of past knowledge and thought, solutions are offered to what is seen as the client's problem. This teaching mode is more associated with "mentoring" than with coaching.

On the other hand, the politics of revelation begins from identifying the nature of the emotional issues facing the client. This generates new thinking between client and coach. The thinking will both be conscious and unconscious, both finite and of the infinite. It will be of the moment and related to the context of the client viewed holistically. The politics of revelation is orientated towards discovery of what has, hitherto, been unknown. Salvation trades in the known.

Very occasionally, the client will have an "epiphany", a blinding insight never before available. The chances of this are enhanced when the politics of revelation are being pursued in the session together with the coach's mental disposition, as this could lead to transformational insight.

The unconscious and the infinite in the coaching session

Lurking in every executive coaching session, every role consultation, and, indeed, every social relation, is the presence of unconscious thinking. That presence can be like an unattended absence, but it is always there, for it cannot be wished away.

The quality of the coaching process will also depend on the conscious thinking of both the consultant and the client, but that will depend on how assiduously unconscious thinking, on the part of the two, is being attended to. This is to work on the hypothesis that the conscious mind and the unconscious mind are in a symbiotic relationship, each reliant for its existence on the other.

Another hypothesis offered here is that people select themselves for a coaching session because they have attained the limits of their comprehension in how they are performing their role. This may be just a vague formulation, or just the wish to have someone to talk through their problems of work, but it can lead to a life-enhancing move on their part. Attaining the limits of comprehension is an achievement of mental courage on the part of the individual, because the complex environmental reality of the business world is recognized, together with their felt, comparative absence of authority to discharge their work roles.

To be sure, the limits of comprehension may be expressed in terms of stress and strain, which is a blanket diagnosis. To enter executive coaching could be a positive move, because it starts with an acknowledgement on the part of the individual of the falseness of narcissistic solutions that have served them so well in the past, coupled with a desire to find new strategies based in reality thinking and not in psychotic thinking that could take them through to a considered future. To state this succinctly, potential clients are experiencing rumblings of their existential state of being and recognize that they have to find their own authority to become something different. Executive coaching offers an opportunity to clients, whether self-referred or not, for these existential problems to be addressed, though not necessarily directly.

The unconscious plays a greater part in our conscious minds than may be recognized. The belief held in this exploration is that the consciousness and the unconscious mind are symbiotically related, though this is often ignored, or denied, by many writers. What is known is that the unconscious mind, with its particular form of thinking processes, offers scanning powers that are superior to conscious visioning (Ehrenzweig, 1967). Every poet, artist, and creative person intuits this.

Furthermore, neurobiologists have established that humans can process fourteen million bits of information per second. "A "bit" is the smallest atomic element in information, is weightless, colourless, has no size, and can travel at the speed of light (Negroponte, 1995, p. 14). But, the bandwidth of consciousness is much too narrow to register all the information humans routinely receive and act on, for it is only around eighteen bits. This means that the vast bulk of information humans use to make decisions must be derived from unconscious thinking (Gray, 2002, p. 66).

Simply stated: consciousness is self-reflective subjectivity that is possible because of mind, which owes its existence to the brain. While the former is intangible and exists only in imagination, the latter is tangibly composed of a multitude of neural networks. It is the interaction and inter-relatedness of these neural networks that gives rise to mind. Because of mind, which generates all our thoughts, ponderings, intuitions, imaginings, dreams, and "is our window . . . to existential mystery, the awareness of death, the poignancy of the human condition" (de Duve, 1995, p. 245), human beings have brought that cultural experience called civilization into existence. Without mind and its thought there would be no business enterprises, as they are known. Someone, or group of people, must have conceived of a business venture in the first instance. This idea is then turned into a real project.

Mind arises from the brain, which is composed of neural networks, and there is a difference between how these neural nets operate. In this, difference can be discerned between the mind of consciousness and the unconscious mind. The conscious and the unconscious can be seen as a continuum of mind. When the conscious mind is operating the neural nets are tight and focused. The thinking associated with the three Rs, reading, writing and arithmetic, is a prime example. The mind is dealing with mathematical symbols and words in a logical relationship. The thinker is very aware of self and is reflective. The thinker works with ideas in a linear fashion. The boundaries of knowledge systems are solidly defined and mental activity takes place within them. When humans are asleep and dreaming the neural nets relax and the unconscious mind is fully operating. The dream is imagery and relies on metaphor. Whereas consciousness is self-reflective, the unconscious mind is not, and is imbued with a sense of "other worldliness".

The dream is surreal and images and ideas are juxtaposed, defying everyday logic. The links and connections between the dream images are multi-branching and display lateral thinking that would be impossible in waking consciousness. The dream is characterized by merging and condensation, with activity in the dream taking place between sub-systems of knowledge. Between these two contrasting worlds of consciousness and the unconscious, there is one, that of reverie, free association, and day-dreaming, when waking thoughts are less structured. Fewer words are used, more metaphor and the connections between them. There are more open boundaries between the recognized domains of knowledge and the whole process is less egocentric and enmeshed in the imagery of the thinking process (Hartmann, 2000).

On the basis of this description, the working hypothesis is that the unconscious mind is the source of creativity (and destruction) because it puts into disarray the cultural schemata human beings live by and, therefore, questions the neat, logical concepts of the categorized, ordered, daily mental world.

This was illustrated by Einstein, when he replied to the question: *what is involved in the psychology of invention*? In a detailed answer he said that words and language do not seem to play any role in the mechanism of thought. Rather, the physical entities, which act as elements of thought, are certain signs and images, which are more or less clear enough to be reproduced and combined. These mental images of the object of thought are emotionally manipulated in the imagination. The emotional basis of this rather vague play is the desire to arrive at logically connected concepts. Once this play is established, Einstein describes the laborious search for words that are analogous to the logical connections implicit in the emotional play with images. Following this route, he arrives, ultimately, at his mathematical formulation. Einstein started from an emotional state expressed in images and sensations to arrive at a purely intellectual and highly abstract conception. In short, emotion is the mother of invention through the transformation of thinking, and father is the unconscious (Matte-Blanco, 1988, pp. 96–99).

A useful metaphor for executive coaching is that it is a crucible for the transformation of thinking taking place between two people. Crudely, the client arrives with one story of how they are behaving in their role in their work system and leaves the cycle of coaching sessions with a revised or, probably, a deeply transformed story. That story will have been transformed as a result of the overt working through the domains that Brunning identifies, but also through the ability of the coach, in the first instance, to be in touch with the unconscious and the infinite. This is another element in the mental disposition of the coach. This "creative metaphoric approach" relies on the ability to plumb the unconscious and the infinite.

The unconscious is "won from the void and formless infinite" (Milton, *Paradise Lost*), which Bion identified as the source of the unconscious (Bion, 1965, p. 151). Mathematically, infinity does exist. This is the unknown. It is no-thought from which thinking is brought forth that can become thought as it enters the domain of the finite. In the coaching session the partnership of client and coach can help each other to be present in the unconscious and the infinite so that they can jointly develop new thinking and thought; to make finite what has hitherto been infinite.

Reverie and dream in the coaching process

The unconscious and the infinite can be accessed through reverie. Reverie tends to initiate through silence when coach and client are stuck and cease to have words. They are on the brink of the unknown.

The topic might be an issue, a problem, a role relationship, conflict in the work system or a puzzling organizational procedure. There can follow a period where both ruminate on the dimensions of whatever is being talked of (the neural nets of the brain are less tight). This may lead to new working hypotheses entertained by both client and coach.

The idea of reverie may not be important to the client in the beginning, but the client will learn to value it as much as the coach. Reverie usually takes place when whatever is passing through the mind is voiced as a free association; it is to exercise the imagination fully, to be available for unconscious thinking and infinity.

Dream, when used systemically, can be of value in the coaching process.[5] The conventional way to use dream in a dyadic situation is to delve into the psyche of the client. While this is totally appropriate in the psychoanalytic dyad that is directed at enquiry into the psyche, it is questionable in the executive coaching process. Why? Because in the coaching session the coach is working with the client to help them understand their work situation systemically, paying attention to the relevant social factors, to understand how they are exercising authority and to formulate goals and strategies for themselves, rather than to focus on and change their client's pathological, intrapsychic patterns of thought, feelings, and behaviour. This demands a holistic, systemic perspective. Consequently, in thirty odd years—to make a personal statement—I have never made a personal interpretation to a client, except in the early, apprentice years. The client can use their own authority to make their own interpretations.

Focusing on the systemic dimensions is possible through dreaming, for the dream can be seen as making a comment on the eco-niche of the individual in their role. By "eco-niche" is meant the immediate social world of relationships as they are affected by the economic, ecological, and other social forces of the larger environment, indeed the cosmos.

The dream, as pure unconscious, will be the result of loose neural networks. It can be argued that dreaming is the most basic form of thinking because what is thought, whether image, word, or concept, started from the incomprehensible logic of the unconscious. Even the finite knowledge of quantum physics had its origins in the infinite world of the unconscious. In this context, the social dimensions of the dream can yield new insight. Using dreaming as a tool of cultural enquiry liberates the dream from being gagged and bound by the individual psyche. By free association and amplification the content of the dream is opened up. Through this expansion thinking can be transformed effortlessly. Once this way of using dreams in the coaching session is tried, the results can be quite surprising and the tasks of the coaching session enriched.

In the coaching process the potential knowledge dimension contained in the dream is focused on, rather than the easier-to-comprehend personal characteristics of the dreamer. By picking up the systemic, knowledge qualities of the dream, the coach and client are intimately engaged in transforming their thinking of the work context, which is taking them well beyond where they initially started in the consultation (Lawrence, 1998, 2003).

This mutual exploration relies not only on conscious, finite bodies of knowledge, as exemplified by Brunning's six domains, but also on unconscious, infinite areas of no-knowledge, the unknown, which have been indicated and included in the work.

The final working hypothesis is that it is in these areas of no-knowledge that will lie the seeds of creative authority, which, once worked through consciously, will provide the strategies for the client to manage herself appropriately in her role in her work system.

The creation of the appropriate emotional space for this to take place will be dependent on how well the coach can manage to utilize her own mental disposition of empathy, of thinking, of reverie, the unconscious, and the infinite. It is in honing these skills that the executive coach becomes a better instrument for working with the client.

Notes

1. Personal pronouns are used interchangeably throughout this chapter.
2. The reader is referred to a chapter by Halina Brunning in this book.
3. The reader is also referred to a chapter by Miranda Alcock in this book.
4. Politics is being used here in the sense of influence.
5. See also Social Dreaming entry in the Directory of Resources at the end of this book.

References

Armstrong, D. (1998). Thinking aloud: contributions to three dialogues. In: W. G. Lawrence (Ed.), *Social Dreaming @ Work* (pp. 91–106). London: Karnac.

Bion, W. R. (1965). *Transformations*. London: Karnac.

Bion, W. R. (1992). *Cogitations*. London: Karnac.

Brunning, H. (2001). The six domains of executive coaching. *The Journal of Organizational and Social Dynamics*, 1(2): 254–263.

de Duve, C. (1995). *Vital Dust*. New York: Basic Books.

Dubbane, E., & Lee, A. (1980). Countertransference and the rescue phantasy. Unpublished paper presented to the Canadian Psychoanalytic Society, Montreal.

Ehrenzweig, A. (1967). *The Hidden Order of Art: A Study in the Psychology of Artistic Imagination*. London: Weidenfeld and Nicolson.

Gray, J. (2002). *Straw Dogs*. London: Granta.

Hartmann, (2000). The psychology and physiology of dreaming: a new synthesis. In: L. Gamwell (Ed.), *Dreams 1900–2000* (pp. 61–75). New York: Cornell University Press.

Lawrence, W. G. (1979). *Exploring Individual and Organizational Boundaries*. Chichester: Wiley & Sons.

Lawrence, W. G. (1994). The politics of salvation and revelation in the practice of consultancy. In: R. Casemore, G. Dyos, A. Eden, K. Kellner, & S. Moss (Eds.), *What Makes Consultancy Work* (pp. 87–97). London: South Bank Press.

Lawrence, W. G. (1995a). Totalitaere sindsilstande in institutioner. *Aggrippa-Psykitriske Tekster*, 16(1–2): 53–72.

Lawrence, W. G. (1995b).The seductiveness of totalitarian states of mind. *The Journal of Health Care Chaplaincy*, October: 11–22.

Lawrence, W. G. (1997). Totalitarian states of mind in institutions. In: S. Antrobus (Ed.), *Nursing Leadership* (pp. 137–138). London: RCN.

Lawrence, W. G. (1998). *Social Dreaming @ Work*. London: Karnac.

Lawrence, W. G. (2003). *Experiences in Social Dreaming*. London: Karnac.

Matte-Blanco, I. (1988). *Thinking, Feeling, and Being*. London: Routledge.

Negroponte, N. (1995). *Being Digital*. London: Hodder and Stoughton.

Symington, N. (1986). *The Analytic Experience*. New York: St Martin's Press.

Turquet, P. M. (1975). Threats to identity in the large group. In: L. Kreeger (Ed.), *The Large Group: Therapy and Dynamics*. London: Constable.

CHAPTER FIVE

Layers of meaning: a coaching journey[1]

Jane Pooley

I ndividuals at different levels within both public and private sector organizations are increasingly employing coaches who work outside their organizations. This chapter explores the author's way of developing a coaching relationship, viewing it through different lenses. First, the lens of experience is used to explore how coaching relationships unfold to offer insight into the client's situation. Second, the theoretical lenses of systemic, psychoanalytic, and attachment theories are used to examine the dynamics at work during this development. The life cycle of a coaching relationship is offered as a framework to demonstrate how the relationship can release leadership potential and resources.

Setting the scene

There are many different approaches to coaching. This chapter focuses on a coaching style that has grown out of systemic and psychoanalytic traditions and can thus be placed within the emerging field of systems-psychodynamics.[2] The elements that are primarily examined with this style of coaching are the client in role and the client in his/her organizational context. An understanding of the presenting issues comes about through examination of the client's personal and work history, organizational dynamics, task and role clarification, and the primary task of the organization together with its history and context. The experience and feelings that are generated between client and coach, together with dreams, metaphors, and free associations, are used to enhance understanding. The insights gained and the connections made between these layers of meaning are used to design actions and strategies that link the person, role and organization together towards productive outcomes.[3]

The reasons for the growth of the coaching industry are no doubt as various as the types of organization and individuals that seek this kind of help; however, there are some underlying themes. The growth of the global village, together with the ability to travel, to communicate across the globe in real time, through to changes in electronics, computing, and e-mail, have brought with them a quickening of change in all organizations. This brings with it anxiety and pressure as well as opportunity.

There is more overt pressure to perform in most, if not all, organizations than existed even five years ago. The manifestation of this is the ethos of performance management, with more frequent appraisals and shorter judgement cycles. Some organizations have recognized the pressure and have offered their employees access to external coaches. It is thus important to understand the particular nature of the organizational context in which the coaching relationship is positioned.[4]

The client's search for meaning

So, what are the clients looking for? Clients often express a wish to reflect on ways of working with complex and, for them, fast-moving organizational systems. There is a concomitant need for them to take account of their own needs and those of their colleagues. They may be looking for a neutral space where judgement is absent, risks can be taken, and connections and thoughts considered and understood, sometimes when the loneliness and isolation of their task has become apparent to them. These feelings invariably increase when boundaries and roles become uncertain, and are also driven by the fact that workplace performance and assessment have become increasingly public acts.

Requests for coaching can also arise when the client wishes to establish and achieve clearer goals in a wider sense of role and professional effectiveness and, indeed, simply to look at ways that the business can be changed and developed. Sometimes these issues have been clarified through feedback based on appraisal systems and have been built into development plans.

Clients invariably seek a "safe place" to consider questions of work–life balance. Clients also seem to be looking for ways to connect their personal and workplace cultures, beliefs, and ethics, perhaps looking for the *existential primary task* (Miller, 1993) to give them meaning.

Looked at in this way it is clear that clients enter the coaching relationship with hope; hope that is born out of a wish that something new or different can emerge that will relate to all aspects of their lives and enhance their functioning and prospects. This need to work with hope (and its bedfellow, despair) is at the core of the coaching relationship. Put another way, the mobilization of a paired relationship, in which hope and despair can be contemplated, is the basis on which the coaching relationship is built. The task of the coach is to work in this paired relationship without colluding in flight, fight, or dependency (Bion, 1961). Holding the "home" organization in view is therefore essential to the task.

The demand for coaching can also be understood as a request for dependency from clients who feel they need an anchor in what they experience as fast-moving turbulent organizational waters. They are often unaware that rapid movement and change has disturbed their capacity to create for themselves, and for the people they manage, a containing environment where anxiety can be held.[5] While clients often present with a list of issues on which to work, the coach's role is to understand what may be behind these issues, so that both the obvious and the hidden can emerge during the coaching relationship. The task is to develop the process of making meaning in order to heighten the capacity to address presenting issues more accurately. In this way, fantasies can be explored without prejudice and creative thought, work satisfaction, and heightened productivity can emerge. However, it is important to see the dependency on the coach within the paired relationship as a stage in the development of the relationship, not an end in itself, or this would be a retreat from organizational relatedness.

A key principle in this method of coaching is to encourage clients to forge new understanding in order to make choices based on greater clarity about themselves, their role, and their environmental context. Reed and Bazalgette (2003) succinctly describe this in their role work on role consultation as "finding, making and taking role".

Executive coaching, like any other relationship, goes through stages in its development; it has a life cycle. At all stages anxiety is aroused in relation to the connection being formed; issues of judgement, concerns about the trustworthiness of the space. Will I be changed? Do I wish/need to change? How can I leave? At each stage in the "here and now" of the coaching relationship different experiences are available for examination and thought that throw light on organizational development issues. Let us now examine in more detail aspects of three key stages: beginning, mid-life, and ending.

The beginning stage—establishing trust

A client,[6] David, came seeking advice on whether or not he should stay in the high profile job that he was not enjoying, or whether he should join another employer, having been headhunted on several occasions. In the introductory meeting he talked about difficulties with a peer and how this relationship was preventing him from developing his department's work. He had formed a judgement that a colleague "had it in for him".

In such a situation an introductory meeting is set up to give the clients space to talk about the concerns they have, and for them to gain information about the coaching relationship. Time, frequency of meetings, ways of working, confidentiality, and the background of the coach are some of the issues that are typically discussed. At the end of the introductory meeting the client either decides to set up four initial appointments or to consider the meeting in their own time, making contact when they have decided how, or whether, to proceed. This open-ended exploration sets a tone for the working relationship between client and coach; a relationship of respect and equality and with openness about how the work will be conducted.

In the first four sessions the presenting issues are discussed in the light of the obvious connections and meanings and with a curiosity about those that are not so obvious. Sometimes, the coach will ask for a personal/professional biography, which will often throw light on the patterns of events and relationships in the past that may be informing the "here and now" work relationships.[7]

> In his introductory meeting, the potential client, David, was more than usually interested in the coach's background, issues of confidentiality, whether he could be seen outside working hours, and how his organization would be invoiced. Of course, these are necessary preoccupations. However, the intensity with which they were probed was unusual. David seemed more interested in them than in the issues that had brought him to seek coaching. This alerted me to the need to be both transparent and robust in explaining the ways I worked and to clarify my expectations of clients as well as theirs of me. Accordingly, we discussed terms and conditions in detail, as well as the possibility of working with biography as a way of illuminating the presenting issues. In working with a client whose state of mind was highly anxious and suspicious there was clearly a need for me, the coach, to create a containing environment in which boundaries could be set in order for my client to move into a more enquiring state of mind. He decided to have four initial sessions and we agreed that progress should be reviewed in the fourth session. However, I also hypothesized that the lack of trust could be a particular issue within his organization, as indeed it is the case in many organizations today.

The ritual of allocated sessions and regular reviews creates a sense of purposefulness and a structure in which to set and measure progress against the agreed aims and objectives. An active framework is created that embodies the coaching relationship, and gives the client a message of autonomy as opposed to one of dependency. In the early stages of a coaching relationship the coach is creating a framework for a working relationship, which would normally include listening, offering feedback, and challenge. Each client has different preferences and tolerances in these respects, and it is the coach's responsibility to "tune into" their client and create an environment that is safe enough for risks to be taken, paying particular attention to language and to the context of the client's working environment. It is imperative for the coach to hold in mind the organizational culture and specific context in which clients are working. This helps to consider the presenting material as not just personal but as an explanation of some aspect of the organization that is being played out through the client's experience.

> The client (David) held a senior role in the prison service. In a prison, secrets and lies, corruption and suspicion are inevitable dynamics. These are some of the dynamics that underpin criminal activity and are bound to be brought into a custodial context. It was not surprising therefore that such a state of mind was also presenting in David and thus needed the attention of the coach.

> David talked of a disciplinary process that he had gone through in a previous job when a prisoner had accused him of bullying. This had resulted in him being suspended from work for over a year while an investigation took place. I set and held tight boundaries until David felt contained enough to explore this issue and to separate his present experience from his past experience. There was much material that left him feeling vulnerable. It was particularly important to David that his coach was able to witness his experiences and make careful links to them and to his current reality. In this way he could begin to consider what belonged where from past and present. He could also identify which part of the organizational dynamic was being pushed into him and why, and over time he could understand and use these insights in his work. David began to be able to think more clearly; he then found that he could hold multiple realities in his mind, leaving him freer to make choices and consider options. Using the idea of time past, time present, and time future was a useful way of enabling him to move from an apparent rigid frame of mind.

The notion of time introduces movement into the system of mind and therefore access to new possibilities (Pooley, 1994). Traumatized people often become stuck in time, not able to access memory of the past or dream about their future. This state of shock, literally holding breath, presents itself in smaller measure when clients experience a difficult event or are under great strain; finding ways to activate both memory and desire free the mental system. Very simply, this process can begin by paying attention to rituals, such as the ritual present in the coaching session. Certainty about the behaviour and reliability of the coach begins these stabilizing ritual processes. The experience of an earlier session that the coach remembers, of the coach's availability in the here and now of the present session, and the image of a session planned for the future, begins the process of freeing a conceptual space. This is particularly useful for clients who experience themselves as being lost within their organizations, often experiencing them as uncontaining and chaotic.

The question of where the line is between coaching and therapy is an important one to ask, but it is not easy to answer straightforwardly. The word therapeutic means healing art. Coaches might be said to be working with "dis-ease", as opposed to with "disease". That is, with a client who has identified something in their professional system that is not fitting or working as well as they could wish. The clients enter coaching to "heal", mend, or in some way or another address the presenting issues. If the coach's task is to address underlying, often unconscious, dynamics in individuals and in organizations in order to build sustainable systems with the capacity to adapt and change, then it is essential to use knowledge about people, groups, resistance, defence mechanisms, emotional worlds, and so on. In this sense it is a "therapeutic" relationship, where personal material is not off limits, but is worked with in so far as it affects work performance.[8]

There are some basic parameters and frames in the coaching relationship that draw a useful boundary around both task and role. The starting point of a coaching relationship is that it sets out to extend and widen the conceptual frame and to name and identify the fields of vision that clients are using to understand their situation. At the same time, self-realization comes about through working with the emerging relationship between client and coach. From such new awareness comes the possibility for the client to improve an aspect of their work, to change something in order to enable themselves, their team or organization, to become more effective. It is, therefore, part of the coaching process to agree desired outcomes that are specific and measurable and to specify how this will be checked; for example, via 360 Degree Feedback interviews.[9] The coaching journey has a focused end point. This is about work, about the client's role, and about developing the client's understanding of the organization. Objectives are reviewed and new outcomes agreed, but the testing and measuring of progress in relation to the "back-home" business context makes a clear distinction from most other therapeutic interventions, which are not primarily aimed at improved work performance, having more diffuse goals, such as greater insight or well being. Nevertheless, the coaching relationship is a journey of discovery, where unexpected thoughts, connections, or indeed, insights, are always waiting in the wings. The distinction comes about in the testing of these new insights in the workplace, and using the feedback from this to develop further understanding.

Attachment research can be of help to the coach on this question (Main, 1996). Research in this area focused on infant–parent relationships and highlighted how, through these early experiences, people develop templates for relating to adults and peers. The research shows that repetition is likely to occur in adult relationships when the person has been unable to consider how their early relationships impacted on them. People can be helped to see *how* and then to reflect on *why* those patterns may be repeating in adult life. These early attachment relationships inevitably reappear in the context of the work setting as well as in the home setting. For further examples of working with these patterns see chapters by Stapley, Spero, and Alcock.

For some clients, coming to terms with this kind of material can free them to understand why they often get stuck in unproductive, and often repetitive, relationships of power by responding in habitual ways. It is also what Bion (1961) describes as "valency". It offers the coach an understanding of the role that they could take up in relation to the client in order to counterbalance projections from previous relationships.

As organizations change, attachment relationships can often become transient. Horowitz (2004) describes these as the "butterfly phenomenon": individuals do not tend to stay in one role for long, as they used to do; in addition, frequent changes in reporting relationships will inhibit the development of group working relationships. A secure base (Bowlby, 1988)—a place where both physically and emotionally people experience consistency and safety—is often unavailable to them. The creation of such a base requires attention to the physical—availability of a quiet consulting room, suitable furniture, agreement to switch off mobiles, clear time boundaries, etc., and attention to the emotional—a non-judgemental approach, a reliable and consistent attitude, etc. When people feel confident in having such a base, they know that the relationship is trustworthy and robust enough to manage difficulties and differences and can contain strong feelings of anger, anxiety, and other arousals. Clients are then much freer to behave in ways that are less defensive, open to opportunity, creativity, and exploration. There is, however, a danger that coaching may be sought out in order to replace the secure attachments that are lacking in many modern organizations. There may be a danger of developing inappropriate dependency on coaches, and for that matter on consultants. In such cases the coach–client relationship could become encapsulated, or "wall off" the individual from the "toxicity" of the organization and prevent the development of new ways of relating to others in it (see Krantz, 2001 on the issue of organizational "toxicity").

It is important to keep the relationship of the client to the organization open and lively. Thus, it is vital to have an appropriate degree of challenge and constantly reflect on the meanings to the organization of particular dilemmas under consideration.

This first stage, therefore, is about setting a scene, creating a space in which to think. This is not just a neutral environment, it is a space and a relationship from which new ideas and meaning can emerge, and while "safe", it is not wholly comfortable. Attention to this level of engagement sets the tone for what follows.

The mid-stage—the search for perfection

Having established the basis for a working relationship, this next phase is characterized by an engagement with, and exploration of, what is being presented and what is being experienced by both the client and the coach. This widening and deepening of the discourse is at the heart of this stage of development.

This approach to coaching works from, and respects, the human dimension of the organizational experience, as opposed to the technical or financial dimensions. The focus is to bring to the attention of clients how their personal feelings and responses in themselves may be influencing decisions and actions. The ownership of both the problem and the solution stays with the client. In this respect the coach is taking up a position of "not knowing", and using that frame for a competent exploration of the unsaid and unthought (Halton, 2004). This apparent paradox is fundamental, in that the coach is working through interest and influence rather than hierarchical authority and knowledge. The coach is not necessarily an expert in the technical issues of workplace; clients can teach the coach what they need to know. Indeed, it is important that the coach sees the world as the client sees it, or the "organization in the mind" of the client (Armstrong, 1997). The coach will, however, have expertise in understanding and working with human processes. Within this framework, the client is more likely to retain his or her own sense of influence, identity, and purposefulness.

Once the environment is set and the client is both comfortable enough, and anxious enough, to engage in exploring some of their preoccupations, play becomes possible. It is important that this is not taken as being frivolous, or as a flight from complexity. That is not the intention, and a watchful eye needs to be kept on these defences present in both the coach and the client. However, when fantasies, dreams, and nightmares are taken seriously and invited into the relationship, dialogue and exploration at new levels can commence. Shifting the register in this way gives clients another framework in which to find expression and new ideas. Clients who are supported in their ability to day-dream, to try out possibilities and explore flights of fancy, to externalize hopes and anxieties, are in a truly playful space. The capacity to symbolize inner thoughts and feelings through play is as vital in adulthood as it is in children. Unconscious conflicts and dilemmas can safely emerge in this space and the drive towards concrete thinking and total clarity, where the solution is idealized perfection, is avoided.[10]

> A Finance Director, Jack, was preoccupied with the inability of the Board, on which he sat, to address the, to him, obvious demise of one arm of his company. He had not been able to convince his colleagues that radical steps needed to be taken if the company was not to be threatened by this failing directorate. Why, he wondered, could they not see what was blindingly obvious to him? As his coach, I felt Jack's stuckness and was aware that it was important to stay with his preoccupation. (In this stuck space the coach will not only experience some of the dilemmas that the client is holding, but also some of the emotional responses to the situation. These can be a clue to both the underlying causes of the dilemma and its solution.) I knew that Jack

enjoyed playing chess, so invited him to imagine that the company's balance sheet was, in fact, a chessboard. Using this metaphor, I invited Jack to consider which parts of the company would be represented by which piece and why? Where would they be placed on the board? What moves in the game would represent the current situation? What moves could be made in order to arrive at a different end point? And so on . . . Coach and client "played" with these ideas for some time, and both were quite engaged in the "game". Jack suddenly said, "If I were the bishop and moved next to the knight (representing Andrew, his colleague in strategic planning) I could show him that we need a new angle on this. I need to work with the knight (Andrew) so together we can get a handle on this and get our moves co-ordinated. I was standing on the outside looking in and felt as if I was knocking on a door and no one was listening. I will go and talk to Andrew and do some work outside of the board room to prepare the way."

While this insight seemed obvious to me it was only available to Jack by his move into a different, yet familiar mind space. It was by drawing on his knowledge of and joy in chess that he was enabled to explore options in a playful way and recognize that he could take action and move from his sense of hopeless impotence.[11]

Here the notion of "good enough" is relevant. A risky concept to introduce in a world that is searching for perfection and "total win", but none the less a useful reminder of the personal power that can be unleashed from raising to consciousness that which is unconscious (see also the chapter by Gordon Lawrence). Winnicott taught, from his extensive observation of infant and parent early relationships, that being a "good enough parent" *is* more than good enough (Winnicott, 1965). In fact, the search for perfection paradoxically works against creating an environment where a child can learn to take risks, get things wrong, survive being left alone, learn that despair and hope go hand in hand, and come to think for him/herself and about others. It is only in an environment that can accept mistakes that people learn to tolerate and digest their experiences and to think and reflect without being compelled into knee-jerk reaction.

The coach is *not* primarily concerned with the psychopathology of the client. The coach *is* concerned with identifying the factors in the organizational system in which the client is working that are eliciting particular experiences and patterns (Armstrong, 2004). Are there particular dynamics around the function and task of the organization that heighten certain defences and ways of doing things? Are there particular current constraints or challenges to the business function that push the organization's culture into particular ways of delivery? Are there significant issues in lines of authority and accountability that require unpicking to free the client's capacity for thought and subsequent action?

In order for clients to feel safe enough to take risks, to think about what they are presenting, they need to experience their coach as someone who not only has the capacity to listen and be present, but is also able to understand what is often not being said in words or actions or to reflect back and move into different layers of understanding. The coach needs to demonstrate a capacity to wonder about the meaning behind the obvious. Naming the un-nameable gives clients an experience of being understood at quite a deep level.[11] For example, looking beyond the obvious reasons for the client who is systematically late, or who regularly leaves on their mobile, or who brings gifts, recognizing that these all have possible and multiple meanings that are worthy of exploration.

> An MD, Peter, who had grown up with an excessively critical and chastising mother, had managed life by determining to be "the best" at most things he took on and he had, in great part, succeeded. He began to bring the coach bags of chocolate from his factory on each visit. These were kindly given and the coach was happy to receive them. However, when the coach invited the client to look at his motivation for these gifts, they began to see that Peter was ensuring that the coach would not turn on him and chastise him; his hope was, in this seeming act of kindness, to keep the coach "sweet". In understanding this, and recognizing consciously his need to be best, and to keep relationships "sweet", he was able to harness his energy and enthusiasm for the business in ways that were less driven by unconscious anxiety. Peter was showing how his organizational culture related to its people. This insight was valuable in later work, when the coach and client recognized that the giving and receiving of gifts was militating against working with resistance and allowing differences to emerge in the corporate culture.

Creating a safe space, with clear boundaries, is only part of enabling containment. Awakening to the fact that thinking can only take place when the client experiences in the "helper" the ability to accept projections, without turning them back, and to understand fear without belittling the experience is also vital (Klein, 1955; Segal, 1991). A useful coach is one who has the capacity to accept that clients will have feelings and emotions that they are not ready or able at that moment to own for themselves. The coach's task is to hold this, reflect on the experience, and hand it back when an appropriate moment emerges. In order to be adept enough at working in this way coaches need to have a good degree of insight into their own inner worlds, so that client's and coach's material do not get confused.

The coach can see these dynamics most acutely at points of transition, as when clients are moving jobs or working through a reorganization, possibly making changes in their personal lives at the same time. Each person has different thresholds for tolerating change and different ways of managing these life events.

This mid-stage of the coaching journey is characterized by the creation of a working relationship between coach and client that tolerates the capacity to both know and not know; to find answers to questions in surprising spaces and to work with the idea that there is often new meaning to be found underlying the presenting issues in the client and in their sphere of influence. Searching for these meanings raises the clients' capacity to work with complexity and to find strategic solutions that attend to all parts of the system in focus.

End stages of coaching: termination and evaluation

Working towards termination of the coaching relationship also links to issues that clients will have to negotiate in their organizations. Anger, regression, yearning for what was and what might have been, are all themes relating to loss that can be relevant to gaining insights into how change and endings affect clients and their colleagues and how they can be better managed in an environment of rush and pressure.

> Shelia, an HR professional, came into coaching to explore why she was not being successful in interviews for new roles outside her company.

Among other things, the coach and client worked on her interview strategy. She began to understand how important it was to meet prospective employers and consider what they might need her to understand about them. As well as selling her skills, she needed to enter into a relationship with them by being interested both in them as people and in the company's history, strengths, and dilemmas. Shelia had been so overwhelmed by her own sense of failure and her personal preoccupations that she had retreated into self-absorption. The coaching sessions were used to help her become more curious and less introverted. Shelia soon gained a promotion and became global HR director of a large multi-national. However, when she was in the process of leaving she retreated into her self-absorbed state. She decided against having any kind of leaving party and just wanted to walk out of the door without saying goodbye to anyone. This after twelve years in the company! Coach and client looked at this urge and understood the dangers she felt in facing the rituals of leaving: in that moment she would not only be facing the warmth and goodwill of her colleagues, but also facing the things that were left undone or that were not tied up in some way. She came to recognize that by working openly with her handover and with the leaving process she would be supporting her colleagues to take on some of the aspects of inter-relatedness that this company was struggling with. Shelia had understood that her self-absorption was also inherent in the culture of the company where individuals were privileged over teamwork.

This example illustrates how the avoidance of proper endings, which is part of the chaos of the "new organizational order", can be worked on in the coaching relationship.

One of the ways that the systems-psychodynamic approach to coaching differs from other models is its basic tenet that to emphasize and work only with the positive is counter-productive and unrealistic. Approaches that focus solely on success, without considering the potential blockers to success, both conscious and unconscious, individual, group, and organizational, are at best oversimplified and naïve, at worst dangerous. The complexity of the client's situation requires the consideration of both apparently positive and negative features. As Argyris reminds us (1985), failure to recognize and work with resistance can have disastrous consequences (Hoyle, 2004). Skilled leaders do not rely on pushing harder when they discern resistance; instead, they attempt to understand the meaning behind the resistance as a source of data from which organizational change can be posited. Retaining this spirit of enquiry and curiosity enables clients to find pathways that create opportunity rather than build up defensive systems. A crucial aspect of the systems-psychodynamic approach to coaching is the ability and sensitivity to discern where resistance to change is sited. If clients are to bring about change in their organizational system, they need to understand where the anxiety lies, and what structures or resources are needed to contain it in order that it will not overwhelm or incapacitate the change programme. Understanding these issues helps clients create their own containing environment, and to develop insight into the human systems in their organization. Strategic planning can then take account of these matters. The reader is referred to an excellent paper by Krantz (2001) exploring this issue in depth.

Evaluating coaching takes the form of reviewing what has been achieved against the agreed aims and objectives. This process is worked on at review points throughout the coaching relationship and new objectives are set as the client's capacity to think deeper and wider grows. This dialogue goes on in tandem with the experience of the relationship between coach and client. Feedback is invited and given both ways. At the end point the total picture is in view, an evaluation of what has emerged during the coaching work can be made, together with discussions as to how new insights can be utilized within the workplace.

One expected outcome would be a shift from problem and obstacle focus to opportunity focus, a move from blame to curiosity; an ability to understand that the dilemmas may not only, if at all, reside in the individual but in an aspect of the organizational culture. As a result of working in this way, clients are able to consider the specific role that they hold in the organization with greater confidence and clarity and have a clearer sense of how to approach issues of both personal and organizational change.

Another less obvious but crucial outcome would be an increased capacity for clients to play with ideas. The loosening of the constraints of anxiety helps clients to take hold of agendas, and to be more dynamic and proactive in how they work with them. Clients and coach often use 360 Degree Feedback to measure some of these movements and to throw light on blind spots that may need further work. It often happens that clients gain promotion, or take on additional responsibilities, or develop their insight and sphere of influence, over the coaching period.

Coaching can build the clients' capacity to use their own emotional intelligence (Goleman, 1998). It brings them into the strategic frame as people with passions and desires alongside the organizational system and the context in which it operates. By bringing person, role, and system together, so that each informs the other, the client is able to infuse their role in the organization with more rigour and focus.

This approach enables clients to move between layers of meaning to understand presenting issues, hence to diagnose more accurately where to intervene both within their own lives and their own organizations.

Notes

1. This is an abridged version of a longer chapter by Jane Pooley originally published in *Working Below the Surface: The Emotional Life of Contemporary Organizations*, edited by C. Huffington, D. Armstrong, W. Halton, L. Hoyle, and J. Pooley, Karnac, 2004.
2. See *The Systems Psychodynamics of Organizations* (2001), edited by L. Gould, L. Stapley, and M. Stein.
3. See also a chapter by Halina Brunning in this book.
4. See also a chapter by Clare Huffington in this book.
5. See a chapter by James Krantz in *The Systems Psychodynamics of Organizations* (2001), edited by L. Gould, L. Stapley, and M. Stein.
6. All case examples described in this chapter are composites from a variety of different sources and no individual client's confidentiality has been compromised.
7. To read more about working with client's biographical material see chapters by Halina Brunning, Lionel Stapley, Marlene Spero, and Miranda Alcock in this book.
8. See also a chapter by Halina Brunning in this book.
9. See also a chapter by Richard Kwiatkowski in this book on the use of 360 Degree Feedback.
10. See a chapter by Gordon Lawrence in this book.
11. For another example of working at the level of emerging meaning, see chapters by Halina Brunning and Laurence Gould.

References

Argyris, C. (1985). *Strategy, Change and Defensive Routines*. London: Pitman.

Armstrong, D. (1997). The "institution in the mind": reflections on the relation of psychoanalysis to work with organizations. *Free Associations*, 7(41): 1–14.

Armstrong, D. (2004). Emotions in organizations: disturbance or intelligence? In: C. Huffington, D. Armstrong, W. Halton, L. Hoyle, & J. Pooley (Eds.), *Working Below the Surface: The Emotional Life of Contemporary Organizations*. London: Karnac.

Bion, W. R. (1961). *Experiences in Groups and Other Papers*. London: Tavistock.

Bowlby, J. (1988). *A Secure Base: Clinical Applications of Attachment Theory*. London: Routledge.

Goleman, D. (1998). *Working with Emotional Intelligence*. London: Bloomsbury.

Halton, W. (2004). By what authority? Psychoanalytic reflections on creativity and change in relation to organizational life. In: C. Huffington, D. Armstrong, W. Halton, L. Hoyle, & J. Pooley (Eds.), *Working Below the Surface: The Emotional Life of Contemporary Organizations*. London: Karnac.

Horowitz, S. (2004). The discovery and loss of a compelling space. A case study in adapting to a new organizational order. In: C. Huffington, D. Armstrong, W. Halton, L. Hoyle, & J. Pooley (Eds.), *Working Below the Surface: The Emotional Life of Contemporary Organizations*. London: Karnac.

Hoyle, L. (2004). From sycophant to saboteur—responses to organizational change. In: C. Huffington, D. Armstrong, W. Halton, L. Hoyle, & J. Pooley (Eds.), *Working Below the Surface: The Emotional Life of Contemporary Organizations*. London: Karnac.

Klein, M. (1955). The psychoanalytic play technique: its history and significance. In: *Envy and Gratitude, Vol. 3, The Writings of Melanie Klein*. London: Hogarth (1975).

Krantz, J. (2001). Dilemmas of organizational change: a system psychodynamic perspective. In: L. Gould, L. Stapley, & M. Stein (Eds.), *The Systems Psychodynamics of Organizations*. London: Karnac.

Main, M. (1996). Introduction to the special section on attachment and psychopathology: II: Overview of the field of attachment. *Journal of Consulting and Clinical Psychology*, 64: 237–243.

Miller, E. J. (1993). *From Dependency to Autonomy: Studies in Organization and Change*. London: Free Association Books.

Pooley, J. (1994). A systemic study into the meanings of time and temporal constructs in family life. Unpublished thesis.

Reed, B., & Bazalgette, J. (2003). *Organizational Role Analysis*. London: Grubb Institute.

Segal, H. (1991). *Dream, Phantasy and Art*. The New Library of Psychoanalysis 12, London: Routledge.

CHAPTER SIX

The six domains of executive coaching[1]

Halina Brunning

Introduction

In this chapter I would like to present my own model of coaching, tentatively called "the six-domain model". This model is framed within the systems-psychodynamic thinking that presupposes an interconnection between three important elements: the Person, the Role, and the System. The basic definition of systems-psychodynamics, with specific references to organizational consultancy, features in the Introduction to this book.[2] The following original sources had influenced my thinking and helped me to distil this model into a coaching intervention: the work of Klein (1946), Menzies (1988), Bion (1962), Obholzer and Roberts (1994), Miller and Rice (1967), Armstrong (1997), and Stein (2004) in relation to the impact of psychoanalysis on organizational thinking and consultation. In addition, I have also been influenced by the writings of Malan (1997), White (2000), and Talmon (1993) in relation to a brief therapy intervention that found its way into my thinking about coaching. Last, but not least, the writings of Cronen, Pearce, and Tomm (1985) and Heron (1990) helped me to think about the presence of multiple contexts. All of these authors are somehow present in my proposed model of coaching.

The reason for including this particular model in the section of the book entitled "The Anatomy of Coaching" is to enable coaches and clients alike to conceptualize and visualize the various building blocks of the coaching process and to make the tracking of progress easier by identifying the domains of work and by making explicit the interconnections that may exist between them.

I examine this proposed model against one extensive case study and in a number of shorter case vignettes. I will also reflect on how the client's personality and life story interact with the coaching process and how differently this interaction is managed in psychotherapy.

The six domains of executive coaching—a proposed model

The six-domain model of coaching presupposes an interconnection that exists between the Person, the Role and the System. The Person elements refer to the client's personality and life story on the one hand and the actual choice of professional role on the other hand (see Figure 1). Additional aspects such as client's skills, competencies, abilities, and talents, as well as aspirations, career progression, and future career options either support or militate against the Role element and may interact well or adversely with the formal elements of the organizationally given role. The System, within which the client performs the current organizational role, then becomes the stage for the unfolding drama. Personal challenges, doubts, insecurities within the client's intrapsychic environment, as well as the organizational challenges and changes that exist within the client's system, both within the immediate work environment and in the world around the organization, may collectively give rise to a request for executive coaching.[3] Furthermore, it could be suggested that behind each of these proposed six domains exists an additional extensive body of knowledge, with which the coach should be cognizant and able to draw on these important additional resources while offering executive coaching (see Figure 1).

Thus, my proposed model of executive coaching is hopefully dynamic, flexible, and sensitive to the client's needs as these relate to his/her past, present, and future. This model could also be used as a diagnostic tool to help the coach and the client locate the

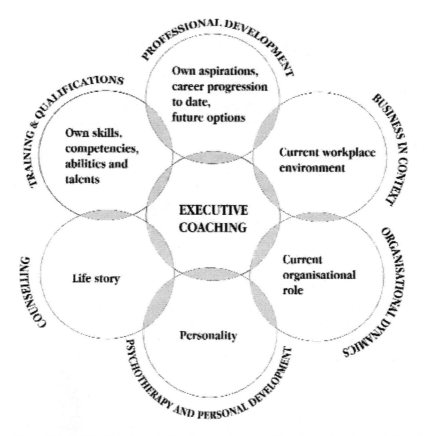

Figure 1. The six domain model of executive coaching in action (copyrights Halina Brunning, 2001, diagram by Kristof Bien).

most appropriate focus of work. For example, if it were concluded that *client's personality* seems to be the crucial factor in the way he/she performs the current organizational role, or was the main reason behind persistent conflicts in the workplace environment, then perhaps further work would require *not* more executive coaching, but psychotherapy. If, on the other hand, a recurrent theme, say, that of loss, had become identified and considered essential for the client to address, perhaps a period of counselling would be more appropriate than more executive coaching. Conversely, if the coaching process identified that the client had specific skills shortage or threw into doubt his/her career choice, or the trajectory

of future career development, then additional training, or professional and career guidance might well be more appropriate to
undertake than to continue with executive coaching *per se*. This
model also enables the client to consider new possibilities *beyond*
the immediate executive coaching framework, such as: planning a
career shift, considering whether to undertake a period of psychotherapy, or to abandon a particular role in pursuit of other life objectives.

Whatever the actual outcome, these six domains are the building blocks of the executive coaching process.

Arising from the above description of the model I propose that
these six domains are contemporaneously present during the executive coaching sessions and constitute a legitimate and appropriate
focus of work:

1.   the client's personality;
2.   the client's life story;
3.   the client's skills, competencies, abilities and talents;
4.   the client's aspirations, career progression so far and future
     direction;
5.   the client's current workplace environment in which he/she
     performs;
6.   current organizational role.

What often leads a client to seek the help of an executive coach
is a particular issue, or disruption, a doubt or an aspiration experienced or witnessed during the performance of their current organizational role. No organizational role is ever undertaken, either
consciously or unconsciously, without deep psychological reasons
for choosing it (Obholzer & Roberts, 1994). To have to address the
role performance in isolation from the other aspects of the client's
life would be to impoverish the process of coaching.[4]

It is also possible to envisage these six domains as if they were
a set of six cogwheels, all interlinked and in continuous motion,
with the ability to affect the movement of the neighbouring cogs,
such that if there was a disruption or rupture in the domain of
"current organizational role" then the neighbouring domains
would also be affected, and vice versa. It is also possible to envisage a *harmonious* as well as a *disharmonious* influence that might

exist between these domains. It could be argued that some organizational roles and some work environments are likely to be more conducive to good work performance, some personalities and some life stories might predispose a person-in-role to work more effectively, or less effectively, under different sets of external conditions and circumstances. I hope to illustrate these assumptions in different case studies and vignettes in this chapter.

As an entry point the coach needs to negotiate with the client relatively free access to relevant data and information, so as to deepen the discourse that takes place within the session.[5] I found that a good way to negotiate a contract with the client is by making direct references to the "six domains" diagram. Having previously agreed the nature of the contract with the sponsor or line manager of the new client I would bring this diagram to the first coaching session and introduce my way of working within the executive coaching framework. Making overt references to these six domains enables me to invite the client to broaden their own outlook and consider bringing relevant material from all aspects of work and life, past, present, and future. The aim of this process is to enable the client to reach new learning, new perspective, and achieve a better integration of salient aspects, all of which may have a bearing upon their current organizational role or their future career.

In order to apply this model successfully the coach would need to be reasonably knowledgeable in the sphere of human systems, psychology, organizational and group dynamics, the impact of change, and individual development, both psychological and professional: in other words everything that constitutes the content of the circles of the diagram. What is not necessarily required is *an in-depth knowledge* or practice of psychotherapy, counselling, personality testing, career guidance, skills and professional training, detailed knowledge of the client's work environment, etc. However, as already stated, the coach needs to be well aware of the impact of these elements upon the client's life and work and to utilize these as additional referral routes, if appropriate.

Paradoxically, while applying this model the most important activity the coach and the client undertake together is not so much "getting stuck" in one domain, but trying to become *meta* to all domains. This, if applied creatively and responsibly, could become transformational in the client's life, can bring a discovery of new patterns and lead to a new integration of meaning. Through the process of systems-psychodynamic coaching the client is invited to integrate new learning, conclusions, and insights arising from detailed work undertaken in each of these six domains. The resultant higher level of understanding is carried out within a paradigm of experiential learning (Stein, 2004). I believe that from this higher level of understanding new freedom to act and to behave differently may arrive.

The case study below illustrates one such attempt at integration of meaning using the six-domain model of coaching.

A case study

I wish to illustrate this point by using an example from executive coaching sessions with a manager working in the National Health Service (NHS) within the UK.

> Margaret,[6] a young ambitious professional, became a manager of a large clinical service area within the NHS. Management appealed to her and although she was not entirely new to it, she was keen to develop herself further in this role. She was already attending learning sets and management training courses. After discussion with her own line manager, a few sessions of individual coaching for Margaret were negotiated with me.
>
> During the first session Margaret described her plans, ambitions, and aspirations. The nature of the first session was practical and its aim was to help Margaret to achieve clarity with regard to the first few necessary steps towards her own aspirations and goals in relation to her current role within the organization.
>
> The second session was very different. Margaret started by declaring that she did not really know what we should be talking about, as apparently nothing really urgent occurred to her. However, after a moment, she chose to talk about her current workload. In the first instance, I asked her to illustrate her current workload on a flipchart and to draw histograms of relative height, so as to illustrate relative aspects of her current work. I then asked her to draw corresponding histograms to illustrate *the emotional*, as opposed to *the factual*, weight associated with various aspects of her work. The next step was to invite her to suggest possible hypotheses about any connections that might

exist between the factual and the emotional weighting she associated with various aspects of her work. Immediately, a pattern had begun to emerge. Margaret noted that there was a correlation between some aspects of her current work and the degree of emotional pressure that she was experiencing.

These were the aspects that Margaret found most emotionally exerting:

- managing conflicts where no clear line management existed;
- dealing with another organization while being employed by her current organization;
- supporting and redeveloping her staff;
- strategy.

I asked her to consider whether there was anything that might have connected the above aspects of her work. In response, Margaret identified the following:

- managing conflicts;
- managing her own anxiety;
- staying in control;
- being strategic;
- trying to stay in a "win–win" situation.

Noting that she simply *restated* the above list, I asked her to conduct a further analysis of the above list. She managed to reduce the list to just one important underlying issue: *trying to control her own anxiety*.

As this had become the focal issue, we then talked about various strategies she could adopt in order to control her anxiety. For example, she could normalize her experience on the assumption that anxiety is commonplace within the NHS and is especially rife at times of organizational transition[7], etc. Her own longing to have a strategy for everything was understood as an attempt to control her own anxiety, not just about the "here and now", but also about any future events. This led us to discuss the reasons why Margaret always wanted to stay in control and was so keen to conceal that she may be faltering, even if it could be fully explained by the relative novelty of her position and her untested management role. Margaret was clear that she did not want to show her vulnerability and uncertainty to anybody. She also understood that her need to stay in control at all costs was at times exhausting and emotionally draining to her. She did not wish to allow herself to appear uncertain, or vulnerable and was not clear as to the kind of behaviour that she would need to exhibit in order to show either of the above.

At this point of the session, I asked her to think in terms of a befitting metaphor that could describe this particular attitude. Margaret was invited to illustrate her thoughts by drawing a picture. Margaret drew a swan. She described the image of the swan as "effortlessly gliding on the surface of the water, while under the water the swan was furiously paddling in a way that was invisible to the spectator".

This telling symbol of her own struggle enabled us to seek meaning in the "above the water" and "below the water surface". These two positions above and below the surface correspondingly indicated what is within the public domain and can be seen as well as what is within the private domain and cannot be seen. Short discussion ensued about the significance of these two positions in Margate's life. I asked her why was it so risky to allow any of the private elements to be demonstrated at work, i.e., within the public domain. In other words, what was *the worst* that could have happened, should Margaret ever show her true feelings at work? Margaret pondered for a moment and offered two examples from her private life when she *did* in fact show her angry feelings, a reaction that was an exception to the rule. She recounted an episode from a recent life event, when she was justifiably angry with some of her friends.

At this point it became important to identify what consequences Margaret observed or experienced as a result of her decision to show her angry feelings. She came to the conclusion that the outcome of that particular situation was very positive, as her friends recognized the strength of her feelings and convictions and offered her considerable help and support.

Margaret was asked whether she could expect similar effects at work, should she ever allow herself to show her true feelings. We debated whether this was more to do with her preferred personal style of interaction, or was it expected of a contemporary woman in management that "feelings were *off the agenda*"?[8] Margaret promised to think about it in relation to her own management position and life in general and bring her conclusions to the next session.

The session was nearly over when Margaret looked at her own drawing of the swan and said, "It looks more like a duck than a swan!" This led me to ask if a duck would have been a more appropriate symbol to illustrate her aspiring management role than a swan. Margaret laughed, saying that a duck was far less "split" between the private and the public presentation of itself than a swan. The swan, she agreed, appears to pay a heavy price for the image of superficial perfection that it tries to convey. Unexpectedly, Margaret asked, "Should I try to be more like a duck than a swan?" This enabled me to link up the theme of this session with the emerging meaning Margaret appeared to have ascribed to both symbols. The second session was, after all, about trying to understand how the factual workload of Margaret's job corresponded with the emotional meaning she associated with various aspects of her management role. Was Margaret's attempt to appear calm and in total control, as if unaffected and without emotions, the reason why some of her management tasks had a heavy emotional burden attached to them? I did believe that, if she were able to experiment with being more "duck-like", rather than "swan-like", she might have felt less exhausted and less stressed at work.

The third and last session took place a month later. Margaret reported that the idea of "the swan" (which was later replaced by "the duck") had been a very powerful reminder of the two positions she could occupy at work. The first position was slightly idealistic and perfectionist, delivered at a high cost to herself; the other position was much more realistic and thus sustainable. In the period between the second and the third session she was often checking whether her reactions at work represented the "swan syndrome". Margaret felt that this theme also influenced her way of seeing herself in her professional role and allowed her to question whether a full-time management position was really appropriate for her. At the conclusion of the third session she was veering towards the idea of developing herself in a part time management role, with a good balance between her public and private life. Interestingly, the original "split" between the public and the private (as described above) has been the most influential concept in the work we did together. This theme appears to have connected the six domains of her life and work and additionally highlighted and integrated a number of salient issues in her life.

Analysis and interpretation

I shall now attempt to illustrate how the six domains of executive coaching, as featured in Figure 1, were present throughout the three sessions of executive coaching with Margaret.

During the first session we focused on Margaret's current organizational role; that of a newly appointed manager of a large clinical service area. We took into account the wider organizational context in which her role was performed. She, like many of my

clients, worked within a continually changing organizational environment that was in the middle of yet another major reorganization.
Interestingly, her employing hospital, like all public sector organizations, was in the process of implementing new legislation about
flexible working conditions, and so the split between public *vs.*
private time was not just Margaret's own issue, but it also reflected
a wider organizational context and therefore had a systemic meaning. Some time during the first session was devoted to the analysis
of the context (*domain e*, Figure 1) in which she aspired to develop
her management role (*domain f*, Figure 1). The focus of the first
session, however, was on her aspirations, career progression, and
its future directions (*domain d*, Figure 1) with some references to her
current skills and competencies and any shortfall she may need to
identify and address (*domain c*) in order to meet her aspirations.
Margaret's personality (*domain a*) and various elements of her life
story (*domain b*) were implicit in the first session but became a
prominent source of new connections and learning in the second
session.

Between the second and the third session a degree of integration
appeared to have taken place within Margaret's view of herself. She
realized that she expected perfection of herself, whereas, in effect,
"good enough" was exactly that: "good enough".[9] This had the
effect of releasing her from the impossible demands the work had
made upon her life. Margaret reached a decision that she needed to
combine a part-time management role with more free time to
pursue her own life. At the time we parted there seemed a higher
degree of congruence between the various aspects of her life and
work. Margaret was also very clear as to what she needed to do in
order to stay "on course". My meeting with her, some years later,
seemed to confirm that she *had* stayed the course and had managed
to integrate her life with her work, paying particular attention to an
appropriate work–life balance to the benefit of both domains.

Coaching and life story, some reflections

Another of my recent clients quite spontaneously told me her life
story during our first session. This was useful to my understanding
of the importance that her career played in her life and why the

prospect of retirement was such a difficult step for her to contemplate. During our second session, she told me that soon after she shared her life story with me she felt as if a heavy burden had been lifted off her shoulders. Powerful as it is, the telling of the life story may not, in itself, be sufficient to create the desired change in the client. The telling of the life story needs to be empathically received, profoundly understood and connected with intellectually and emotionally in a way that will allow the client to "re-author" his or her own life and create new layers of meaning (Pooley, 2004; White, 1995). This process may well belong to the domain of psychotherapy, but if it also creates new possibilities and allows new perspectives and new learning to emerge, it also fits comfortably into the realm of coaching and the paradigm of experiential learning (Stein, 2004).

I believe that coaching is much more effective and transformational if it is delivered at the point where the client struggles with a number of issues and when these different contexts in effect overlap. These different contexts can simultaneously resonate within *the life story* and *the work environment domain*, where an experienced coach may be able to detect the likely existence of the same threat or conflict. A number of case studies in this book make this assumption.

This assumption can be illustrated by a vignette of a manager,[10] who was devastated by her inability to manage the hostility she encountered as a result of a recent organizational merger. As a service manager in a human service organization she had successfully negotiated transfer of her entire department from a disbanded organization to another system, only to encounter enormous hostility within the new organization. I have described this case in depth elsewhere (Brunning, 2003), and illustrated the impossibility of the task the manager was facing when the organizational envy and hostility she encountered in the newly merged organization disabled her and made it difficult for her to hold on to her own authority in the role. Detailed examination of her background and some reverie[11] led to a hypothesis that her Jewish background and the hostility she remembered from her own country of origin, from which she had emigrated many years earlier, was unconsciously stirred up by the current scenario of the two organizations merging. As one organizational culture oppressed and dominated the other, she suddenly found herself in the midst of the devalued minority. This had a profoundly disabling effect upon her role performance. She began perceiving herself as being, yet again, "an unwanted immigrant", lost and without support, suspended in a persecutory hostile environment.[12]

This story is a good example of the incomplete conversion of "the beta-elements to the alpha-function", as hypothesized by Bion (1962), with the effect that the necessary process of neutralizing and metabolizing what an individual perceives as poisonous, toxic material (Krantz, 2001; Stein, 2004) cannot be accomplished without external help. In this case, the coach linked the various domains of life and work and was able to demonstrate to the client that her deep distress and discomfort was most probably related to the way in which she unconsciously allowed her own departmental staff to project on to her their own distress, feelings of loss, and of being overpowered by the new organization. It was further hypothesized that, by virtue of the valency of her own life story, she was able to give voice to the complex feelings related to the death of their cherished organization that symbolized a particular way of working and that stood for their collective identity. Her sense of isolation was the result of her staff's desire to move on with the new organizational reality and her inability to do so due to the overpowering sense of loss that she felt on her own and her staff's behalf. Thus, the complex feelings related to the domain of life story, work role, and the organizational environment contained the same threat. Furthermore, *the same threat* was unconsciously being perceived by her at the level of the current working environment (e.g., the merged organization) as well as also being present in the client's own life story (emigration, following hostility and ethnic threats). Dealing with and examining the fusion of the obscured, yet deeply felt meaning attached to both the work context and the life context of the client led to the transformation of the meaning to the point that it became available for use, workable and neutralized as a nontoxic personal conclusion. This process might have been closely related to psychotherapy, but it was *not psychotherapy per se*, even though the effects might have been *therapeutic*. The prevailing aim here was to enable the client to perform her work role more effectively.[13] With regard to the client just described, coaching enabled her to leave the newly merged organization in which she could not function and to seek a different organizational frame for her future career.

Occasionally, it may be necessary for the clients to realize that their role within the organization is quite beyond salvation and so parting of ways might be a more appropriate and a desirable outcome for both the person and the organization.

Working with the client in this multi-faceted way is a complex process as it delicately hovers between different layers of meaning the client brings for examination while offering a chance of integration. The emerging meaning becomes the subject of co-creation between the client and the coach, with the overriding aim to create a higher, more containing, and more enabling layer of meaning from which the client may be able to see and act differently in the future. This work requires delicate poise, containment, sensitivity, and professionalism as well as clarity of purpose and a clear differentiation and distinction between the realm of coaching and psychotherapy. At no time must this endeavour be confused with applied psychotherapy: it exists solely for the purpose of helping the client to perform his/her organizational role better and to position the client closer to the organization (see: Gould, 2004; Huffington, Armstrong, Halton, Hoyle, & Pooley, 2004) even if an occasional outcome may well be the client's departure from the organization in search of a better fit elsewhere.

Sometimes the focus on several seemingly unconnected, yet fused contexts in the client's life (Cronen, Pearce, & Tomm, 1985) offers the opportunity to integrate the underlying meaning present in all contexts. This can be illustrated in the following vignette.

The encounter was one of a peer consultation (co-coaching) between myself and a colleague. We were consulting to one another on issues of professional relevance to both of us. The first session started, as planned, by my colleague identifying her own past and current qualifications, training and professional courses undertaken in support of her professional role. This revealed that *on her own initiative* she undertook numerous training events, well in excess of the average level expected by her professional body. Curiosity led me to inquire why she found it necessary to undertake so many lengthy and costly training events. What was the driving force behind all this training? This produced a fascinating brief life history, which identified that within her own family of origin enormous importance was placed upon continuous learning, training, and skills acquisition, where professional awards, new titles, and qualifications were greatly valued. Over the years, she accumulated what was well beyond the expected level of continuous professional development (CPD) for her own profession. So, the roots of this pursuit were clearly found within her own family, rather than imposed by her professional body. Yet, *absent* from her description of training courses and numerous acquired qualifications was any sense of having "finally arrived" at a point of readiness, at which it would have been appropriate for her to feel pleased and ready to put this extensive knowledge into an integrated practice. Furthermore, there was not even a clear point of arrival suggested upon the horizon.

This led us to question where the validation to practise comes from: does it come *from within or from without*? During this challenging discussion my colleague had a sudden realization[14] that throughout her professional career she must have pursued the route of *external validation*, e.g., one that relied solely upon having her professionalism and her readiness to practise confirmed upon her by several external and formal authorities and organizations and that, despite all resultant qualifications, she never seemed to have fully arrived at a point of having reached the *internal validation* of her own readiness to practise. This realization had a profound effect upon her. She decided that the point had already been reached to begin to exercise her own authority to fulfil her professional role without the need for any additional confirmation. She decided not to pursue yet another lengthy and costly training course. Instead, she began to work in a way that allowed her to internally *re-author* (White, 1995) her accumulated extensive knowledge. She began to put this considerable and impressive knowledge at the disposal of her clients and for the benefit of her own profession. She was also planning to write, as well as to practise.

These two examples illustrate that for an effective intervention within a consultative/coaching frame, it may be necessary to examine the fusion of the two contexts; e.g., the life story and the work role; i.e., the person and the role. It is possible to hypothesize that similar unresolved schemas, conflicts, and issues that operate at the personal and professional layers (the person and the role) will similarly affect and undermine the performance in both domains (life and work). In their respective chapters in this book, Jane Pooley and Clare Huffington bring these two layers of emerging meaning into a completed circle, whereby the organization is also involved and can benefit from this changed meaning. This takes place *either* by the virtue of changing the internal perception of the client (as in the case study described by Jane Pooley's metaphor of the chess player) *or* by the virtue of the organization-wide intervention, as in the example of the investment bank in Clare Huffington's second case study, where the executives of the investment bank agreed to take a fresh look at the meaning behind their existing procedures and policies.

Perhaps a more appropriate diagram would then look like Figure 2.

Coaching and personality, some reflections

In the chapter on the development and application of psychometric techniques, Richard Kwiatkowski describes how a Jungian approach to personality classification found a lasting beneficial and influential role within the coaching industry. In this chapter I wished to illustrate how the six-domain model would differ in application if the client's personality, rather than life story, were the dominant focus of work. This can be illustrated in the following vignette.

I was working in a coaching framework with a client, who came with her MBTI type (see chapter by Kwiatkowski on personality testing in relation to coaching) having already been given to her as

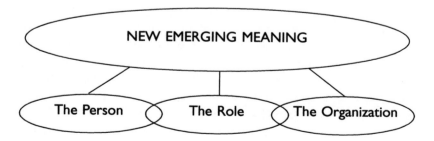

Figure 2.   New emerging meaning.

a result of attending a prior learning set. My client was an experienced public sector manager and the reason for her referral was a request by her sponsor, fully supported by the client, that she needed help in her interaction with her own staff. She gave me her MBTI type as INTJ. This type is known as Introverted Intuition with Thinking, and it may well demonstrate itself in human interactions as insightful, logical, thoughtful, innovative, visionary, but also as single-minded in pursuit of a task or objective and unappreciative of others' contribution (see Hirsh, 1998; Myers, 1998).

In working with this client, given her previously diagnosed personality type and associated problems, it became clear that we needed to focus on her interactive style, rather than to work with the unfolding meaning of her life story. In order to help her engage with her team in a more effective way, we began our work under a banner of trying to teach her how she might *engage their hearts and minds*, on the assumption that her preferred style would only find appeal to the *minds* of her staff or not engage them at all. She noticed that her staff members were usually hostile or resistant to any new ideas and innovations, which she enthusiastically brought into the service. She found it difficult to understand why nobody within her department shared her enthusiasm for innovations. I worked on the hypothesis that she found it difficult to show her genuine enthusiasm to her staff because she experienced each innovation more as *a technical idea* than as a visionary possibility fused with emotional connotations. She certainly found it difficult to demonstrate to her staff her vision, together with associated feelings. Consequently, they were left feeling "cold" and uninvolved, the technical explanations having fallen short of the staff's needs for engagement with the vision. All they saw was yet another management change programme and refused to get involved with it.

Early in our work I drew a symbol of the heart on one part of the flipchart and a symbol of the brain on the other part of the same flipchart. I invited my client to tell me how she would customarily introduce a new change initiative to her staff. As she demonstrated her typical style, I wrote the words she actually used on the flipchart. It came as no surprise to her (or me) that all of the words she chose were within the "mind" and not a single word was within the "heart" category. It was therefore important to demonstrate to my client how the same message would sound if it were to appeal to the hearts and the minds of her staff. I demonstrated this by using other words to describe the same change initiative. Following my modelling, she practised and rehearsed a new speech a number of times and agreed to use in real life key words that carried the specific "heart" symbolism. She practised between coaching sessions to some effect and with a corresponding improvement in the style with which she interacted with her staff. Interestingly, during a subsequent three-way debriefing with her sponsoring manager, my client was able to demonstrate not only her new behavioural change, but also an in-depth understanding of how and why she needed to change her interactive style. At another review session, some months later, my client reported surprisingly profound and lasting changes in her interactive style and in her general attitude towards work. I was impressed with these changes, given her particular personality type.

Coaching and psychotherapy, some reflections

In order to allow clients to make connections between various levels of meaning (Brunning, 1998; Pooley, 2004; White, 2000), as an executive coach I might use various therapeutic and counselling skills and techniques. However, at no time do I actually enter the domain of counselling or psychotherapy *per se*. Subsequently, in the first case study it was of no great concern to note that there was a considerable split between "the public" and "the private" domain in the life of my client. So long as this split was noted and understood as a recurrent theme, we did not need to trace its aetiology and try to change the pattern of associated behaviour, as might have been the case in psychotherapy.

Correspondingly, I may encourage my clients to take up various roles, or to experiment with different nuances to their main work role in between sessions, as in the above vignettes, but I do not actually engage in skills training as such. Having said that, it should not be excluded that, as a result of executive coaching, the clients may be tempted to pursue further training, counselling, or even psychotherapy at some stage of their development, or to act on newly acquired insights with profound effects.

The practitioners of executive coaching differ considerably in the extent to which they are happy to embrace various domains within the coaching framework. This book illustrates different positions practitioners can take as they tend to privilege one domain over another. Consider, for instance, that Lionel Stapley starts every new executive coaching contract by inviting his new client to tell his or her life story, so that the more contemporary problems, such as those experienced within the context of the current role performance, could be better understood and seen as rooted in the client's childhood and in the relationships with parental figures. I am, however, of the view that there is no need to start each executive coaching relationship with the retelling of the client's life story, as long as the existence of the story is openly acknowledged and access to it negotiated from the outset of the contract. Additionally, attention must be given to a respectful and appropriate reception of the story if and when it is offered within the context of executive coaching.

In her chapter, Miranda Alcock gives an example of an executive whose childhood-based psychic pain had caught up with him late in life and resurfaced unexpectedly in his work role. Marlene Spero similarly describes a client whose unresolved Oedipal issues took over some of his work-related interactions. In neither of these cases did the authors actually engage in psychotherapy *per se*. It is possible, however, to see that this way of working and framing of the focal issue might have been a logical step to undertake by practitioners with a psychoanalytic psychotherapy training background, and correspondingly, should not be undertaken by anybody without such a background or training.

Conclusion

The overt aim of executive coaching is not necessarily to help the client to reach a better personal integration, to deepen personal insight, or to change self-perception, *per se*, but to enhance the client's work performance. However, if all six domains were to be recognized as equally valid aspects of the coaching process, the clients may well experience changes that go beyond the improvements of their current role performance and some transformation of meaning may also occur.

What, then, are the unique features of coaching practice delivered from a systems-psychodynamic perspective? I would argue that it is not so much working with the unconscious processes *per se*, but the creation of an enabling framework where the transformation of meaning that links the person, the role, and the organization can take place. This could have profound, positive, and re-energizing impact upon all three: the person, the role, and the organization.

It is my belief that if we, as executive coaches, were able and willing to address *the whole person* within the organizational and the human contexts, we would be working for our client's best interests and also be demonstrating the right organizational and management principles in action.

Notes

1. This chapter is based on an earlier paper originally published in 2001 in the *Journal of Organizational and Social Dynamics* (OPUS).
2. See also Gould, Stapley, & Stein (2001), *The Systems Psychodynamics of Organizations*.
3. This issue is discussed in depth in *Working Below the Surface: the Emotional Life of Contemporary Organizations* (Huffington, Armstrong, Halton, Hoyle, & Pooley, 2004). See also chapters by Laurence Gould, Jane Pooley, Marlene Spero, and Miranda Alcock in this book, each offering a further elucidation of this theme.
4. The reader is referred to a chapter by Laurence Gould in this book on the importance of the client's developmental life stage in coaching.
5. The reader is referred to the chapter by Jane Pooley in this book on the stages of the coaching contract.
6. This is not her real name. Client's permission for publication has been obtained.
7. See James Krantz (2001) on the impact of organizational change upon individuals.
8. See Kathleen Pogue-White in *The Systems Psychodynamics of Organizations* (2001) and a chapter by Angela Eden in this book about the emotional cost of the struggle of women in contemporary organizations.
9. Also, see the chapter by Jane Pooley.

10. All vignettes are of real clients and their permission for publication has been obtained.
11. See chapter by Gordon Lawrence on the role of unconscious thinking in coaching.
12. For a fuller discussion of this case and about working with metaphors in consultation see also Brunning (1999, 2003); for a fuller description of impact of organizational change upon individuals and groups see also Krantz (2001); for working with "the tragic position" in coaching, see Gordon Lawrence in this book.
13. See also the chapter by Jane Pooley, "The layers of meaning: a coaching journey".
14. See the role of "epiphany" in Lawrence's chapter.

References

Armstrong, D. (1997). "The institution in the mind". Reflections on the relation of psychoanalysis to work with organizations. *Free Associations*, 7(41): 1–14.

Bion, W. R. (1962). *Learning from Experience*. London: Heineman Medical.

Brunning, H. (1998). Working briefly with meaning. *International Journal of Psychology and Psychotherapy, Changes*, 16(4): 274–283.

Brunning, H. (2001). The six domains model of executive coaching. *International Journal of Social and Organizational Dynamics*, 1(2): 254–263.

Brunning, H., (2003). Organizational merger—a dance of constructive and destructive elements. *Organizations and People: the AMED Journal*, 10(1): 2–8.

Cronen, V., Pearce, W., & Tomm, K. (1985). A dialectical view of personal change. In: K. Gergen & K. Davis (Eds.), *The Social Construction of the Person*. New York: Springer-Verlag.

Gould, L. J. (2004). Fraternal disciplines: group relations training and systems psychodynamic organizational consultation. In: L. J. Gould, L. Stapley, & M. Stein (Eds.), *Experiential Learning in Organizations* (pp. 37–61). London: Karnac.

Heron, J. (1990). *Helping the Client—A Creative Practical Guide*. London: Sage.

Hirsh, S., & Kummerow, J. M. (1998). *Introduction to Type in Organizations*. Palo Alto, CA: Consulting Psychologists' Press.

Huffington, C., Armstrong, D., Halton, W., Hoyle, L., & Pooley, J. (2004). *Working Below the Surface: The Emotional Life of Contemporary Organizations.* London: Karnac.

Klein, M. (1946). *Notes on Some Schizoid Mechanisms.* In: *Envy and Gratitude, vol. 3, The Writings of Melanie Klein.* London: Hogarth, 1975.

Krantz, J. (2001). Dilemmas of organizational change: a systems psycho-dynamic perspective. In: L. J Gould, L. Stapley, & M. Stein (Eds.), *The Systems Psychodynamics of Organizations* (pp. 133–155). London: Karnac.

Malan, D. H. (1997). *Individual Psychotherapy and the Science of Psycho-dynamics.* London: Butterworth.

Menzies, I. (1998). *Containing Anxiety in Institutions. Selected Essays, Vol. 1.* London: Free Association Books.

Miller, E. J., & Rice, A. K. (1967). *Systems of Organization.* London: Tavistock.

Myers, I. B. (1998). *Introduction to Type* (6th edn). Palo Alto: Consulting Psychologists' Press.

Obholzer, A., & Roberts, V. Z. (1994). *The Unconscious at Work; Individual and Organizational Stress in the Human Services.* London: Routledge.

Pogue-White, K. (2001). Applying learning from experience: the inter-section of psychoanalysis and organizational role consultation. In: L. J. Gould, L. Stapley, & M. Stein (Eds.), *The Systems Psychodynamics of Organizations* (pp. 17–43). London: Karnac.

Pooley, J. (2004). Layers of meaning: a coaching journey. In: C. Huffing-ton, D. Armstrong, W. Halton, L. Hoyle, & J. Pooley (Eds.), *Working Below the Surface: The Emotional Life of Contemporary Organizations* (pp. 171–190). London: Karnac.

Stein, M. (2004). Theories of experiential learning and the unconscious. In: L. Gould, L. Stapley, & M. Stein (Eds.), *Experiential Learning in Organizations* (pp. 19–35). London: Karnac.

Talmon, M., (1993). *Single Session Solutions.* London: Addison-Wesley.

White, M. (1995). *Re-authoring Lives.* London: Dulwich Centre.

White, M. (2000). *Reflections on Narrative Practice.* London: Dulwich Centre.

CHAPTER SEVEN

Inside-out and outside-in: the use of personality and 360 degree data in executive coaching

Richard Kwiatkowski

Overview

In this chapter I am going to describe how, in developing a coaching relationship, I have used other sources of information, beyond the usual verbal or, indeed, written, information normally provided by clients. The two methods I have used most frequently are personality measures and 360 Degree Feedback; what one might term "inside-out" and "outside-in" sources. I will begin by describing, briefly, something about these sources and what I consider to be their advantages when used in a coaching relationship. I will then present a case study, reflect on it, and briefly consider Brunning's recent model of coaching as a way of examining what, consequently, was and was not explored with the client.

For some readers of this chapter, and in particular those of a psychodynamic, relativistic, person-centred, postmodern, or even constructionist persuasion, the notion of including external data may perhaps sit uncomfortably with their underlying epistemological position. By the end of the chapter, I hope to show that, notwithstanding the basically humanistic, and perhaps even psychodynamic, perspective that I personally tend to employ, personality instruments can be helpful in understanding certain aspects of personality, and in structuring engagement, communication, and thinking with the client, while 360 Degree Feedback presents a powerful way of engaging with the client's reality and priorities.

There *is* a reality within life and work that exists beyond that of an individual's own single perspective, and both the use of personality instruments and 360 Degree Feedback are methods of enquiry that allow an individual to access some important data about the outside world; for example, in beginning to understand how internal predispositions may influence reaction to external reality, as well as engaging with how social aspects of the world help define or even construe an individual in their relativistic context.

Personality instruments

I have most often used the Myers–Briggs type indicator as a personality instrument so I shall present my use of it here. In this chapter I am going to describe the use of the Myers–Briggs Type Indicator[(r)] or the MBTI[(r)]. For ease of reading, from now on I shall omit the reference to it being a registered trademark and assume that readers know this to be the case.

Based on the seminal work of Carl Jung, the Myers–Briggs Type Indicator (MBTI) is probably the most widely used personality instrument in the world; perhaps because of its non-judgemental nature it is popular within a variety of organizations. Over 2.5 million people per year complete this instrument, under carefully controlled conditions, and receive feedback and interpretation as to its meaning. It is used for a variety of purposes, including enhancing self-awareness (one reason why I use it in coaching), enhancing communication, understanding customers, working out and utilizing learning preferences, providing a common language for discussing differences, in relationship counselling, and in team building.

A full description of the instrument is beyond the scope of this chapter, but I will describe what I consider, for our purpose, its most salient characteristics, so that the reader can get a sense of how and why this instrument, and the data that it produces may be of use in coaching.

The MBTI makes certain assumptions about the nature of personality. One assumption, which is fairly common in the psychological literature, is that personality is a relatively enduring set of characteristics that predispose individuals to behave in particular, and broadly understandable (and perhaps even predictable) ways across a variety of contexts. The behavioural manifestation of underlying personality characteristics may be modified by various factors, such as transient physiological states, social context, culture and so forth, but the supposition is that there exists something enduring that we can term "personality", and that we can become aware of it.

Another underlying assumption of the MBTI is that people are naturally (and probably related to genetic or neurophysiological factors) one sort of "type" or another. For example, someone might prefer to interact with a small number, rather than a large number of people; in childhood they displayed this characteristic and in adulthood the same characteristic remains, though, obviously, tempered by experience and, one hopes, enhanced by social and interpersonal skills. One interpretation of this, by the person concerned, might be that if asked whether he or she were an intro-vert or an extrovert, the individual would say that fundamentally he or she was an introvert. This parallels the notion of type theories in general; fundamentally, you are one or the other. The MBTI is thus a *type* rather than a *trait* theory. What this means is that people are identified as being on one side of a dimension or another. By analogy, you would be classified as right- or left-handed, rather than 95% right-handed, which might occur if one used a trait approach. This, in contrast, would seek to assign a numerical quantity to various categories. This example, however, only serves to illustrate the fact that we do not always exhibit the same behaviour. For instance, a right-handed person does use their left hand for some tasks; they tend not to be so skilled, but they *can* use their non-preferred hand. In this formulation of personality, we also focus on preference; people have clear and specific preferences, but they can, at times, behaviourally exhibit the other side of the trait. In general, it is not so smooth or natural, it often requires conscious effort, and frequently more energy, to do something in a manner opposite to that which one prefers. I shall return to the notion of preference later.

There are a number of advantages in using a personality instrument *per se*: the first is that of clarity of dimensions. We all naturally have a set of constructs that we use when examining personality. In many cases these are essentially lay dimensions of personality that we have developed, and may never be actually articulated or consciously examined. Sometimes, they are useful and sensible; for example, we may be able to use, quite accurately, the notion of the level of anxiety a particular individual is displaying at any one time in tempering our interactions with them. On the other hand, some of these "implicit personality theories" may actually be rather hopeless. For example, the belief that someone who is fat is jolly, or that someone who is blonde is impractical, or that all lawyers are dishonest, or all dentists are sadists. In contrast, in using the MBTI we have a number of very clearly understood and well-defined dimensions of personality, which have been established through observation and research spanning nearly sixty years, and which correlate highly with other measures of personality, including various measures of the "big five". These are the five underlying personality dimensions that seem to subsume all other personality dimensions: Openness, Neuroticism, Conscientiousness, Extroversion, and Agreeableness. (For an explanation of their derivation please see Barrick & Mount (1993), for the relations between MBTI and the "big five", please see Bayne (1993).)

A second advantage is that of confidence: people are categorized according to type, and if on a personality instrument, such as the MBTI, someone scores themselves particularly clearly in terms of their preferences, then one can be reasonably certain (and the research evidence and statistical data exist to back up this supposition) that they actually are that particular type, or, perhaps more accurately, actually possess those aspects or attributes of personality.

But no instrument is infallible: as with any psychometric instrument, another advantage of using the MBTI is that we know in some detail about its characteristics and properties. Thus, we can calculate the amount of that error, or "noise", inherent in a particular scale. For example, if a preference is not fully clear you need to seek extra information. This contrasts with the assessment of personality made by (most) people; some people are accurate judges of character, skill, or personality, but the research evidence indicates that most of us are not, despite our fond imaginings. Thus, a psychometric instrument is likely to have a number of technical and objective advantages when used in this way.

A further advantage is that the MBTI is particularly humanistic and non-judgemental in its orientation. It does not make any assumptions about what is the "best" sort of personality; it accepts that there are "gifts differing" (Briggs & Myers, 1980) and that, given a certain level of underlying competence, all sorts of people can undertake all sorts of jobs or tasks successfully, but would perhaps tend to perform them in rather different ways. Therefore, if used properly, it is an extremely affirming and positive measure. The same extends to the type descriptors themselves, as these are couched in positive terms and this allows people, particularly on first contact with the instrument, to be more receptive to them and their implications.

The MBTI is easily understandable; it consists of four pairs of personality characteristics (see below). These pairs, in combination, produce one of sixteen personality types. It is, of course, over-simplifying the world if one assumes that everything about an individual is contained in their type, but no competent person would make such an absurd claim. On the other hand, I have frequently heard variations of "the description of me was extra-ordinarily accurate" during debriefing, which I take to mean that the client readily recognized key aspects of themselves in the description.

Finally, the MBTI facilitates communication; if a group of people have all been exposed to the MBTI they will be able to share a language with which to discuss their individual differences. It is a positive language, it is well articulated, and it enables diversity to be discussed in a non-threatening way, all of which can be of tremendous benefit in understanding other people as well as oneself.

In using the MBTI, it is important to emphasize the fact that people determine their own personality preference. I may have used the MBTI with hundreds of people in my career and certain sorts of characteristics seem to me to be fairly easy to distinguish, but it is not my judgement that is important, but rather that of the individual concerned. Thus, as well as completing a questionnaire and receiving a score, I would provide my client with multiple opportunities, both before and after filling out the questionnaire, for them to assess themselves against these dimensions, and to decide if the questionnaire is "correct". This might be carried out through the client reading the description of the various characteristics, so that they can assess themselves on a continuum, to sort themselves into categories, reading descriptions of different types and suggesting which fits them most closely, looking at lists of development activities and wondering which of these is most applicable to their own situation, undertaking structured exercises in a group, observing the different ways people with different characteristics interact, or react, speaking with like minded people, and so forth. While I do not wish to labour this point, I would like to emphasize that my use of the MBTI is by no means deterministic, but rather developmental, as it starts from the assumption that people can have insight into fundamental aspects of their own personality.

Although it is impossible to do so to any depth in this chapter, I have attempted to provide a brief taster or summary of the personality dimensions, which the MBTI uses in the table below.

As mentioned already, the MBTI is a Type Theory, which means that it gathers information about people according to particular dimensions, and then classifies them as being of one type or the other. For example, the notion of introversion and extraversion, as first hypothesized by Carl Jung (1921), examines where an individual gets their energy from. Extroversion is denoted by the letter E, and introversion by the letter I. Briefly, the other dimension pairs: sensing is denoted by the letter S, and intuition by the letter N, thinking is represented by the letter T, and feeling by the letter F, while judging is J, and perceiving is P (see Table 1).

It needs to be stressed that the use of the letters to denote different types is deliberate, and I believe, is also deliberately commonplace in much of the writing about the MBTI. The use of the letters helps people to understand that ordinary everyday language is not being used. As an example, if we asked structural engineers about stress, they would understand exactly what we meant, if we asked doctors about stress, they would understand exactly what we meant, if we asked opera singers about stress, they, too, would know the exact meaning of the term. The point here is that what seems like an ordinary everyday English word actually has

Table 1.   A summary of type theory and its effects.

Type	Description
	Where does your energy come from?
E	Through external stimulation Interacting with other people Extrinsically
I	From deep within yourself Through staying interested in things Intrinsically
	What sort of information do you prefer?
S	The concrete and real The here-and-now Related to the practical world
N	Possibilities and ideas The future Related to ideals
	On what basis do you make decisions?
T	Rationality and logic Thinking and evaluating Considering things
F	Values and beliefs Emotions and reactions Considering people
	How do you prefer to live your life?
J	Keeping things ordered Planfully Without surprises
P	Keeping things open At the last minute Keeping things new

a specific, technical, but *different* meaning for each of these professional groups. In the same way, we are in this context using terms like extroversion or introversion in a strictly technical sense.

360 Degree Feedback: a brief introduction

Three hundred and sixty degree feedback is an increasingly popular tool among a wide variety of organizations and is used within both the private and public sector. Many middle and senior managers now routinely expect to be assessed annually, or biannually, not only by their bosses, but also by their peers and subordinates. In some organizations this has been extended in a number of interesting ways; for example, by having all staff subjected to 360 Degree Feedback, or else by including customers in rating named and known staff (e.g., by the clients of a law firm), or unnamed and relatively anonymous individuals (e.g., following a call to a Call Centre), or even extra organizational entities (e.g,. statutory bodies) in the process.

In a well designed 360 Degree Feedback process, both the target individual who is being assessed and those rating him or her are properly trained in the process. Thus, for example, they will be aware of the need to use good data, to rate each dimension separately to avoid "horns or halo" effects (the tendency to allow one characteristic—for example how much you like someone—to influence a host of others; so that no differentiation is really made between aspects of a person; essentially, there is only one big, amorphous factor present). They will also bear in mind the pervasiveness of central tendency (the tendency of most people to use mid points in a rating scale and to shy away from using "extreme" ends, high or low; this limits variance and, thus, the usefulness of, for instance, comparative or developmental data) and so forth. The fact that many people do not know of these artefacts indicates that training is important.

Crucially, in a well designed 360° process, the characteristics on which the target individual is to be rated are carefully designed and may be based, for instance, on a specific set of competencies, precisely developed as applying to people at that level in that organization. They may have at their core current performance indicators, or they may be aspirational, being more closely related to how the organization wants its people to function in a hypothetical future.

The form of 360 Degree Feedback also varies: in some cases very specific aspects of behaviour are assessed, in others, much more general characteristics are looked at; thus, "smiles when greets a customer" might be an item on a checklist to be rated, or a much broader category such as "social skills" might be assessed, leaving more discretion to the (skilled) assessor. For the purpose of this chapter, I present a number of fairly typical competencies, with some particular ratings.

What are the advantages of using 360 Degree Feedback, first for the individual and second for the individual in the context of an organization?

We can, I think, do no better than consider this comment from Robbie Burns (1786):

> O wad some Power the giftie gie us
> To see oursels as ithers see us!
> It wad frae mony a blunder free us,
> An' foolish notion:
> What airs in dress an' gait wad lea'e us,
> An' ev'n devotion!

Through 360 Degree Feedback that power is given to the individuals to examine themselves in the mirror of their co-workers' views. It is very difficult to continue to maintain that you are "the most skilled communicator" in the whole organization if your boss, your subordinates, and your peers rate you as "poor" on this very characteristic. As in this rather extreme example, the target individual will have to understand what this difference in perception and rating actually means. One recalls the JoHari window, which identifies four areas of self knowledge:

1. Area open and public (known to self and known to public);
2. Area blind (not known to self, but known to others);
3. Area hidden (known to self, but not known to others);
4. Area unknown (unknown to self and unknown to others).

Since in almost every 360 Degree scheme the responses are anonymous, people are inevitably encouraged to say what they would not, or could not, say face to face, thus "hidden" areas may be exposed.

This exposure to data is, in my view, at the core of the power of the technique: simply through the fact of feeding back information that has previously almost certainly been hidden, or obfuscated, target individuals will need (at the very least) to make some changes in their thought processes, their self-perceptions, or their self-awareness, in order to understand what has happened and the meaning of the data to them. At the extremes, the process of receiving such powerful feedback can spark off the beginnings of some very radical change.

Depending on your background and training (and probably your personality) this last statement may seem obvious and logical, or troubling and dangerous. Some people can respond to new information by incorporating it in existing schema of thought; for others even slightly discrepant data can lead to psychic upheaval. Most well functioning individuals (i.e., the sort of people whom one will tend to see for a coaching intervention) are relatively well adjusted and will be able to deal with the feedback they receive appropriately. For many, it will not be a surprise. They will metabolize the information. That is not to imply that change will not take place: but it may be gradual and gentle, rather than dramatic or traumatic. However, the fact that feedback always has the potential to impact negatively on people, or to harm them in some ways, indicates that it must be carefully handled.

In the context of an organization, there are a large number of benefits to be derived from using 360 Degree Feedback, as shown in Table 2. This is largely self-explanatory and is taken from the Department of Trade and Industry (DTI) website. It was developed through a joint initiative funded by the British Psychological

Table 2.   Reasons for using 360 Degree Feedback

Increased individual self-awareness
Increased understanding of the behaviours required to improve both individual and organizational effectiveness
More focused development activities, built around the skills and competencies required for successful organizational performance
Increased involvement of people at all levels of the organization
Increased individual ownership for self-development and learning
Increased familiarity with the implications of cultural or strategic change

Source: From "360 degree feedback, best practice guidelines" (BPS/DTI/ CIPD/SHL (2001))

Society, The Chartered Institute of Personnel and Development, The Department of Trade and Industry, and Saville and Holdsworth, a major psychometric test developer and publisher.

Thus the involvement of people throughout the organization in assessment, and their awareness of the importance of specific competencies to the organization, means that at an organizational level, 360 Degree Feedback can have significant organizational advantages.

More aware organizations will use 360 Degree Feedback systematically, utilizing these same appropriate competencies for selection and development and, increasingly, through linking the outputs to structured training, placement, coaching, mentoring, cross functional, experiential, and other opportunities.

In passing, I should note that there is a good deal of debate as to how 360 Degree results should be presented. On the whole, I am not in favour of presenting "averages", for the following reasons: first, information is lost on the pattern of results (for example, peers may "love" an individual, but subordinates may "hate" them); second, regression towards the mean can imply that a fairly average score has been achieved, but this may mask important, significant and unsystematic variance; and third, the use of averages, sometimes to several decimal places, suggests a level of accuracy that is often simply not justified by the underlying data. To be told that you've been rated at 3.56 on leadership is actually fairly meaningless, but may have a spurious "scientific" credibility associated with it, in the minds of the unwary client. For an interesting and readable recent summary of 360 Degree processes and their research base, the reader is referred to Fletcher and Baldry (1999).

To summarize, 360 Degree Feedback allows a glimpse of the outside world, from others' perspectives, to be made available to the client. The use of a personality instrument is almost the opposite, as a way of codifying the inside looking out and offering a way of examining individuals self-perception of their own personality, as well as by providing a systematic and valid structure within which to understand it.

Having briefly described the MBTI and 360 Degree Feedback I will now try to demonstrate how these have been used in a case study. The reader interested in trends in organizational change and the assessment methodologies that organizations may consequently deploy in the future is referred to Kwiatkowski (2003).

The case study

Because of issues of client confidentiality, as well as commercial sensitivity, I am going to present a hybrid case. All of the incidents and conversations recounted here have actually taken place over the years, but not necessarily with the same client, nor in the organization as described.

Biographical and background information

Peter Jones (the name of the client has been changed) was a regional manager in a major European distribution business. He was in his forties, earned a generous salary, which included bonuses and share options. He had joined the organization a few years before we met, having previously worked for a rival, though a smaller, organization. He was well known at his level in the industry and was considered very competent. His original qualifications had, unusually, been in accountancy, and he did not have a degree. He was married, with three young children.

Reason for consultation

Despite the fact that he was considered extremely competent within his own organization, and had achieved or frequently exceeded his specific targets, there were concerns expressed by members of the Board that he was not, in effect, maximizing his full potential. There was a "high-flyer" scheme operating in the organization and Peter had been placed within the "talent pool" three years previously. Despite being identified as a "high-flyer", his performance, while good, had somehow "not quite made the grade" as yet. There was a strong feeling that he should be operating at a more senior level within the organization by now, that his internal drive was high, that he undoubtedly had ability, but somehow his "personal impact" was missing. This seemed to relate to how he came across, rather than any lack of specific expertise.

He had been described by one of his colleagues as an "extremely sociable book-keeper". And, informally, this was also how the Human Resource Director described him to me.

Initial contact

We met in Peter Jones' office. It had proved rather difficult to organize the initial meeting, as a previous meeting had been re scheduled. Our first meeting lasted only twenty minutes and was very much a planning meeting.

Peter appeared smartly dressed, polite, sociable, and apparently healthy. He was pleased that his organization had provided the possibility of coaching. It later turned out that he had some positive views about coaching based on friends' experiences.

We started by speaking in rather general terms about the business and some of its current challenges, as I had worked with other organizations in the sector. He seemed to find this industry "small talk" reassuring, but we very quickly moved on to talking about him. He, alongside most of the management team, had recently been through a 360 Degree evaluation programme. This was the first year that such a programme had been used. Although written feedback was provided, there were no other obvious consequences for those assessed. However, it was "understood" that from next year, results from the 360 Degree Feedback process would be factored into staff's annual appraisals, salary increases and bonuses would be partially dependent on achieving specific ratings, and there would be a combination of individual targets and minima at each level. There was also the implicit threat that the 360 Degree process would be used to monitor performance improvement. Peter was happy to use his 360 Degree Feedback results as part of the coaching process, as he wanted help to interpret it and also was keen to influence ratings in subsequent years, saying, "My bonus will depend on it."

After initial discussion, he agreed to complete the MBTI in preparation for our first formal session. The organization was willing to pay for four sessions in total, the timing and frequency of which, were to be left entirely to us to negotiate. In addition, the Human Resource Director wanted to receive a report about how the coaching had progressed. I agreed that I would submit a short report, which would of necessity be very general, and that the wording would first be agreed with Peter. I also made it clear that if Peter did not wish to divulge any information, then I would support him in that action. Nevertheless, I still expected to be paid, whatever the outcome. The HR Director agreed to this in writing, by letter.

Session 1

Peter brought the results of his 360 Degree Feedback profile to his first coaching session as well as the MBTI. We started the session by discussing in general terms what he expected to get from coaching, as well as taking a brief history. Peter said he had given this a great deal of thought. He had recently received his 360 Degree profile, but had not had the chance to discuss it with anyone, except briefly with his wife. He was not sure how accurate the process was, because he felt that the people consulted did not really have enough data to go on, and so much of the time were actually guessing. He did seem ambivalent about the process and while he was initially reluctant to do so, he eventually did express some annoyance with the organization, which had gone through a potentially far-reaching 360 Degree programme, but, in his view, had simply " dumped" the results upon their staff without providing any support or direction to those receiving feedback.[1]

Fundamentally, he wanted to know whether he had a future with the organization, or if he should consider leaving, as he did not seem to be advancing as quickly as he thought he should be.

I cite here only the most important dimensions of his 360 Degree results, as identified by Peter, and, for the sake of clarity I will also summarize the results of his peers, subordinates, and boss. I would like to stress that in feeding back 360 Degree material I would always provide more detailed information than this, while, of course, respecting and protecting the anonymity of the raters who provided the raw scores.

Leadership

	Below Average			Average			Above Average
	1	2	3	4	5	6	7
SELF					✓		
PEER		✓					
SUB				✓			
BOSS				✓			

Communication

	Below Average			Average			Above Average
	1	2	3	4	5	6	7
SELF				✓			
PEER			✓				
SUB						✓	
BOSS							✓

Technical knowledge

	Below Average			Average			Above Average
	1	2	3	4	5	6	7
SELF				✓			
PEER							✓
SUB							✓
BOSS							✓

Coaching/mentoring

	Below Average			Average			Above Average
	1	2	3	4	5	6	7
SELF				✓			
PEER		✓					
SUB						✓	
BOSS					✓		

Personal impact

	Below Average			Average			Above Average
	1	2	3	4	5	6	7
SELF				✓			
PEER				✓			
SUB				✓			
BOSS			✓				

Results orientation

	Below Average			Average			Above Average
	1	2	3	4	5	6	7
SELF							✓
PEER	✓						
SUB						✓	
BOSS							✓

Peter's MBTI Type was rated as ISTJ (Introverted, Sensing, Thinking, Judging) by the questionnaire. We went through the process of self-rating, and examination of the dimensions; he seemed satisfied that this was a true reflection of his type, and that he had "always been like this".

I gave him a copy of *An Introduction to Type in Organisations* (Hirsh & Kummerow, 2000) to take away with him. In the session we examined his initial disappointment with this "type" because he thought that the organization had preferred Extroversion rather than Introversion as a characteristic. He engaged with the notion that we all had "gifts differing", that there were many different ways of achieving the same end, many different ways of being a leader, and that context and ambition (a word he had used with some emphasis) were important.

In *Introduction to Type in Organisations*, Hirsh and Kummerow describe the typical contribution to an organization of someone who is ISTJ. Somebody with ISTJ profile was characterized by

> getting things done steadily and on schedule, concentrating on details and careful about managing them, having things at the right place at right time, can be counted on to honour commitments and follow-through, and work within the organizational structure comfortably. [Hirsh & Kummerow, 2000, p. 10]

Under leadership style it suggests that people who are ISTJ

> use experience and knowledge of the facts to make decisions, build on reliable stable and consistent performance, respect traditional hierarchical approaches, reward those who follow the rules while getting the job done, and pay attention to immediate and practical organization needs. [*ibid.*]

Under the section describing possible development they suggest that people who are ISTJ

> need to pay attention to a wider future ramifications of problems in addition to present realities, may need to consider the human element and communicate deserved appreciation, they need to try fresh approaches to avoid ruts, may need to develop patience for those who communicate differently or who bypass standard operating procedures. [*ibid.*]

Peter recognized nearly all of these facets as applying to him.

We then moved on to an initial viewing of his 360 Degree results. The most obvious factor in all the 360 Degree ratings was how poorly his peers had rated him. He commented on this and agreed with the suggestion that he would try and work out what the underlying reasons might be, and in addition, he would seek information, based on past experience, but it also on information that he would now gather from people in his current organization, as to what the threshold levels were for advancement in the organization, as judged through the rating scale employed in the 360 Degree Feedback. This task was tailored to his MBTI (ISTJ) results and some clues from the session as well as patterns in the 360 Degree data. In other words, by using the information we already had we could formulate an activity, to take place between sessions, which would move forward key issues. In this case, his ready acceptance indicated that I had "read" the data, and the cues provided in the session, appropriately.

Session 2

During the second session, Peter was very keen to describe what had happened when he had been searching out information from his peers about how he was perceived, and seeking to establish what the threshold levels of performance were, in order that he could "get ahead" in his organization.

He reported, with some surprise, that everybody hugely respected his technical expertise and knowledge of the area. If anything, some had told him, the rating was an underestimate. He was seen as a significant professional figure, both within his organization and beyond it; but this was clearly limited to his technical competence ratings. However, people liked working for him, as he saw it, due mainly to the fact that he was able to bring about huge increases in knowledge and expertise in them in a very short period of time. This he saw as the reason behind the high ratings that he received under the "Coaching/mentoring" dimension of the 360 Degree Feedback process.

He was also unusually surprised by the fact that most people had emphasized to him the political nature of decision-making processes within the organization, something he was not attuned to before. In addition, he had, for the first time, had some very open and frank conversations with people at his own level in the organization, especially concerning how he came across to them.

The main theme of these conversations was that people did not really know him as a person. Because his presentation was rather quiet and technical, his personal impact was much less influential than it should have been. In particular, a strange process of projection seemed be occurring with his peers: because of his technical expertise and his introverted nature, he had been labelled as a "geek", a "boffin", or a "pointy head" and almost everything that he said or did was now seen through this filter. It was as though having a lot of technical knowledge was not seen as a "sexy" characteristic within the organization. Furthermore, during his conversations, managerial peers had "confessed" to having qualifications and technical knowledge that they had deliberately kept quiet about.

In thinking about the culture of the organization, Peter had come to the conclusion that either he could be seen as an "expert" or he could be seen as "a strategist" (and perhaps a "leader"), but that it would be very difficult for people to see him as both. This might well be an obstacle to his progress in the present organization. He was also able to acknowledge that having technical expertise and mastery made him feel very good about himself, but, in contrast, venturing into the political and more ambiguous world of the senior levels within the organization made him feel rather uneasy. Once again, he was able to make some clear links both to his personality type and his upbringing. The amorphous and ambiguous world of politics had always seemed illogical and impractical to him; he had focused instead on doing a "good job".

He was particularly surprised when he spoke about the "results orientation" category in his 360 Degree Feedback with his colleagues. He viewed himself as rather driven, not to say competitive: he was an active squash player and was often either champion or runner-up in his local league. He felt that he brought that same dynamism and energy to work, but his peers, in particular, had obviously had not perceived him in that way. Again, he had been bold enough to speak directly to several of his peers about this issue. What he found was that they remembered, particularly in terms of his performance in meetings, that he would raise a number of difficult, specific, and often unanswerable technical objections, at a late stage in the proceedings. In keeping with his ISTJ profile characteristic, in his conversations with his peers, he had asked them for examples to back up their ratings; although, as I had cautioned him, he did not go as far as to ask people directly to disclose their ratings of him. He was surprised that a number of people volunteered their ratings spontaneously, and that they had remembered specific examples.

Peter was able to combine his understanding of the MBTI with the Feedback that he had recently received in his organization with aspects of our discussion to suggest that what he was doing, from his own perspective, was making sure that a project or idea would really work. He realized that from his peers' perspective, however, this was viewed negatively and interpreted as simply putting a damper on things.

He further described how, perhaps due to his introversion, coupled with his technical expertise, he would spend a good deal of time thinking retrospectively through suggestions previously made in meetings, particularly if he had heard them for the first time at that meeting. He tended to evaluate them, examining specific instances that might test the idea and then he'd compose a form of words that would allow him to communicate succinctly and precisely the limits of the idea put forward at that previous meeting. Sometimes he had not thought through his position sufficiently by the end of the actual meeting where an idea was raised, which meant that he had to raise it afresh at a subsequent meeting, when, in the view of others, the project was considerably more advanced by then and many seemed to assume that those issues had already been agreed. This clearly created resentment and partially explained why he was seen as "retarding the process".

Although he attended a number of pre-meeting discussions in the past, he was now beginning to understand that they were part of the "political process", where people canvassed opinions and sought to persuade colleagues of their own particular viewpoint. He had not really understood the point of these discussions, and had tended to dismiss them as "idle and irrelevant gossip", thus missing connection with the "human" rather than the "technical" aspects of the organization. As a result of the coaching discussions, he began to recognize that he should use these meetings to gather data and to put forward any objections at an early stage. If he was to do it early on in the process, there would be fewer surprises for his colleagues and he would have more time to formulate a final position. Specifically, he suggested that he could put forward initial objections shortly after the pre-meeting approaches, and when this initial discussion was being held. If he felt particularly pressured one tactic he could use could be to excuse himself, ask for more time to think it through and then to get back to the other person within a short period, say 24 hours, with a thought-out position.

We agreed that self-presentation should be the first point for Peter to focus on, particularly in relation to his peers.

Peter agreed to carry out this planned course of action, as well as to keep a logbook of his actions and other people's reactions. We agreed to meet three weeks later. The other part of his "homework" was to find out about specific courses focusing on personal impact at senior levels.

Session 3

Peter arrived at the third session in a positive frame of mind. He had been surprised that attending to his behaviour outside meetings had seemed to make the actual meetings run more smoothly. He had diligently kept a notebook recording of what he had said, what he had done, and how people had reacted to him, etc. In general, his colleagues seemed to have been much happier being told of difficulties and problems prior to the meetings, so that they could adjust their proposals accordingly, rather than at the end of the meeting itself, or in a subsequent meeting. Peter laughingly suggested that "saving face" seemed to be a key aspect of "how management was done" in this organization.

Much of this session was spent discussing specific aspects of his behaviour. However, towards the very end of the session a completely new topic arose. I would characterize this by using Peter's own words, "Why am I doing all this?" He spoke about how little time he had with his family; while they were materially well-off, none the less he had lost sight of why he was doing what he was doing. One might see it as an "existential crisis", but "crisis" would be very far from how it was presented in the session: Peter talked about it in a thoughtful and careful manner, with very little emotion, without any sense of desperation or confusion.

The session finished, from my point of view, in a bit of a rush. A whole range of issues had been mentioned, and while on the behavioural level things seem to be going well, behind this, suddenly, a much more fundamental (as I thought) aspect of Peter's life had been raised.

Reacting to this, I made some remarks about him needing to see the bigger picture to understand what the totality of his life was about and how his position in the organization and his career to date fitted in with the larger scale understanding that he had of himself and his life. I had previously thought about asking him to consider his skill in coaching and mentoring. I felt that by focusing on this he would gain two important benefits; first he would enhance and deepen his conversation with those around him, and this would serve as a positive reinforcement, and second, it would help Peter to implicitly or tacitly begin to understand on a personal level what a longer term coaching or mentoring relationship for *him* might be like. I thought that such a relationship would be beneficial to him, but that the ground needed to be prepared first. With the end of the session imminent, and feeling as though too many big issues had suddenly appeared, I reverted to saying this. But as I said it, I was aware that he was frowning; in disagreement or in thought, I had no way of knowing. I added something about the importance of meaning in our lives, and found myself asking him to consider between our sessions what was really important to him in his life.

Session 4 (final session)

The final session occurred a whole month later. Peter seemed pleased to see me; he had made a number of interesting decisions.

He had secured, with the knowledge and approval of his organization, a highly respected mentor from another organization within the overall group. He had additionally booked himself to attend a course about "presenting with high impact", run by a famous actor at a well-known business school.

He wanted to spend the last session going over his 360 Degree Feedback again. When we discussed it, an interesting shift seemed to have occurred, for the data was now clearly about him. I realized that when we had discussed it previously we had both been talking about the information as though it referred to a third party, and not a person present in the room. He definitely seemed more present and connected.

He spontaneously, and quite openly, told me about other personal aspects of his life that he felt had had an impact on his performance. He had also decided that he would like to receive ongoing coaching, but that at this stage he wanted someone with more industry-specific skills than I had to offer. He was particularly interested in supply chain or demand chain management and he asked me for a referral, which I provided for him.

I referred to the existential questions about life and meaning that he had raised at the previous session. Peter laughed and said that he was perhaps going through a difficult patch at the time. He hadn't realized, he told me, almost teasingly, that he had been identified as one of the first people to go through an "assessment centre for high potential", out of which a structured development plan was going to be put into place. On exploring this it turned out that he had been worried that he had been referred to me because he had already been "found wanting" by the firm. His new construction was not that despite his hard work he was being doubted, but that his potential was being recognized. His previous "existential" comments were rather brushed aside when I returned to them; though he listened attentively and even took a note when I spoke about other people's experience of the search for meaning, and sources of practical help and advice.

We parted amicably, and he suggested that he would like some of his "people" (his phrase) to be helped to understand their 360 Degree Feedback through some sessions with me; he enquired as to what my rates were, and how he could contact me.

The coaching process and links to 360 Degree Feedback and personality as measured by the MBTI

In working with Peter, I was able to tailor, to some extent, the way in which I presented information to suit his personality. In my experience, if you do this, the rapport building with the client is established faster, and communication is heard much more clearly. For example, I expected that because he had a clear preference for *sensing* (S) he would be impatient with general statements, which he would view as vague and wishy-washy. It was thus important to ground my comments in concrete reality, and, if possible, provide Peter with specific examples. Since his preference was for *introversion* (I), it was important that I allowed him time to think and space to speak, and that I allowed him time between the sessions to consider what we had talked about, and give him a chance to complete any agreed activities in his own way.

From other people's assessment of him, through the 360 Degree process, I had certain expectations of where disparities of perception might lie. It turned out that these were fairly accurate and additionally seemed important to him, which meant that he was motivated to work on them.

In "Type Theory" it is hypothesized that one of the functional pairs is "dominant"; that is, broadly, that it is most favoured or most powerful. It tends to be used for most of the time. The "dominant" function for someone who is ISTJ is S and the "inferior" function, the one that is used least and is least familiar, is N. Type Theory further tells us that the "inferior" function may emerge at times of stress. I should have been more prepared, given Peter's MBTI Type, for his intuitive (N) side to emerge in an extroverted and unstructured way, as it did, when he spoke about needing to know the meaning of what he was doing. Because this function is the least favoured for people with an ISTJ preference, it is likely to seem somewhat chaotic, and may be distressing to the individual, though it did not seem to be in this case. Notions of "the bigger picture" and of meaning may emerge, as they did here. It is because he was temporarily "in the grip" of his "inferior" function that, I suspect, he was able to accept my general, not to say somewhat vague, final remarks at the end of our third session; normally, I suspect, he would have sought clarification and expected evidence and examples. Once the period of stress had passed, perhaps due in part to the specific actions that he had been undertaking, the extroverted intuitive concerns were not in the foreground any more, and had thus faded from his awareness.

I was also able to tap into, successfully in this case, some of Peter's naturally skilled behaviour, that is his ability in coaching and mentoring his own staff, based on clear perception of their needs and of skill gaps, of being able to plan systematically how to bridge that gap and of showing great patience. We talked about it in a reflexive way, so as to seek to guide him, perhaps utilizing unconscious identification processes, to apply those particular skills to his own position.[2]

Finally, using the MBTI, it was possible to establish certain facets of his personality quickly and accurately and to develop a shared language more explicitly. In addition, time was saved by not having to probe and examine any differences between self and other perceptions, particularly of performance related dimensions of organizational importance, since the 360 Degree tool had provided that information already. Thus, at the very least, a great deal of time was saved, especially given that only four sessions of coaching were commissioned.

However, the question remains whether, by using these tools, I was imposing particular structures on our encounter that were not necessarily there to begin with. Was a self-fulfilling prophecy being generated and acted upon? We have all had the experience, often when encountering an attractive theory or framework for the first time, of finding that we make the data fit our new version of reality.

That said, theories and models are valuable for a number of reasons, including those suggested for the MBTI above, as they summarize and codify complex fields in understandable ways and facilitate exploration and examination, as well as providing shared meaning and language. For all these reasons, I think that while a structure was indeed imposed by the presence of the 360 Degree process and the MBTI upon my coaching interaction with Peter, it was a helpful structure in so far that it allowed speedy progress despite the brevity of my involvement of four sessions and brought into play external and internal reality in an ordered and systematic way. I have already suggested that a problematic aspect of this approach is the possibility of concretization. However, against that, the benefit of calibration in ideographic and normative terms is not to be underestimated. In addition to using psychometrics it is of crucial importance to listen to and be attentive towards the person present in front of you. As Casement (1985) and others suggest, clients will, even in a time-limited encounter, provide various hints, clues, and cues of other matters that may also need addressing. The strength of the relationship and the level of rapport are inevitably key in surfacing deep or important issues; however, this discussion is well beyond the scope of this chapter.[3]

Links to Brunning's coaching model[4]

Halina Brunning's model of coaching seems to me to be very helpful in this case in reflecting on the areas we worked on and those not brought explicitly into the coaching process. I would suggest that many facets of the model were touched on in our exploration with Peter, though I did not use the model explicitly with him.

Through the fact of having 360 Degree Feedback available, both his role in the organization and his training needs were necessarily and explicitly brought to the surface and examined. Similarly, his professional development was plainly being addressed, both in his terms and, interestingly, in those of the organization. Again, aspects of his personality and personal development were unambiguously addressed.

The model is helpful in seeing the parts of the enterprise that were neglected in this case study. In working with Peter, perhaps because of the time-limited nature of our contact, and certainly partly due to the client's presentation, his own "life story" was neglected. As Smith (1999) describes, using Langs' notion of frames and the expression of unconscious messages within them, Peter brought this aspect of himself into the conversation rather dramatically, first by bringing his existential need for validation and meaning into the session, and subsequently, when that information did not destroy our working relationship, by bringing more personal disclosure into the next session. In so far as this material was brought to the sessions at all, it indicated that some trust and confidence in the relationship was present. However, the fact that it did surprise me may well indicate that while the brief history was being taken in the first session, it is likely that a variety of clues to problems in this domain had already been offered, but that I had not properly heard them. In a more traditional counselling encounter, the comments about the organization leaving the recipients of the 360 Degree Feedback process to digest their own feedback data might have paralleled his trepidation about what might happen to material that emerged in our work together. The fantasy may have been that he might have to, once again, hold something unpalatable for himself without there being a safe container available. Brunning's model would have been very useful to have "on the table" in looking, however briefly, at the beginning of our work, at the boundaries, and in mapping out the thematic areas of the encounter.

The model very usefully cautions us against the seductive nature and the lure of concretization. In having a piece of paper with a personality profile written on it, or of a complex, complicated and "scientific-looking" 360 Degree Feedback report, it is all too easy to focus on these artefacts, as if they somehow "represented or reflected reality", rather than focusing on the nature of the relationship between the two people present in the room. In many ways, that is the only reality that we can ever directly work with, and work on.[5] I think, in retrospect, that despite the tremendous usefulness of the tools, and the time and energy they saved, in this case, I should have gone beyond them: I was perhaps unwittingly seduced into thinking that "personality" or "perception" were things, rather than processes. Let me briefly elaborate: Peter's preference towards the concrete influenced me, and, indeed, I tailored my communication with this preference in mind. However, given the very concrete and results-driven culture of the organization, it became all too easy to operate in a concrete rather than an abstract way. So, personality and 360 degree relationships may have become construed as "things". Stepping back, I can see that that path was easier to embark on, rather than overt counter-cultural work, and while four sessions were only enough to start a process, one can wish that another facet of the encounter had been more explicitly addressed; that is to say, the reliance on the concrete. But again, instinctively, four sessions with a transient outsider are unlikely to have a serious impact on decades of cultural development, so my instincts may well have been appropriate.

Let us now consider other aspects of the model: the client's aspirations and career progression were touched on at the beginning of the process, but were then taken as read. It was assumed that the actions taken, and subsequent steps, would enhance Peter's standing in his organization and lead to his advancement. He did, increasingly, have an understanding of the political dimensions of the process, and his career goals were well articulated and clear. In this case no follow-up appointments were made, and with certain self insights and concrete behavioural plans in place (as well as a mentoring relationship, etc.) I felt hopeful that change had been initiated. I heard (informally and not directly from Peter) that he had been promoted and shortly afterwards head-hunted into a very senior position in a niche consultancy. I took this as confirmation of some change, but certainly not evidence of direct causality!

Returning to Brunning's model, the client's current workplace environment and organizational role were not explicitly addressed; a huge number of shared assumptions and meanings were present but not explored. We had briefly talked about the industry at the beginning, but that was simply, I suppose, a way of assessing my initial credibility. Some of the markers of this were entirely non-verbal; for instance, the fact that we both wore smart business suits and had shiny shoes! The shared language used at that time, that of profit, margins, supply chain management, channels to market, return on investment, and so forth, indicated that we both understood the language and the organizational context of a commercial organization. Thus, we had a shared understanding that, luckily, did not seem to be inaccurate; certainly there were no "jarring moments" in our conversation in this arena. Thus reassured of my *bona fides*, we were able to progress.

Finally, while I hope that I have described what happened in this case in an accessible way, I need to stress that I have been a psychologist for over twenty years and have been involved with these techniques for well over half that time. I would urge readers to obtain good training, mentoring, and supervision. Last of all, let me reflect on my reflection; in writing this, as ever, I have put something of myself into it, reflecting what I have learnt, but, naturally, also wishing to present myself in a favourable light, particularly due to the permanence of the written word. On the other hand, it is also scary to be so revealing; first, because what one might say may cause others to view one unfavourably, and second, that one's reflections may seem banal rather than appropriate. I eagerly anticipate reading and hearing about possible links and common threads that fellow contributors, perhaps unknowingly, share in this book.

Notes

1. This is, indeed, very much contrary to good practice; those using tests or instruments have a duty to those on the receiving end to ensure that, at the least, they do no harm. The provision of feedback, or at least the opportunity to avail oneself of feedback, is a basic fact of proper test usage. Both test publishers and relevant professional bodies have codes of conduct concerning test usage—for examples, please see websites for the American Psychological Association, British Psychological Society, Consulting Psychologists' Press for professional associations; and Saville & Holdsworth Ltd, Oxford Psychologists Press, and the Psychological Corporation for responsible test publishers.
2. See a chapter in this book by Gordon Lawrence on the role of unconscious thinking in coaching.
3. See chapters by Jane Pooley, Miranda Alcock, Marlene Spero, and Halina Brunning in this book.
4. See chapter by Halina Brunning in this book.
5. See chapter by Gordon Lawrence in this book.

References

Barrick, M. R., & Mount, M. K. (1993). Autonomy as a moderator of the relationships between the Big Five personality dimensions and job performance. *Journal of Applied Psychology*, *78*(1): 111–118.

Bayne, R. (1994). The Myers–Briggs versus the "Big Five". *The Psychologist*, *7*(1): 14–16.

BPS/DTI/CIPD/SHL (2001). 360 Degree Feedback, best practice guidelines. DTI Website, accessed June 2003.

Briggs, K. C., & Myers, I. (1980). *Gifts Differing*. Palo Alto, CA: Consulting Psychologists' Press.

Brunning, H. (2001). Six domains of executive coaching. *International Journal of Social and Organizational Dynamics*, *1*(2): 254–263.

Burns, R. (1786). "To a louse, on seeing one on a lady's bonnet, at church". Etext accessed 2001, project Guttenberg mirror site, UK.

Casement, P. (1985). *On Learning from the Patient*. London: Routledge.

Fletcher, C., & Baldry, C. (1999). Multisource feedback systems: A research perspective. *International Review of Industrial and Organizational Psychology, 14*: 149–193.

Jung, C. G. (1921). *GeR: Psychologische Typen*. Zurich: Rascher Verlag. English translation, *Psychological Types; or, The Psychology of Individuation*. London: Kegan Paul, Trench, Trubner, 1923 [revised London: Routledge & Kegan Paul, 1971].

Hirsh, S. K., & Kummerow, J. (2000). *Introduction to Type in Organizations* (3rd edn), European English Edition. Oxford: Oxford Psychologists Press

Kwiatkowski, R. (2003). Trends in organizations and selection: an introduction. *Journal of Managerial Psychology, 18*(5): 382–394.

Myers, I. B. (1980). *Gifts Differing*. Palo Alto: Consulting Psychologists Press.

Smith, D. L. (1999). Communicative psychotherapy without tears. In: E. M. Sullivan (Ed.), *Unconscious Communication in Practice* (pp. 3–16). Buckingham: Open University Press.

PART III

APPLICATIONS OF SYSTEMS-PSYCHODYNAMIC COACHING

CHAPTER EIGHT

"Getting off on the right foot": coaching young adults

Laurence J. Gould

Background

It is conventional wisdom that one's first or early experiences, in whatever venue, situation, or circumstance, often define the path one will initially take and reverberate, psychically and behaviourally, long after. "Getting off on the right foot" as a novice manager, therefore, or in whatever other work role one may take, can be of critical importance for both the young adult and the organization. Given this, it follows that the process of developing and bringing along young managers[1] is an important strategic human resources task, which, if accomplished thoughtfully, will be handsomely repaid over time.

While it is certainly true that most, if not all, sizable organizations, at least in the USA, have some form of training programme for new managers, many of which are quite successful, I believe that they can be enhanced even further if they explicitly take into account the developmental issues that young people are struggling with as they take up managerial roles for the first time. It is this aspect of the "training" of young managers that I focus on in this chapter, by presenting a case that exemplifies many of them.

Specifically, the hope is that those who have the responsibility for such programmes, and in particular those who are mentors or coaches in such programmes, may benefit from a deeper consideration and understanding of early adult development.

A model of coaching: brief overview

I approach the work of coaching from what I characterize as a Person–Role–Organization (Developmental Stage) perspective[2]— denoted as PRO (DS). In practice, this means that I work at understanding a client's needs and issues through an exploration of the *interaction* between their personal characteristics—P—(with a focus, among others, on the role in their family of origin, their needs, strengths and weaknesses, defensive styles, attitudes regarding authority relations, and an in-depth assessment of their motivations, *dreams*[3] and aspirations); the role—R—he/she occupies (e.g., its nature, boundaries, complexity, clarity, how the organization perceives and values it, etc.); and the nature of the organizational setting—O—(e.g., its culture, dynamics, structure, etc.). Further, and quite critically in my model, these dimensions are explored in the context of the client's stage of adult development (DS). In this regard, my guiding hypothesis is that whatever potentials the client brings to the situation, the impact on them of their role and the organizational setting are either amplified or inhibited, developed or constricted by the interaction of these dimensions. I believe it is only through such a multi-factor conceptualization that one can develop a fuller appreciation and understanding of the client's experience and behaviour, which one hopes will translate into growth-promoting coaching that facilitates more effective performance, increased gratification, and a more nuanced appraisal of the client–organization fit.

My aim, therefore, is to outline the approach I utilize, which is systematically informed by the developmental perspective summarized below, and apply it to a case that, in my view, illustrates how such understanding can enhance all aspects of work with young managers as they begin to occupy work roles in the early stages of their careers.

A note on early adult development

Starting in the late 1970s, a substantial body of contemporary work began in earnest with the publication of a number of books that attempted to conceptualize the adult life course from a psycho-dynamic/psychoanalytic perspective. Notably these were: *Adaptation to Life* by George Valliant (1977), Levinson, Darrow, Klein, Levinson, and McKee's *Seasons of a Man's Life* (1978); *Transformations* (Vallant, 1977) and, a volume called *Adult Development* (Colarusso & Nemiroff, 1981; Gould, 1982). These significantly carried forward several prominent earlier inquiries regarding the stages of life by Erikson (1959), Jung (1971), and Jacques (1965). My views of early adult development are largely drawn from these sources, with Levinson and his colleagues' work as the descriptive, conceptual fulcrum. Rather than summarizing and synthesizing the views of early adult development by these authors, I will concentrate on Levinson's work regarding the period he terms the *novice phase*[4] of adulthood, since this defines the population I focus on in this chapter.

According to Levinson, the process of entering adulthood is considerably more lengthy and complex than the ways it has usually been conceptualized. This view takes form concretely in Levinson's dividing it up into three distinct but continuous and overlapping periods, which he terms respectively, the *early adult transition* (roughly age 17–22); *entering the adult world* (roughly age 22–28); and the *age thirty transition* (roughly age 28–33).

A simple, but useful way of thinking about these periods is to consider them from the point of view of the primary tasks (Gould, 1999)[5] that characterize each, which, if accomplished in a reasonably successful manner, facilitate continued growth and development. In this sense, Levinson's approach is similar to Erikson's (1959) epigenetic stage model. Below, I briefly provide an explication of the tasks of each of the three periods, with greater elaboration of the second.

The early adult transition (approximately age 17–22)

This period represents the boundary between pre-adulthood and early adulthood. It is a significant transitional period, and it may be noted that, in this regard, Levinson's thinking was considerably influenced by Winnicott's (e.g., 1971) work on transitional phenomena in infancy and childhood. For example, coaches and mentors can serve functions similar to Winnicott's "good enough mothering", which, during the *early adulthood transition*, facilitates, among others, the critical development of an increased and robust sense of "me" and "not me", and "play" as a form of exploration, imagination, and creativity in behaviour, fantasy, and reverie. Finally, if conditions are reasonably felicitous, the period that follows, as with all significant developmental transitions, is marked by greater stability, a heightened capacity for containing uncertainty and its attendant anxieties, and a move toward differentiation and a consolidation of the self.

Entering the adult world (approximately age 22–28)

Normatively, and most notably, separating from one's family of origin and other significant relationships in the late teens and early twenties, is characterized by a heightened process of decathecting them and, concomitantly, gradually forming attachments to new peers, love objects, and important authority figures.

In outline form, the tasks of this period, stated simply, can be subsumed under three major headings: (a) exploring the possibilities that the world has to offer, and one's suitability for competently engaging them; (b) testing some initial choices and the authenticity of one's interests and desires, and, (c) organizing whatever choices are made in what is, at least, an initial, rudimentary *life structure*.[6] However, it needs be emphasized that the first two tasks are inherently at odds with each other, which is a major source of tension[7] during this period. That is, staying open to possibilities, and functioning in an exploratory mode is, in essence, the antithesis of making provisional choices, and commitments, and moving toward stability. Having said this though, it is also clear that even seemingly binding choices at this age have a provisional quality, since one is still young enough for even major changes and shifts in love and work to be realistic and feasible, even if they are quite difficult and painful to accomplish.

The age thirty transition (approximately age 28–33)

While it is not the focus of the developmental issues of the population I focus on in this chapter, to round out the discussion I will summarize the highlights of this period, as well. According to Levinson, the primary task is to revisit and reappraise one's initial *life structure*. By this age one will presumably have accumulated a sufficient portfolio of experiences to be able to make some more refined judgements about the adequacy, gratifications, and suitability of decisions made and the path one has chosen. If, as Levinson does, one considers that the twenties and thirties comprise what he terms an *era* in the life cycle (i.e., *young adulthood*, as distinct, for example, from the eras that follow: *middle adulthood, late adulthood*, and *late, late adulthood*), he views the developmental essence of the *age thirty transition* as an opportunity for a mid-era correction. This can potentially range from a radical, discontinuous transformation of the *life structure* to incremental, but significant, and more gratifying refinements.

A hypothesis regarding the coaching of young managers

In addition to the my general model of coaching, outlined previously, before turning to the case itself I would like to adumbrate the particular challenges and caveats of coaching young managers by offering, as a starting point, two linked, working hypotheses:

• Perhaps more than at any other stage of development, a major task of coaching is to engage young managers in a process of helping them to discover, at a deeper level, whether their work/career choices and the roles they have taken up suit their interests, needs, capabilities, passions, and emerging aspirations;

• it is in this sense that coaching, while critically informed by a developmental perspective at all phases of life, takes on a particular significance in young adulthood, since decisions and choices made during this time may set in motion a work/career trajectory that, for better or worse, often reverberates far into the future. The coach, therefore, can play a critical role, not only in the narrower sense of helping young clients "get off on the right foot" in their organizational work roles, but also, perhaps more critically, in one's life vocation altogether.

The case: coaching and assessing MH[8]

Introduction

I met with MH for a total eight hours for the purposes of coaching and assessing his dilemmas in taking up the role of a Fellow in a Public Sector Leadership Training Programme sponsored by a retail clothing organization, which I'll call Global Village Clothing (GVC). The goal of the programme was to "provide business and organizational skills to socially-orientated, high potential young leaders". The programme, therefore, was not conceived as a management training programme in the traditional sense, but rather because of GVC's wish "to give something back to society by way of contributing to the accomplishment of socially-orientated goals by developing a cadre of competent, sophisticated young leaders". This is a critical and quite apposite point in connection with the case of MH, which I will take up in greater detail later in this chapter.

However, before turning to the nature of the coaching work itself, and the organizational context, I thought it would be useful to outline briefly some considerations related to the nature of this specific assignment, which, while atypical in certain ways, foregrounds what I believe are many of the issues I wish to address in connection with coaching young adults.

As noted, MH was a Fellow in GVC's Public Sector Leadership Training Programme. Coaching and mentoring were an intrinsic aspect of the Programme, during which each Fellow, with three other peers, met bi-weekly with their assigned coach for a group session. Individual sessions with the coach were also available on an "as needed" basis, and could be initiated by either the coach or the Fellows. Confidentiality about the Fellows' progress or performance was strictly maintained by the Programme, but it was the operating units to which the Fellows were assigned, and rotated through, that had the responsibility for formally evaluating their performance. Aside from these periodic evaluations, they could also provide the Training Programme with their views or concerns about the Fellows at any point, if they felt that it would add to their development.

On rare occasions, when serious issues about a Fellow arose and the training director felt that these could not be effectively worked on within the boundaries of the Programme, as was the case in this situation, she thought it useful to have an outside person both assess the Fellow and provide additional, intensive coaching. This process was transparent, in that the Fellow in such instances was told that an outside consultant would be asked to make an assessment, based on their work together, and report back to the training director. So, the obvious dilemma in working with MH, which certainly had an initial impact, was that I needed to develop an appropriate balance between the dual, but opposing, tasks of assessing him, given the difficulties that led to the recommendation that he receive outside coaching, and providing effective coaching itself. Not surprisingly, knowing that he was being assessed, and that I would write a report providing my views about him, he was initially, and not unreasonably, guarded. I took this issue up with him directly at the outset, and I believe that he developed enough trust over the time we met to become sufficiently candid and direct, making it possible for us to work constructively together.

Highlights of the assessment and coaching

Given my PRO (DS) approach, I've organized this section into separate sub-headings. Under each I provide an overview of my assessment and work with MH, and then provide a brief overall summary integrating these three dimensions, P, R, and O, with the issues related to developmental stage interpolated as appropriate. I conclude with some general remarks and recommendations.

MH the person

Overall, I experienced MH in much the same way as the training director initially described him to me. He was charming, ingenuous, very bright, articulate, and engaging, which made it quite easy to understand why he was selected for the programme. His accomplishments, especially for his age and stage of professional development (a twenty-four-year-old, recently minted MBA), were quite impressive. I questioned him in detail about these, and felt that, for the most part, he was appropriately realistic about his own role and contributions, generally gave credit to the others with whom he worked, and to those who provided him with mentorship and guidance along the way. He impressed me with his devotion and idealism, and, while justifiably proud of his successes, his recounting them to me, the above notwithstanding, was marked by more than a bit of grandiosity. He also displayed a great deal of certainty, had strong views that he was not reluctant to give voice to, and was not, as a result, all that self-reflective. To put it slightly differently, he was not unduly plagued by doubts or second-guessing, which often made it difficult for him to learn from others, despite his avowed desire to do so. And while his accomplishments were certainly impressive, his certainty and confidence had more than a hint of bravado.

These characteristics: certainty, grandiosity, youthful idealism, self-righteousness, and a lack of self-reflection, provide a good example of why I stress as strongly as I do the critical necessity for bringing to bear a developmental perspective. Such attitudes and behaviours are quite normative and age appropriate, and to my mind reflect as much about MH's stage of development as they do about his personality *per se*. On the one hand, they provide a necessary and adaptive defence against the daunting prospect of taking on adult responsibilities, and on the other they virtually define a conventional and conceptually centrist view of the mind-set requisite for taking creative leadership. However, even for his age, he was a bit naïve and immature—but only a bit. (I can't help thinking, by comparison, what I was like as a twenty-four-year-old. I'll let you draw the obvious conclusions.) It is also easy to see, without this perspective, why many of the people with whom he interacted experienced him as cocky, arrogant, and "full of himself", and, as a result, often developed a distinctly mixed appraisal of his leadership potential.

Further, he was not really interested in the nuts and bolts of organizational life, and found them largely irrelevant to his interests (he told me that he felt the same way about his MBA experience). This attitude came across quite clearly at GVC, much more than he recognized and, in part, accounted for some of his difficulties. For this reason, I put considerable emphasis on the fact that successful organizations required competent management, as well as leadership, and that even those with a strong entrepreneurial leadership bent—which is how he thought of himself—needed to understand how organizations function, even if they themselves were not interested in details. I think he took in this message quite well, and began to appreciate that it would be foolish to squander an opportunity that potentially could be quite useful in helping him to realize his public service aspirations more fully, but that did not, as yet, have a well-defined focus.

As we continued to work, he also seemed to recognize that he did not handle many situations well, that it took him a long time to catch on to how a large, hierarchical organization functions, and that diplomacy and sensitivity to the views of others were important aspects of forming the alliances and collaborative relationships necessary to be effective. He acknowledged, in this connection, that while his experience at GVC was often quite painful, he felt (and I think genuinely) that it was a very important lesson for him. I also based my assessment, in part, on his having openly, and without any prompting on my part, recognized that, by contrast, his peers, being somewhat older (the closest in age was twenty-seven, and the oldest twenty-nine), who may have initially faced the same or similar dilemmas in their assignments, seemed to MH to handle them with considerably greater maturity and diplomacy.

I note the above to provide some balance in understanding the source of his difficulties, and the way he came to be perceived. I would add, though, that there were several other factors that I also believe played a role in exacerbating them. MH, as I noted, clearly had an impressive number of significant achievements, and was accustomed to being greatly appreciated, admired, and treated as someone who was quite special and gifted. It was a shock to him, therefore, that after the glow of being accepted into the Programme wore off, this was not his experience at GVC. Quite the contrary, he felt generally misunderstood, unappreciated, and unfairly criticized, and, as a result, deeply hurt and angry—reactions he had rarely experienced previously. In this connection, I also agreed with the training director's assessment of what she characterized as his "selective memory". He did not want to hear anything that was at odds with what he wanted to do, and when such instances occurred, as they often did, he experienced all of the feelings noted above. Further, he almost always (especially early on in our work) expressed these in an intemperate, self-justifying way. But while these reactions reveal how he contributed to his own difficulties, it was hardly the whole "story". That is, even if many of his responses could be discounted as a function of his immaturity, attitudes, personality, and behaviour, manifested in a lack of appropriate interpersonal sensitivity and competence, I believe that others needed to be seriously considered as reflecting a more complex, systemic picture, which I will describe in the next section.

Finally, MH, at least initially, was indeed "full of himself", and his attitudes, both subtly and directly, like that of many very talented and exceptional young people, are likely to frustrate their elders and drive them to distraction, whether they be parents or supervisors (this was a common complaint about his peers as well, but to a lesser degree). There is no question in my mind that he was self-absorbed, but in a way that entrepreneurs often are—even young ones—which is commonly mistaken, and not without some reality, as contempt for and/or disinterest in what others do, which seemed, at times, to have been the case. However, a not uncommon assessment might very well have written him off as a narcissistic personality disorder, unduly pathologizing developmentally appropriate behaviour, even, at times, "over the top". Further, in a related manner, it seemed to me that there was a pervasive, implicit attempt to induct him into a rather conventional view of a "good manager/leader" (temperate; a team player; more obedient than otherwise; having "appropriate" respect for authority; and, uncritically adopting the values and culture of GVC, etc.), rather than helping him to develop his considerable entrepreneurial/leadership potential. Here, we begin to see evidence for an emerging hypothesis regarding a mismatch between the Programme's espoused goals, and the way they were enacted in a culture seemingly at odds with them. One may speculate that, perhaps at a less than conscious level, many of the line managers were also envious of the rich, developmental opportunities GVC provided the Fellows.

GVC's Public Sector Leadership Training Programme

The above appraisal led me directly to a more serious consideration of the role of the Public Sector Leadership Training Programme at GVC and the role of its Fellows, which I believe, in addition to the utility of taking into account normative trends in adult development, provide an additional and critical, systemic perspective on the nature of MH's difficulties.

Both my discussions with MH and a review of the Public Sector Leadership Training Programme materials led me to conclude that he was not very clear about the role of being a Fellow, in that the stated goals of the Programme, as well as the details of its structure and activities, seemed to me too general to offer useful guidelines for taking up this role. MH directly confirmed this view by telling me that he and his peers felt the Programme's goals had been neither effectively communicated to them nor, more importantly, to the rest of the organization. When I inquired more closely about this, he gave as major examples, two types of episodes or interactions.

- First, he said that he was often called an "intern". To him this clearly implied that his role was perceived to be more like that of a trainee, and not a Fellow, in what was billed as GVC's most prestigious Programme designed to facilitate the development of the "best and the brightest" for service in the public sector. Further, to the extent that some people did appreciate this fact, they had little in-depth understanding of what this meant in practice, and as a result did not know how to relate to him, nor what they could usefully offer. So, in his view, their responses to him ranged from the sympathetic, interested, but not particularly helpful, to treating him "like an office temp". On two occasions, for example, he was asked to crunch numbers and create some very basic spreadsheets.

- Second, he reported that many of the people he was told to speak with had little idea who he was and why he was there. From his perspective, the result was similar to that noted above. He said, in effect, that "many of them were not sure what to talk to me about, nor what to do with me in their units."

These experiences left him feeling anxious and abandoned, and he dealt with them by falling back on a familiar and previously successful pattern: he pursued his own interests as best he could, assuming, without giving it much conscious thought, that as a Fellow he had the authority to shape his role in a manner consonant with his needs. A case in point was a meeting he had initiated with the chief designer of the women's sportswear division, to whom he offered his services, feeling that the creative aspect of this work would be much more appealing and broadly in keeping with his own interests. But, when he was admonished by the training director for doing this, because he didn't discuss it with her before proceeding, he felt hurt and bewildered once again. Ironically, the chief designer was quite impressed, and would have been happy to have him join her group. The training director vetoed the assignment.

This episode, I believe, highlights quite succinctly the multi-level nature of MH's situation in that it brings to the fore both the systemic issues (e.g., lack of clarity about the Fellow role in the Programme, and the parallel lack of clarity about the role of the Programme in GVC) and aspects of his developmental level and personality, which got him into difficulty and earned him a reputation of being immature, insensitive, and a "loose cannon".

This view was subsequently corroborated by the training director herself, who felt that she was caught between two masters—the Board and senior executives with whom she and the Fellows had little or no functional contact, and the managers of the operational units, who were her peers and on whom she depended to collaborate with the Programme by taking the Fellows on board, bringing them along, and evaluating them. She acknowledged, as well, her own sympathies with the stated goals of the Programme, which was why the position was originally so appealing to her when she accepted it ten years earlier. (At the time she was a relatively young comparative literature lecturer who was finding the academic life increasingly unsatisfying and confining.) It is hardly a surprise, therefore, that in many ways, in a manner almost identical to that of the Fellows, she also felt chronically frustrated and "in the middle". However, she realized early on that for the Programme to survive she had to simultaneously present it in a manner that was in keeping with the organization's definition and bow to the realities of the line managers' perceptions, behaviour, and attitudes, since she had no direct authority to require their compliance in relation to the Fellows. It was in this sense that she felt MH put the Programme in jeopardy by his insensitivity and lack of even a rudimentary awareness of the politics, although she subsequently acknowledged in our feedback discussions, that she had never been candid and direct with MH about this aspect of the situation.[9]

Conclusions

I felt that I was able to work in some depth with MH to assist him in understanding and more fully appreciating the difficulties he had by putting them into a meaningful framework. I think that doing so made it possible for him to begin to sort out the situation he had become embroiled in, as well as assisting him to develop more realistic expectations, in the time that remained, as to how he could best make use of the rich resources that were available. I also felt that while he was still in considerable pain about what had been happening to him at GVC (more, I am quite certain, than he could acknowledge, even to himself), his self-awareness and ability to be reflective were heightened, and he was determined to make the most of his remaining time as a Fellow. He also very strongly felt the need to redeem himself in the eyes of the training director, whom he both liked and admired, and whom he felt he had let down by his behaviour, thereby making her life more difficult, and thus hurting the reputation of the Programme, which, he came to appreciate, was somewhat tenuous.

In this connection it may be hypothesized that the *primary task* (see n. 5) of the Programme had, over time, been covertly transformed from accomplishing its stated goals to insuring its survival in the GVC organization. This is a critical point in clarifying the relationship between the Programme and the GVC organization: that the guiding spirit of the programme was to contribute to the Fellows' development, in the service of more fully and competently realizing their socially-orientated aspirations, rather than the Fellows being there for GVC's benefit. That is, the espoused goals notwithstanding, implicitly acting *as if* the Programme's task was to create a pipeline to bring along a potential new cadre of talented future corporate leaders and managers.

In sum, my hypothesis was that MH was certainly the "right" kind of person for the programme, but probably too young and immature to take full advantage of the opportunities it offered. Given the complexities of the situation as I have attempted to outline them, I believe that navigating the GVC system was simply too daunting for him, as I think it would have been for a great many people his age. Even three to five years at this stage of life make a considerable difference in developing the necessary maturity and readiness to optimally benefit from the opportunities provided by what was a relatively unstructured Programme. This difference is most obvious in the other Fellows' relative maturity, and their ability to manoeuvre, and position themselves effectively, as well as having the capacity for containing the inevitable anxieties, irritation, and frustration (which MH didn't), given the thicket of mixed messages, contrary expectations, and lack of clarity about purpose and goals of the Programme and its place in the organization.

Having said this, on balance, I felt quite strongly that MH had what it took (intelligence, drive, creativity, initiative, dedication, passion, and ideals) to make a contribution as a potential socially-orientated leader, and that his difficulties and youth aside, I recommended a continuing investment in his development. Further,

I suggested that he needed to be supported, in whatever way possible, to finish the Programme on a positive, redemptive note. I believed that doing so, certainly in the long run, would be important for his continuing development and morale, as well as providing good value for the Programme and the organization.

Summing up

It is my hope that, among other issues I've raised in presenting this material, you will, at the very least, consider the usefulness of explicitly bringing the client's developmental stage into your coaching work, and especially so when working with young, entry-level managers. Doing so, as the case material suggests, potentially adds a great deal of richness and depth to the coaching task, without which inadvertent collusiveness between the coach and the organization, as well as painful mismatches between the person and the role, are more likely to occur. If not addressed directly, these may have powerful, negative, long-term, psychological effects for any individual who has "got off on the wrong foot" at a developmentally critical and vulnerable period in life. In such instances, their potential contributions as future leaders, blessed with a dedication to social ideals, vitality, and creativity may be lost, inhibited, subverted, or derailed at a considerable cost, not only to them, but to society and its institutions.

Notes

1. I am using the term "management" generically to encompass any significant work role, or function (e.g., leadership).
2. In an excellent paper, Brunning (2001) conceptualizes, quite comprehensively, six major domains of coaching, and while she does not explicitly mention the client's life stage in her case example, one of her domains—the "Life Story"—is suggestive in this regard.
3. According to Levinson, Darrow, Klein, Levinson, and McKee (1978) the *dream* is defined as follows: "In its primordial form, the Dream is a vague sense of self-in-the-adult-world. It has the quality of a vision, (and) an imagined possibility that generates excitement and vitality (p. 91)." (See note 4.)

4. Those concepts and life stage descriptors used by Levinson, Darrow, Klein, Levinson, and McKee (1978) are italicized.

5. I utilize this concept of *primary task* analogously to Miller and Rice's (1967) usage, as applied to organizations; i.e., "the task that an enterprise must perform if it is to survive" (p. 25). I view as primary those developmental tasks that an individual must perform in order to meet optimally the emerging challenges of psychological survival at any given stage.

6. Levinson, Darrow, Klein, Levinson, and McKee (1978) define the concept of the *life structure* as the "basic pattern or design of a person's life at any given time". They argue that it provides a way of looking at the engagement of the invidual in society, which "requires a consideration of both self and world, and the relationships between them".

7. "Tension" is used descriptively, and not as a negative state. Rather, the ability to manage it, and contain the corollary anxieties, creates the optimal conditions for growth.

8. To ensure confidentiality, the initials of the client, the name of his organization and several other identifying details have been changed.

9. When I discussed with her the reason for not doing so, she said that she was too anxious to confront the line managers, and as a result she often did not defend the Fellows when they had difficulties, even when it was appropriate to do so. This situation left her feeling angry, fragile, guilty, and ashamed, for which she blamed the Fellows who "caused" them.

References

Brunning, H. (2001). The six domains of executive coaching. *Organizational and Social Dynamics, 1*(2): 254–263.

Colarusso, C. A., & Nemiroff, R. A. (1981). *Adult Development: A New Dimension in Psychodynamic Theory and Practice*. New York: Plenum.

Erikson, E. H. (1959). Identity and the life cycle, *Psychological Issues, 1*(1): 1–171.

Gould, L. J. (1982). Adulthood comes of age. Book review of *Adult Development: A New Dimension in Psychodynamic Theory and Practice* by C. A. Colarusso and R. A. Nemiroff. *Contemporary Psychology, 27*(8): 649–650.

Gould, L. J. (1999). A political visionary in mid-life: Notes on leadership and the life cycle. In: R. French & R. Vince (Eds.), *Group Relations, Management and Organization* (pp. 70–86). Oxford: Oxford University Press.

Jacques, E. (1965). Death and the mid-life crisis. *International Journal of Psycho-Analysis, 46*: 502–514.

Jung, C. G. (1971). The stages of life. In: J. Campbell (Ed.), *The Portable Jung* (pp. 3–22). Viking Portable Library.

Levinson, D. J., Darrow, C. N., Klein, E. B., Levinson, M. H., & McKee, B. (1978). *Seasons of a Man's Life.* New York: Alfred A. Knopf.

Miller, E. J., & Rice, A. K. (1967). *Systems of Organization.* London: Tavistock.

Winnicott, D. W. (1971). *Playing and Reality.* London and New York: Routledge.

Valliant, G. (1977). *Adaptation to Life.* Boston: Little Brown.

CHAPTER NINE

Role consultancy: an application in the field of sports psychology

Lionel Stapley

Introduction

In this chapter I use a case study from my work as an Organizational Consultant in the field of sports psychology. Halina Brunning has identified various domains of coaching that are fully set out in her chapter. This case study is primarily concerned with the work environment domain and the domain of the life story of the client as it relates to and is mobilized by organizational dynamics.

Being a leader or manager in any organization can be an extremely lonely position. This is patently true for managers of football clubs. The demands on football managers are such that, from time to time, many experience situations that bother them professionally and personally. Quite often such situations are experienced around issues of leadership and authority. A frequent result is an adverse effect on the performance, not only of the individual manager, but also of those working with them and, ultimately, the whole team.

The view taken here is that these are not individual problems that can be solved by, for example, the manager attending a course.

Rather, they are organizational problems that have their roots in the relationships between manager and team members, Board members, or other staff. Consequently, the individual manager is required to be seen as a person-in-role in an organizational system. Thus, any attempt at gaining a deeper understanding of the situation needs to take into consideration the wider organizational system. This can be best achieved not by bringing in "new" knowledge, but by utilizing the "current" or experiential knowledge.

The difficulty is, whom can the manager turn to? In theory, it should be possible to try to resolve the problem with a variety of people. However, the very reasons that make it such a lonely position may also inhibit the manager from seeking advice. Thus, the very circumstances of the problem are frequently the reason why it is perpetuated.

Management Role Consultancy (MRC) is a variation of a system that has been successfully developed by OPUS Consultants[1] over the past twenty years to help individual managers by supporting them in a process of development. It is considered important that they have someone neutral to talk to about the issues in their work that bother them. The material for work is the manager's experiences in his own working situation. That is, the manager's perceptions, thoughts, feelings, images, and interactions with those he relates to day by day. In working with this material the consultant seeks to enable the manager to develop his understanding of himself by learning how to analyse, and modify, the way in which he interprets his organizational roles. MRC consists of a series of two-hourly consultations held at regular intervals over a period ranging from one to two or more years. It is a totally confidential service that helps individuals to become more effective, with concomitant results for their organization—in this instance, football clubs.

This sort of consultancy is valuable not only to existing football managers, but is also of particular benefit for those planning to take up the role of football manager. By working at an understanding of their own experiences in football thus far, potential managers will be able to develop themselves for the challenges to come, as was the case with the client referred to in this chapter.

The consultant role

Isabel Menzies Lyth (1989) was of the view that the consultant's responsibility lies in helping insights to develop, freeing thinking about problems, helping the client to get away from unhelpful methods of thinking and behaving, facilitating the evolution of ideas for change, and then helping them to bear the anxiety and uncertainty of the change. Eric Miller (1993) was of the view that the consultant's role was to offer individuals a way of examining and understanding how they get caught up in unconscious processes, so that they can learn to exercise their own authority. And it was that theme of helping people to gain greater influence over their environment that underlaid virtually all his research and consultancy as well as education and training.

I share both of these views, and seek to apply such an approach while working in a Role Consultancy mode. I have invariably found that some of the most unhelpful methods of thinking and behaving adopted by my clients have their roots in the "coping mechanisms" or "defence mechanisms" they have developed in infancy and later in life. If I am to effectively carry out my role as a consultant, I cannot do so without working closely with my clients to establish the origins of their behaviour and the reasons behind them. The next step is to help them to discover the links between current and past behaviour, so that, if they wish, new ways of thinking and behaving can be developed.

In the following case study I shall try to demonstrate how this approach was used with a footballer who was soon to retire from playing football and wanted to become a football manager. Unlike the usual role consultancy, where I work with existing managers, in this situation I was working with a person in the role of player who was being managed within an organizational setting. Here I was concerned with the subject's experience of being managed. Where helpful and appropriate, I shall refer to other case material.

Case study: background information

Most football managers, upon taking up a management role, will have had no formal management development, relying entirely upon the knowledge and skills acquired during their playing careers. Taking up a management role means that they are likely to experience numerous unexpected and new challenges. Unfortunately, they will have no opportunity or time for experimenting and they will immediately have to live with the consequences of any decisions they make. Sometimes, if as a result of such a decision the players lose confidence in the manager, this may lead to a dismissal of the manager.

Contrary to much public opinion, my experience of working with footballers is that they are highly intelligent. It is true that most gave up any attempt to achieve academic success in order to pursue their dream of becoming a professional footballer. For all would-be footballers, their desire to make it as a "pro" encompasses every part of their life from an early age, and little time, or indeed interest, is available for other pursuits. Unlike the majority of people I work with, who are mainly influenced by cognitive learning, footballers are much more likely to be influenced by experiential learning. It also means that the exploration of the dynamics of management has to be based on experiential learning.

One of my earliest field notes from working in the football industry is a recognition that football is both a physically and mentally painful experience. Clearly, I am not directly concerned with the physical aspects, but consider the emotional issues to be paramount in this work. This is the case in all role consultancy work, but I feel that it is even more important in this field. There is a need to work at an understanding of the self so that clients can begin to see how they are likely to react in anxiety provoking circumstances.

Many readers will appreciate the immense pressures and stresses that the demands of football management can promote. There are many occasions when victory and feelings of euphoria are changed in one dramatic moment to the totally opposite situation of defeat and feelings of desperation and devastation. It really is "an emotional game"; consequently, there is a greater need for understanding of emotions and of the ways one reacts when extreme emotions are experienced—be that anxiety or euphoria. For a fuller exploration of emotions see Stapley, 2002.

Even though the consultancy with prospective managers differs from working with existing managers, the consultancy still primarily centres on the "self" of the person-in-role and the way that person affects the dynamics. The material used in the consultancy is their actual experience of being managed and of being a player. Further in the process they may take up a coaching role, which will also provide opportunity for exploration and applied learning. Whatever the situation, the work is about being *a person-in-role* and of exploring the dynamics and emotions experienced in that role.

The client

Sam[2] was a young man who was coming to the end of his playing career. In typical fashion he started his football career at about ten years of age by attending regular training sessions run by a local league club. He later progressed to become an apprentice with that same club and then played as a junior, until contracted as a full professional. He progressed through three other clubs until he was playing at the highest level. When I first met him he was coming towards the end of his playing career and had dropped down a level. He was now looking at the new prospect of life away from playing—his sole desire in life. This was a highly disturbing event and represented a considerable loss to him after some twenty or more years of his thirty-year life. I started working with him in a "management role consultancy" mode as a means of helping him to prepare for taking on a future role in football management.

Apart from the first two sessions, which will be referred to below, there is no formal structure for this type of consultancy. On the contrary, in each session we work with whatever preoccupations the client brings. The aim is always to provide opportunities for learning, rather than teaching. However, as the consultancy progresses, certain management processes, when raised, may be named in order to provide some form of classification and a framework for the client. For example, giving and receiving feedback, issues of authority, motivation, leadership, and management: as these various experiences arise they are named and labelled.

Case material

When carrying out any role consultancy, I start with an exploration of the client's total background, especially their childhood history. In this case too, the first two sessions were used to provide an opportunity to obtain information about significant aspects of the client's experience. I was interested in gaining a picture of the *person-in-role*: about how the client's inner world affects his outer world. As is my common practice, experience of Sam's relationships with parents and other significant authority figures were then explored in greater detail in order to provide information on the development of his coping mechanisms, which Sam was almost certainly not aware of.

To clear up any ambiguity that may exist in the mind of the reader, the role consultancy process is in no way a therapeutic endeavour. It is solely concerned with helping individual managers to fulfil their role by supporting them in the process of professional development. We all develop our own preferred methods of coping, which become second nature to us. As a result, when we are confronted by anxiety we tend to repeat what has worked for us in the past. In the short term, these coping mechanisms provide us with relief from anxiety, but there is a downside, too, because they may also create blind spots in our thinking. The aim of gaining an insight to the development of these coping mechanisms is to enable a consultant to work with clients in order to help them uncover these "blind spots" so that they can develop a better understanding of themselves in their organizational roles.

> In the first session Sam told me that when he was with his teammates he always felt the need to be "helpful". On the field he would always try to encourage others and try to help them by providing passes that would be appreciated by them. Off the field, he would also be helpful by providing teammates with lifts or other forms of help that he felt that they would appreciate. He also talked about his experiences of managers and said that occasionally he found these relationships "difficult". In particular, he felt that they "didn't care a damn" about him. This often resulted in arguments and, in his view, in him being unfairly treated. I should add that, in football, control by the manager is seen as all important and "difficult" players are not received favourably.

> During the second session, when I was seeking greater detail about family relationships, Sam said that he had been reflecting on our last session and intimated that he had a strong feeling that he had not

received the quality of affection from his mother that he so badly wanted of her. As a child, he would frequently become angry and frustrated at this perceived lack of emotional care and would deal with it by turning inwards and shutting himself in his room and remaining there to work hard on his homework. He would spend several hours longer on his homework than other children in an attempt to please his teachers, who would then give him the affection that he so craved from his mother.

During the third and fourth sessions he began to make links between current and past behaviour. In work with clients in other settings, this is sometimes a lengthy and difficult process. In the football setting my experience has frequently been that, even at this early stage, links are not only made but are also experienced with considerable relief, because the client can now understand why they adopt various forms of behaviour.

At least at a cognitive level, Sam made the link that his search for affection, as experienced in his childhood, was also repeating itself with his fellow footballers. He began to understand relatively quickly that by offering lifts and the like, he was "buying" other people's affection. That is not to say that considerably more self-reflective work needed to be done by Sam to further understand these issues and to bring about changes.

This understanding was reinforced by an exploration of the likely effects on his playing career. Provided with the opportunity to work at linking his needs for affection to his experience of playing, he struggled for some time, but then referred to the fact that some of his managers had felt that he was not "greedy enough" and that he always wanted to pass to someone else when he could have taken a shot at goal to the benefit of the team. He began to realize that he had wanted to be seen as "helpful" to his fellow players and to gain their affection for providing the chance to score.

Based on what Sam said about his experience with managers it seemed clear to me that he was often developing a relationship with his managers that was based on unconsciously repeated pattern from his early life. In effect, he was treating his managers *as if* they were his mother and seeing them as uncaring. At this early stage, however, he failed to make any links regarding the psychological transference to his managers. This was something that had to wait for several months. In the meantime, there was a considerable amount of work to be continued on his self-reflective position as we began to explore group and individual management processes and dynamics.

Over a period of several months we constantly explored Sam's relationships with his fellow players and his managers. As we did so, through frequent self-reflection, Sam began to develop a level of self-awareness that enabled him to move from self-centred concerns to being able to understand something of others. This process was considerably affected by the current culture of football management, which was, of course, the only culture that Sam had ever experienced. In particular, it influenced his perception of the role of football manager. At some stage of the process, I had asked what he understood that role to be. His response was much the same as other footballers with whom I worked using role consultancy. In his experience, the role of the manager was to make all decisions and this applied to all managers he had ever worked for. Some managers were seen to be more controlling than others but, as he saw it, all managed in a way where they made all the decisions.

Upon gently questioning this approach, I was met with a very firm response that "the manager must be in charge and must make the decisions". Sam's experience had been this and only this: he had never experienced anything different. As this seemed a particularly unhelpful way of thinking and behaviour for someone who was aiming to become a manager, I sought to explore this notion with him. I started from the position of accepting that as the manager he might be quite brilliant in building his professional knowledge. In football terms, he might even be up to date with all the latest playing, training and fitness techniques; he might even be considered to be one of the best brains in the game. I then asked how he might get all that information into the heads of the players, who were actually getting results. For a long while and with some discomfort Sam struggled for a response. After several efforts to support his previous response, he stated "with difficulty".

I then asked him to consider the possibility that if the team consisted of, say, fifteen or sixteen members, there might be a good chance of achieving an improved and more successful team performance if we used all those brains. Again, Sam struggled with the fact that his current thinking was being challenged in this way. It may help to consider why Sam was struggling. Through the process of perception we compare sense data with a store of internal knowledge, and it is from this awareness that we can begin to understand the problem. The thoughts Sam was having were in conflict with his "internal" world because there was nothing in his store of knowledge to compare this data with. He therefore had to work hard at a process of accommodating new thoughts and making sense of them.

As he did so, my role changed to one of helping him to bear the anxiety and uncertainty of the change. I think it is important to say that my words here do not and cannot do justice to the struggle experienced by Sam over a long part of a two-hour session. However, before the end of the session he was able to begin to explore the possibility that different ways of managing might actually result in a more productive experience, both for him and other team members. I hoped that he could now begin to work with those thoughts that were grounded in his own experience.

This small example perhaps helps to provide a picture of the overall consultancy. It was a long and arduous journey, much of which concerned taking the opportunities, as they arose, to encourage Sam to reflect on his own experience of being managed and to gain an understanding of the affect that this had on him. Reflecting on his experience and feelings about the way he had been managed he became aware that this had been a painful and destructive experience that, in spite of the intentions of his managers, had frequently served to lower his self-esteem, to demotivate rather than motivate him. This was a slow process and at almost every turn the prevailing culture of the football world acted as a sort of barrier that had to be crossed if we were to free Sam's thinking and to enable the evolution of new ideas.

In doing the work it was not unusual for Sam to refer back to his own family dynamics. In this setting I have found it to be exceedingly helpful in my work with Sam, because the football culture is very "macho", and those involved find it hard to talk about feelings in that setting for fear that they will be seen as "going soft". However, they are quite content to refer to feelings in the more "appropriate" setting of the family. For example, the first manager I worked with frequently referred to his son. At one level this was clearly avoidance, but at another level it was most valuable because the experiences explored provided an opportunity to transfer the thinking to the workplace. Having got round the culture "barrier", it was then possible to make direct explorations of feelings. This was also exceedingly valuable in Sam's case as will be shown below.

On several occasions, I tried to take the opportunities presented by Sam to explore his relationships with his managers. For a long time he was stuck with his "splitting", seeing his managers as wholly bad objects who could do no good. When pushed to explain his feelings about his managers, the response would be to the effect "they do not care about me, they treat us all like shit". I eventually got him to explore how he dealt with this and how he felt about it. He explained that at the end of a training session he would go off and train alone, constantly practising shots at goal and other skills. It was easy to note that this was exactly the same behaviour as when he was a child and had locked himself away alone at home with his homework. But for Sam this was the most difficult link to make. It took several sessions over a number of months before he was able to make the link between the way he viewed his mother and the way that he was viewing and reacting to his managers.

Over time, there was a considerable movement in terms of helping him to get away from unhelpful methods of thinking and behaving. I was now able to encourage him to try to see things from the managers' perspective, especially to try to understand why a particular manager acted the way he did. As he grew able to understand himself, he was able to start to understand others. He was now able to understand how emotions would affect the behaviour of managers and to see that they would frequently act out their emotions in an uncontrolled manner. This sort of learning was vital to develop, as his future role as a manager was likely to involve "getting results through other people". This development was helped by Sam's preoccupations with his teenage son, who made him to reflect upon his own "management" style.

Many sessions would start by Sam bringing his current difficulty with his son and we would explore these issues as a way of learning about management. At first this concerned me as being "off task", and yet I also realized that there was rich learning opportunity in examining data that could be relevant to the exploration of management issues. Not least, the whole field of punishment and discipline, authority, responsibility, and accountability suddenly became open to exploration. In this instant, while he needed to "manage" his son, he was also learning about the need for clarity about delegation of authority, responsibility. and accountability.

Session after session would start with Sam's reflections and struggles concerning the way he was using his authority in relation to his son. He was deeply concerned and frustrated about the process and was beginning to realize that to exercise authority is not simply a matter of making decisions. Eventually, Sam came to the realization that his son was not a part of himself, not like his car or computer, which he could use in any way he liked. He realized that his son was, in fact, a separate entity, an autonomous human being, just as he was; a human being with needs and desires, just like he and other autonomous human beings. He realized now that he could not treat him as an extension of "himself". From that point on it was a relatively easy process to apply the thinking to his experience of being managed and to develop an understanding of the needs of other team members when he became a manager.

The learning from his experience of "managing" his son was extensive. It was particularly helpful when football culture was blocking consideration of new ways of thinking. As stated above, a significant part of the football culture is that the manager is the overall decision maker. It is what might be described as a single leader work group as opposed to a team (see Stapley, 2002 for a fuller description). Inevitably, the manager insists on management control and this leads to a black and white approach—a world of right and wrong where the manager is right and everyone else is wrong: a black and white world where there is no conception of grey.

This frequently leads to "blaming" others for outcomes. For example, it is not unusual during a match for a goal keeper to make several brilliant saves during a game; saves that prevent the side from going behind and of being demotivated. However, it sometimes happens that in the dying moments of the game the goalkeeper makes one error that leads to the opposition scoring a winning goal. More often than not the goalkeeper will be blamed for the defeat and severely castigated for his error; his brilliant saves will be immediately forgotten.

Working with Sam's experience in relation to these issues often resulted in support for the actions of managers. Influenced by the football culture, Sam reflected that he would react in the same way. However, once again, a family experience served to permit Sam the opportunity to explore the dynamics of this type of situation. Sam explained that during a recent weekend his son had looked after the other younger children while his wife joined him at an away match. He explained that one of his rules was that the sitting room must always be kept tidy. Yet, when he returned home from the weekend away he found it untidy. We then explored what else his son had done over the weekend and he grudgingly and with much prompting eventually came out with a list of other important things that his son had done very well. It was clear that this one failing had completely dominated his thinking. For him it was a black-and-white world where there was no conception of grey. More importantly, we then started to explore why this was so, but he struggled to make any progress.

At this point, I took him back into the world of football, and asked him to consider the issues concerning the goalkeeper example referred to above. In looking at these circumstances he was able to see the inequity of blaming the goalkeeper, or of himself being blamed if he had missed a goal. More importantly, he was able to understand that the reason why the manager had blamed the goalkeeper was because of his own anger and frustration at losing, perhaps even his fear of losing his job after suffering another defeat. He was able to understand that when a manager had been angry with him the manager was more often than not projecting his own feelings on to him—he was blaming rather than owning his feelings. Instead of the manager owning and understanding his own feelings, Sam was being scapegoated.

Having done this work we were then able to return to the situation we had started with concerning his son. He was now able to understand that it was his disappointment, his anger and frustration that had made him blind to the wider picture so that he had taken this one piece of evidence out of proportion to the total. This moving between family dynamics and work dynamics was a rewarding experience for the client, who was learning that in both areas the current thinking was not at all helpful.

Somewhere at this stage of the consultancy he expressed the view that "it was easy to be an autocrat but to be a manager requires a lot more knowledge and skill". Sam had now achieved a new level of understanding and this provided the opportunity for a deeper exploration of many issues regarding the whole field of management, especially that concerning authority, responsibility, and accountability, as well as punishment and discipline. He was now able to develop new thinking about these matters, which would have such an important effect on his ability to be a successful manager.

I should add that at this point we had been working together for almost two years, and by this stage he had now moved into a coaching role. It had been a fascinating, if at times difficult process, but I felt that we had now reached a point where we were able to work across the boundary in a highly creative manner. My role now was almost exclusively one of working with him to bear the anxiety and uncertainty of change. This also presented considerable problems for Sam, because he was now finding himself outside the football culture. His views and understanding had changed, and these were not in accord with those he was working with.

On many occasions he was appalled at the behaviour and thinking of many of the coaches he was now working with. He experienced the way they behaved as "barbaric", unfeeling, and without any awareness of the dynamics of a given situation. In particular, he would be aghast at the way managers bullied their players and literally destroyed young people.

He now had to learn how he could influence others whose behaviour and thinking was so vastly different from his own. This was a new struggle; it presented Sam with many frustrating and, at times, almost hopeless moments. As ever, in working with him I encouraged him to reflect on his own experience. His first response was that this was a completely new experience. So, how could he reflect on anything helpful? On further reflection, he began to realize that his current experience was a reflection of the road we had travelled—of the total role consultancy experience. He would now start to reflect on how we had worked on various issues and how he had managed to develop new thinking. The model was now his model.

Concluding remarks

As stated at the outset of this chapter, the manager is seen as a person-in-role in an organizational system and any attempt at gaining a deeper understanding of the situation also needs to take into account the wider organizational system. In role consultancy, the approach taken to helping the client is not by the imposing of "new" knowledge but by developing a better understanding of the "current" and experiential knowledge.

As the case material presented here shows, this process relies entirely on encouraging the client to take up a reflective position. This can help them to achieve a deeper understanding of the situations they find problematic. As shown in this case study, the material for work is the client's own experience. Thus, there is no confusion around meaning of "new" material, or difficulty in transferring this knowledge into the workplace. All work is client-centred, utilizing solely the client's material, and therefore is very effective.

It follows, therefore, that the consultant's role is not a teaching role and there is no "new" material that is being supplied. Rather, the consultant's responsibility lies in helping insights to develop, freeing thinking about problems, helping the client to get away from unhelpful methods of thinking and behaving, facilitating the evolution of ideas for change, and then helping them to bear the anxiety and uncertainty of the change. In a nutshell, the consultant approach is to help clients become more effective in diagnosing their own problems and finding solutions through the transfer of skills and insights. Precisely how Sam, or any other client, chooses to take up their role is clearly a matter for him or her. They are free to make their own decisions. What this process achieves is the provision of a deeper understanding of the prevailing dynamics. From a position of greater understanding the client is then able to make new choices, where none previously existed. For example, where Sam saw only one way of managing, as a result of role consultation he was able to understand that there were many approaches he could take.

In addition, the consultant's role is to offer individuals a way of examining and understanding how they get caught up in unconscious processes, so that they can learn to exercise their own authority. For Sam, the opportunity to examine the way that he got caught up in the unconscious processes resulting from his perceived relationship with his mother, both in terms of the dynamics concerning his fellow players and his managers, enabled him to view these experiences in a very different light. Not least, this deeper understanding enabled Sam to act with freedom from this internal constraint and to develop more reality-based relationships.

In many ways, role consultancy might be seen as a process of holding up a mirror for the clients to see themselves as others might see them. The reader is referred to the chapter in this book by Richard Kwiatkowski on the intrinsic and extrinsic factors in building up this coaching mirror.

Role consultancy is a highly effective process that may result in clients changing quite significantly. In a closed world such as the football industry, where change seldom occurs, taking a different approach may result in the individual being seen as an island of abnormality in a sea of normality. As was referred to in the case material, this was part of Sam's experience. In one sense, this created difficulties, as he soon came to realize that others would not readily understand his solutions.

However, the process also provides support to the client by means of continuing development. The process of role consultancy offered to Sam also provided him with a model for diagnosing problems and finding his own solutions. The transference of skills meant that Sam was now able to become his own consultant.

Notes

1. For a detailed description of OPUS, see the Directory Section in this book.
2. This is not his real name; identifying details have been altered to protect client's confidentiality.

References.

Menzies Lyth, I. (1989). *Containing Anxiety in Institutions*. London: Free Association.

Miller, E. J. (1993). *From Dependency to Autonomy*. London: Free Association.

Stapley, L. F. (2002). *It's an Emotional Game*. London: Karnac.

CHAPTER TEN

Coaching as a transitional process: a case of a lawyer in transition

Marlene Spero

Introduction

Executives, like the organizations they work for, are faced with constant change, increasing complexity, uncertainty, and diversity. The greater fluidity of boundaries and structures, the intrusion of the external environment, affect their freedom and autonomy and the capacity to think and act. Roles, relationships, and identity are constantly challenged, and the assumptions on which they operate may be outdated or inappropriate. Executives are often asked to make decisions they don't support and to take more risks. Many experience mistrust, disappointment, and abuse as well as a growing sense of vulnerability. Loyalty to the organization for many has diminished, resulting in a growing ambivalence and lack of commitment. This has been replaced by a growth in narcissistic self-interest and a greater need to depend on personal resources (Amado, 2004).

In addition, organizational development programmes, which have traditionally focused on acquiring new behaviours, skills, and knowledge, have been experienced as being too narrow and distant from the everyday realities and complexity of the lives of these executives. Few of these programmes recognize that unconscious processes "below the surface" can guard against change and result in a repetition of old patterns of behaviour and an adherence to old values. Consequently, many executives find themselves unable to develop new and creative ways of thinking about the challenges that they faced. Coaching can offer a solution to many of these shortcomings, especially if thought of as a socio-psychological and transitional process. Coaching can be designed to meet the specific needs of executives by focusing on different domains of concern, on roles, tasks, authority, and the organizational context as well as the emotions that are stirred up. The aim of coaching is to enable these executives to question, make sense of, reflect in a new light, and reach a new understanding of what is happening around them, and to provide the flexibility, learning, and understanding that is needed to function more effectively in the work place.

In this chapter I

- explore and address coaching as a transitional process;
- explore the role of the coach;
- present a case study to illustrate.

Coaching as a transitional process

The thinking

Transitional thinking takes the view that people and organizations are always in a state of transition, change, and development, and that in order to work with the real life problems of organizations and their members there needs to be a focus on the psychological processes within the individual as well as the social processes that operate beyond his control (Ambrose, 2001). This approach moves us from Freud's biological–psychological understanding of individual behaviour to one that suggests that how the individual engages with his role and organization is a function not only of his psychological make-up but also of his life experiences, from the womb through childhood, adolescence, and adulthood. He will be influenced by his environment, his culture, social class, religion, education, beliefs, values, skills, and knowledge, which in turn will influence his motivation, aspirations, and choice of work. As Pines (1998) states, the development of our subjective self is an ongoing process that is mirrored by and entwined with the other throughout life. We are continually redefining ourselves and our identity. Erikson (1950) describes a series of identity crises that are linked to physiological and psychological as well as environmental changes.

These ideas are particularly pertinent to thinking about people who may have had (out of their own choice or not) to change profession or occupational sector and adapt to a change in values, skills, ethics, and identity. At one level they may feel ambivalent, confused, or experience a loss of self-confidence and the feelings that cannot be coped with may be denied, displaced, or projected on to others. Indeed, survival at work would appear to depend more and more on the capacity of the individual to manage his internal world and the regressive feelings that may be evoked by the working environment.

At another level the structural aspects of the organization, its technology, tasks, culture, procedures, and the wider environment in which the individual operates, will create their own tensions and dynamics influencing how he enacts his role and relates to others. Individual action is made more difficult by the complexity of interdependent relationships between systems and roles.

Transitional thinking is based on the ideas of Winnicott (1951) and Bridger (2001a,b). Bridger realized that the transitional processes in organizational situations resonated with the mother–infant experiences that Winnicott described of dependency, independency, attachment and separation, the period when the infant tests the environment to ascertain his own independence. The one-to-one coaching relationship provides a transitional space, not only in time but also in the mind, evoking many of the unconscious processes that Winnicott alludes to. It becomes a "cover", a transitional object like the "teddy bear", where the executive can explore, question, make mistakes, try things out, learn about himself—a space that is both reality and not reality, in which he can feel safe and unthreatened.[1] He can test out his ideas about the other and the external environment and, most important of all, be himself. The play of the child mirrors the exploration, questioning, and creativity of the client and the coaching relationship, the feelings of attachment and separation, dependency and independency. The coach can create the conditions to help individuals change but cannot force them to change.

The process

Bridger (2001a,b), writing about the problems faced by executives and managers in the process of transition, suggests that they need to:

- relinquish earlier and dysfunctional, but still valued, roles, ideas, and practices;
- create and discover new, more adaptive and viable ideas and different ways of thinking and acting;
- cope with the instability of the changing conditions, both outside and within the organizational system and with the sense of insecurity arising from it.

Bridges (1986) suggests that the individual has to work through a series of stages:

- ending phase—disengaging from existing working relationships, dis-identifying with existing roles and disenchantment;
- neutral phase—taking stock, creating and discovering new ways of thinking and acting that may be characterized by disorientation, disintegration, and a loss of meaning;
- new beginnings—developing new competencies, new relationships, "new turfs", which entails coping with and mourning the loss of old turfs, relationships, competencies, careers, and control.

Difficulties arise when the individual remains too identified with his role, or when the environment in which he works changes but he does not move with it, or if he engages in illusory, rather than realistic, thinking, or when it becomes difficult to relinquish old ideas, rules, and procedures that may no longer be relevant. This may be a defensive response to the anxiety generated by the changes. Marris (1996) connects the experience of dramatic change within organizations with bereavement, when a loss of the whole structure of meaning can occur. Loss and its management, he suggests, is about mourning, working through, and resolution.

The coaching process entails:

- a need for engagement;
- working through the issues and tasks;
- reviewing the process of coaching and disengagement.

The role of the coach

Although the role of the coach may vary from that of being a counsellor, a teacher, a consultant, or an adviser, her primary task is to be empathetic, to be able to put herself in the client's shoes, and understand where he is coming from. She must understand his defences, motivation, capacity for the work, his degree of engagement, his role and "the organization in his mind".[2] She needs to be non-judgemental, non-critical, a good listener, questioning, with a sense of curiosity, and able to deal with ambivalence. She may function as an idealized ego, a model that the client may unconsciously emulate and identify with. The coach will be able to address non-resolved developmental issues that are played out within the working environment and that inhibit the individual's capacities to engage with his various roles. For example, Oedipal issues (relationships with mothers or fathers) that have not been worked through may affect the individual's capacity to relate to authority figures at work or sibling rivalry may be re-enacted with colleagues.

The coach reflects, questions, confronts, and makes interpretations in order to facilitate a new way of thinking, and understanding.[3] She will help the client deal with irrational behaviour and the negative feelings and emotions that may have been aroused, which need to be recognized rather than denied. The coach acts as a "container" (Bion, 1961) for the client's anxieties and projections, helping to process them. She[4] can use her own feelings (countertransference) to understand the feelings that the client is experiencing as well the feelings that are transferred to her (transference) that relate to significant people in the client's life that may be re-enacted at work. She will focus on the task in hand as well as reviewing the dynamics that emerge. As Amado (2004) suggests, the coach acts as a "shadow gardener", helping the individual to grow without him knowing it.

The case—a lawyer in transition[5]

The case illustrates the coaching experiences of a lawyer, David, who worked for Zenith, a financial organization. It traces his transition from a purely legal role to a business role, the changes in values and identity that were required, and the emotions that were stirred up and enacted. The case will illustrate some of the above issues.

The context

Zenith was an old established organization with a strong geographic identity and brand name. Besides its financial services, it had widened its business to include life insurance and health care, and had recently merged with another company with a view to increasing its commercial interests. This had resulted in a major internal reorganization, numerous redundancies, and a questioning of the existing corporate identity and culture. Senior staff had traditionally been "home grown" but the new organization had a policy of promoting high-flyers to key executive positions. The "job for life scenario" was being challenged, and the culture was becoming more competitive and skills focused. The original staff found it difficult to adapt and were feeling demotivated. The HR department saw coaching as a way to resolving some of these problems as well as developing general management and leadership capabilities.

The coaching contract

The contract with the client was for nine sessions to be held every three to four weeks. This was part of a larger contract with the organization in which ten senior executives had been selected for coaching. It was hoped that the effects of the coaching would have a greater impact on the management of the changes that Zenith faced. To this end, an evaluation process was also included as part of the design. Each of the executives was given a series of psychometric tests and a 360° leadership assessment.[6] These 360° assessments had traditionally been used to identify and target behaviours that needed "to be improved" and fitted in with the clients' expectations and the culture of the organization. I was interested to see whether a psychodynamic approach to understanding these shortcomings would be more helpful than a behavioural approach.

Engagement with the new client

The first session was exploratory and aimed to facilitate David's engagement with the process. There was a dual task: first, of telling him about the coaching process and checking out whether we would be able to work together (i.e., to ensure that neither of us had negative feelings towards each other, such as a negative transference that would block the process) and second, of getting to know his background, work experience, and the current issues that he faced. During the session we also reflected on his psychometric assessments.

His story

> David was a very pleasant and welcoming man, somewhat shy and quietly spoken. When I asked him to tell me about himself, he told me about the pressures in his life and his past career. School had been difficult and he felt he had not done particularly well. He had been bullied and had felt quite lonely. He said that making music had been his salvation and he became a serious cello player. He felt more engaged at university and had been successful academically but remained socially uncomfortable. David said that his father, an accountant, always criticized him, and as a result David grew to be very critical of himself. Mother was an infant school teacher and very ambitious for her son. His younger sister was also an accountant. He came from a lower middle class background, which he found problematic at Law School, where he felt that everyone was middle or upper class. This feeling of being socially inferior affected his relationship with the Company Board. He said that he also had difficulties in handling conflict and related this to his Calvinist background. Conflict and confrontation had been avoided within the family and he recalled having to suppress his anger and frustration at home. He was married with two children, with a new baby on the way. He had had a very successful career working in a city law firm, moved into retail, and then to Zenith. He said he was always very driven.

We explored some of the feedback from the psychometric tests. David said he felt that he was well thought of but it was clear that there were certain areas of his personality, behaviour, and leadership that would need to be addressed in the coaching. The results suggested that he was very conservative, somewhat introverted, and prone to self-doubt. He was not sufficiently assertive or confrontational and could be somewhat intolerant of other people's failures. His social difficulties meant that he tended to avoid high profile situations. He realized that he was over dependent on other people's views and when making decisions he would tend to do so in a co-dependent, as opposed to a collaborative, way. He would become very directive and controlling when anxious, and had difficulties getting support for his ideas because of his reserved demeanour. He was also seen to be more interested in immediate rather than long-term objectives. However, he was technically able, practical, and realistic, and his shrewdness in decision-making resulted in his being thought of as trustworthy and competent.

His role

It seemed clear to me that David was under great stress and was in touch with some unresolved issues from his earlier life. Not only was he having to cope with the structural changes in the company and his new senior management role, which had made him very anxious, but the transition from a legal to a business environment was resulting in a conflict of values and the beginnings of an identity crisis. He said he was uncomfortable as head of the legal department because of the speed with which he had been promoted. He was expected to integrate the legal function more closely with the business and had some serious authority issues in relationship to his team and the Board. He was used to a clear hierarchy of authority, but the recent shift to matrix management meant that this clarity had become obfuscated. Equally, the demands of family life were putting extra pressure on him—could he be a good enough father and husband *as well as* lawyer and manager?

The fear of failure concerned him—he had bad memories of failing at school and had also had a crisis in his early career. He was frightened of this happening again. The long-term impact of failure has been noted by many psychoanalytic writers, including Couch (2004). The work environment had become exceedingly competitive and he realized that "keeping ahead" was becoming more difficult because of the pressures on him. I was aware of powerful aggressive feelings underlying his very quiet, if not self-effacing, self- presentation. We reviewed the session and I suggested that he reflected on what we had discussed so that we would, at our next meeting, be able to focus on one or two of the issues that were preoccupying him.

On being in transition

In his new role David had also been invited to take part in various project groups, but it was his relationship with the Management Board that was of concern to him. He found himself interfacing with different systems. He now had a dual reporting line, one to his line manager, Nigel, the Director of Legal Affairs, and the other to Ken, the Operations Director. Managing the boundary between the different systems and the different relationships had become problematic. His loyalties were becoming split as he began to have ambivalent, if not negative, feelings towards Nigel, whose conservatism was holding him back, and very positive feelings towards Ken, whom he clearly idealized. David felt very envious of his skills, knowledge, and creativity. He said he felt uncomfortable meeting with the Management Board—it was as if he was being scrutinized. On the one hand, he wanted to impress everyone and felt highly competitive, but on the other, he said that he felt like a little boy, out of depth, out of his class, and initially silenced from taking part in the discussions. He became confused and unsure. Old memories and feelings were re-enacted, which we were able to explore within the coaching framework.

His new role meant that he was involved in discussing strategic business decisions that were unfamiliar to him, and he began to realize that the assumptions and fantasies that he had about the Board were unrealistic. He felt he was in an ambiguous situation, caught between the two worlds of law and business. As a lawyer, he had been trained to be altruistic, cautious, rule-following, and reflective. He saw these values as conflicting with those of the Board, whose members he found to be self-interested, reactive, profit orientated, and preoccupied with risk. He was faced with differences in values, a new culture and identity. Was he going to be able to let go of the old way of thinking and doing things and engage with the new? Could he make his department more commercial? He felt very transparent and feared that everyone could see his lack of confidence. His need to impress had become a defence against his feelings of insecurity and it seemed to me that his attempt to present a "false self" (Winnicott, 1960) was undermining his capacity to function. David found my comments very helpful, especially when I told him how important it was for him to be authentically himself. He saw me as someone who could help him deal with the emotions he experienced and the systemic issues related to his role. This was a new way of thinking about work.

The team

David managed a team of five and a department of thirty and was finding this role difficult. Most of the team had been with the organization longer than him. He had been promoted to head of his section within a year of his joining the department, ahead of an older lawyer, Tom, who had been with the company for over twelve years. Tom had applied for the post unsuccessfully, but had been very helpful to David in the early months, informally acting as a mentor and helping him deal with the cut-backs and redundancies in the department, which he found very difficult to do. David was very identified with his staff who, like him, had young families. They were quite traumatized by the job losses, which he found difficult to address. He also felt resentful of his initial dependency on Tom. Tom would challenge his authority and leadership and David would become angry with him and feel impotent. When I spoke about Tom being a representation of his father, he found this very containing, and his outbursts became less frequent. He realized that his success had made him feel guilty because he felt more successful than his own father. This had been blocking his performance: the Oedipal drama was being enacted.

His lack of confidence and fear of failure were evident in his difficulties in making presentations to his team and the Board. When I asked him to describe what usually happened, he said that he would become very anxious, and lose his authority and confidence. The team would become disinterested and not support his ideas. Tom would then take over, leaving him feeling humiliated. At a more practical level we explored the design of his presentations, the room layout, and the technical equipment he had used. I would suggest that he prepared a presentation for the next session, which we would then review. We would move from focusing on the task to personal issues, to skills training, and reflecting on his experiences.

With the involvement of the department in more commercial activities, David found that he had to reorientate his team into thinking commercially. The technical roles within the team needed to be reorganized and streamlined to meet the new demands on the department. There was a greater need for coherency and consistency as procedures were confused or not followed through. We mapped out his main areas of work: his responsibilities, tasks, role relationships, and boundaries, both within his department and beyond. It became apparent that he was still very unclear of his responsibilities *vis-à-vis* the Board, and that there was some overlap between himself and his staff in some of the technical areas. He had difficulties in delegating. Our exploration of his role enabled him to see how anxious he had been about becoming the head of the department. This had meant having to give up his peer relationships with old colleagues. He was feeling increasingly isolated, if not slightly depressed, and this was affecting his capacity to exercise his leadership and to think. As Bridger suggests, one of the most difficult aspects of transition is the capacity to let go of what were once meaningful relationships and ways of thinking and working with which one is closely identified, and then to attach oneself to the new. The question of being both a lawyer and a businessman had become problematic to David.

David became more involved in commercial decision making and more questioning of some of the decisions that were made by his senior colleagues. He realized that our exploration of the religious influences on his behaviour had freed him, enabling him to be more confrontational. When the Board introduced new procedures that would have had serious legal implications, he experienced enormous pressure to "turn a blind eye" and to collude with the Board, which left him feeling very stressed and conflicted. Tom became very critical of how he was handling the situation and David felt that Tom might "whistle blow" if he was not technically correct. He became increasingly paranoid and was thrown back into his old feelings of self-doubt. As a result of our conversations he was able to understand his anxieties and realized that he was acting out his anger by burdening Tom with extra work. Tom had reacted by going to David's boss to complain and David felt undermined by this. An exploration of the guilt and hostility that had been aroused in him led to a reduction in his anxiety.

Line relationships—shifting boundaries

The relationship with his line manager, Nigel, remained problematic. His Oedipal difficulties affected all his authority relationships; he felt that Nigel would readily criticize him. However, he soon began to realize that some of the advice offered by Nigel wasn't always relevant to his new situation. Nigel was not commercially minded and had very little idea of how to work with the reactive operations division. On one occasion, when they discussed the question of legal risk, David was told that it was not his job to manage risk, but rather to deal with uncertainties and to clarify the legal position. David wasn't happy with this, because he was now very much more involved with and excited by the thinking within the Board. At the same time he was also aware of his own personal potentially libellous situation, if things went wrong. As Hirschhorn (1999) points out, the management of risk in a world of uncertainty and competition seems to have taken priority over the primary task, whereas risk is a non-sequitor as far as the law is concerned. Nigel's legal advice did not fit the new business situation and David began to realize that he needed to keep Nigel better informed about his "commercial" thinking. Our conversations had led to a change in their relationship and David began to feel that he was being accepted on equal terms as a colleague. I also felt that he began to tell me more and that I, too, was no longer viewed as another critical figure in his life.

His relationship with his own team began to improve once he was able to take up his leadership and authority. He would present new ideas in a very creative way, invite his staff to lead projects, and then follow through to see that these had been carried out. As he became less anxious, his leadership style shifted from being co-dependent to collaborative. He no longer felt threatened. Once David had understood the critical father transference that he had with Tom, he was able to manage and relate to Tom more easily.

Sibling rivalry

Non-resolved Oedipal relationships with parental figures (as above) or sibling relationships are frequently re-enacted in he workplace. David told me that he had difficulties with a female member of staff, Kate, whom he felt was alienating everyone. She was very assertive, would make inappropriate demands, and was very antagonistic towards him. She was the only woman in his team. As with Tom, he felt challenged and responded by undermining her. He said he found it very difficult to deal with women and, in particular, with strong women. As he began to talk about Kate, he said that she reminded him of his sister and their rivalrous relationship as children. He would become enraged and aggressive towards her. He felt he was enacting the same hostility with Kate. Mitchell (2002) makes the point that sibling relationships can be even more pernicious than those with parents, due to the lack of superego control. Kate had had six months' sick leave and was about to return to work. He was very anxious about her return, as he didn't want her back in her old management role. He found her a non-managerial position, which she accepted. He was delighted with how he had managed the situation, saying that six months earlier he would have been unable to do so.

Home and work

Finally, managing the balance between home and work had become increasingly difficult. He had always been very ambitious, and in an early coaching session told me that he was concerned that he had reached a plateau and was not moving on. Being ambitious, he had always strived for new heights, but the demands of two children and another baby were weighing on him. His wife, who was new to the area, did not have any parental support and was also anxious about the new baby. David had to attend school events, which he found conflicted with his work schedules. He would not allow himself to take time off. I realized David needed my permission to do so and he was very relieved when I told him that this was acceptable. He had become increasingly stressed and anxious, but working through his anxieties had enabled him to start thinking about balancing his work and personal life more effectively.

Reviewing the process and ending

As the sessions progressed, it was clear that David was moving on; he was increasingly able to manage himself and the changes that he faced. He was beginning to feel more comfortable with his business role and had built new relationships. He understood things better and, consequently, could present to the Board in a more coherent and forceful way. He would ensure that he got the support he needed for any contentious or political issue, and developed new strategies to work with his team. He built up a new network of relationships and moved from being a technical manager of his team to engaging with the wider management and leadership structure, interfacing with the external systems and being more externally focused. He no longer felt isolated or depressed. As the sessions proceeded, he continued to bring new concerns that he was preoccupied with and to develop a more reflective stance, thinking about and working through the issues that needed to be addressed.

He also began to feel more comfortable with the senior management team, saying that he now felt he was part of the "inner circle". He felt listened to, and received considerable support from senior management, which enhanced his confidence. He would question things that he was not happy with, offering alternative solutions. He told me that he was now making business decisions and felt comfortable in so doing. David also had his job re-evaluated by the Operations Director and managed to get himself rated on a higher payment band in line with operations. This marked the beginnings of his emotional as well as structural separation from the legal department.

In the final review David said that he felt more confident, more relaxed and able to "stand in his own shoes"; he added, "I feel I am making the right decisions." His new role had really stretched him and he had learnt to put himself about and to network. His ability to communicate had greatly improved. He was less afraid of conflict and realized it could also be constructive and creative. He felt more effective and valued as the leader of his team, although he recognized that he still did not delegate enough. He no longer depended on other people's views of himself, but acknowledged that he still had to work on his leadership style.

We spent time reviewing our relationship, making future plans and commitments in order to prepare for the ending of the coaching. He said he had valued the whole process in that I had helped him through a very critical phase in his life. I had been a container for his anxieties and he had grown more confident and seemed to be more integrated within himself. He was very aware of how the external world and the changes had impacted on him, and how he had acted out many of his feelings. I felt that initially he had not trusted me enough to explore the issues that he was confronted with in the coaching. I had been another critical authority figure whom he didn't like seeing his lack of confidence. This changed, as he shifted in his identification with his new role.

Conclusion

Thinking about coaching as a transitional process and holding this in mind made it possible to facilitate David's move from a lawyer into business. He found himself having to let go of some of his old roles, relationships, values, perceptions and ways of working in order to integrate himself with his new role. The move meant a realignment of David's self with the new situation, a need to integrate those parts of himself that were split off, and a need to work through the emotions that were aroused in him. The aim of the coaching had been to review the new situations, tasks, and tensions as they emerged, to develop a new awareness and enable him to act in a more thoughtful way. There was a constant sense of movement, of trying new things out, taking risks and testing out new ideas and ways of doing things.

Although many of David's behaviours and difficulties could be understood from a psychodynamic or cognitive point of view, religion and social class, sociological variables, were also significant influences on his behaviour. These are themes pursued by several writers: Pines (2002) points to how the loss of status and a stable sense of self and identity can contribute to psychological illness, and Craib (2002) suggests that moving up *the social ladder* may be psychically possible, but can be thwarted by the impossibility of moving up *the social level*. David found his lower middle class background problematic, and in particular relating to his seniors, who he sensed came from a higher class. Likewise, David also felt that his Calvinist background had disabled him from dealing with or confronting conflict within his team.[7] He always wanted to please and this was very evident in his relationship with me as his coach. This also had led to passivity in his leadership and in his relationships with his staff.

The psychometric assessments were the "baseline" for the coaching, and the final evaluation referred back to these. However, it seemed to me that many of David's behavioural needs were better understood as "phenomena below the surface" (Huffington, Armstrong, Halton, Hoyle, & Pooley, 2004); for instance, his defensive structure, his critical ego, feelings of ambivalence and hatred, and non-resolved Oedipal relationships. Once he had understood the interrelationship of the past and its continuous presence in his current behaviour, things shifted for him and were reintegrated into his personality. He no longer felt so paranoid and subject to criticism.

I found myself acting as a container of his anxieties, interpreting what was going on for him in a more manageable and meaningful way. Holding in mind that David was in transition, I also paid attention to the task in hand, to the organizational and structural factors that were impacting on him and the emotions that he was in touch with, which inhibited him from functioning effectively. It was his capacity to tolerate and understand the ambiguity and anxieties he felt that enabled him to move on.

Post script: I have since heard that David has left the legal profession and is totally engaged with the business in his new role as Operations Director of the Division. He is one of the youngest to achieve Director status.

Notes

1. See also a chapter by Jane Pooley in this book.
2. See a chapter by Clare Huffington in this book.
3. See a chapter by Miranda Alcock in this book.
4. "He" is used to represent the client and "she" to represent the coach.
5. The names of the client, the organization, and other names have been changed. Client's permission to use this case study obtained.
6. For a detailed description of the use of psychometrics in coaching the reader is referred to a chapter by Richard Kwiatkowski in this book.
7. I have frequently found in my one-to-one consultations religion impinging on the individual's capacity to act. For example, the conflict between socialist and individualistic values of the Muslim working for a profit-driven IT company, or the Italian HR director who felt he could help others to change, but could not change himself because of his strong Catholic beliefs.

References

Amado, G. (2004). Le Coaching ou Le Retour de Narcisse. *Connexions*, 8: 43–51.
Ambrose, A. (2001). An introduction to transitional thinking. In: G. Amado & A. Ambrose (Eds.), *The Transitional Approach to Change* (pp. 1–28). London: Karnac.
Bion, W. (1961). *Experiences in Groups*. London: Tavistock.
Bridger, H. (2001a). Foreword. In: G. Amado & A. Ambrose (Eds.), *The Transitional Approach to Change* (pp. xi–xix). London: Karnac.

Bridger, H. (2001b). An introduction to transitional thinking. In: G. Amado & A. Ambrose (Eds.), *The Transitional Approach to Change* (pp. 1–28). London: Karnac.

Bridges, W. (1986). Managing organizational transitions. *Organizational Dynamics, Summer*: 24–33.

Couch, A. (2004). Personal communication.

Craib, I. (2002). What is social class? *Group Analysis, 35*(3): 342–350.

Erikson, E. H. (1950). The healthy personality. In: *Identity and the Life Cycle* (pp. 51–107). USA: W. W. Norton.

Hirschhorn, L. (1999). The primary risk. *Human Relations, 52*: 5–23.

Huffington, C., Armstrong, D., Halton, W., Hoyle, L., & Pooley, J. (2004). *Working Below the Surface: The Emotional Life of Contemporary Organizations*. London: Karnac.

Marris, P. (1996). *The Politics of Uncertainty. Attachment in Private and Public Life*. London: Routledge.

Mitchell, J. (2002). *Siblings*. London: Blackwell.

Pines, M. (1998). Mirroring and child development: psychological interpretations. In: M. Pines (Ed.), *Circular Reflections* (pp. 41–58). London: Jessica Kingsley.

Pines, M. (2002). Falling in and out of class structures. *Group Analysis, 35*(3): 406–410.

Winnicott, D. W. (1951). Transitional objects and transitional phenomena. In: *Through Paediatrics to Psychoanalysis*. London: Hogarth [reprinted London: Tavistock, 1987].

Winnicott, D. W. (1960). Ego distortions in terms of true and false self. In: *The Maturational Processes and the Facilitating Environment*. London: Karnac, 1990.

CHAPTER ELEVEN

Three-dimensional coaching

Miranda Alcock

I n this chapter I use a case study from my work as an Executive Coach to discuss three key aspects of my approach to coaching. I demonstrate how these three aspects contribute to positive changes in the working life of the client. Clients come for many reasons and the coach responds accordingly. The example I have selected illustrates the type of coaching where personal career progression and skills development may be a direct outcome of the work, but are not the client's initial focus at the point of entry.

First, Open Systems Theory[1] takes into account the influences of the environment, within both the organizational boundary and the wider society, on the way client manages a designated role. Second, early experiences and relationships may influence the behaviour and dilemmas of the client in the workplace. Third, by taking note of the way the client and coach relate during the coaching sessions and by being sensitive to the impact of the client on the coach, it enhances the coach's insight into the issues under discussion. In other words, I recognize transference and countertransference as a valuable source of information within the coaching process.

These three aspects form a three-dimensional arena. One can focus simply on the client, or explore a two-dimensional relationship between person and place. Use of one's own feelings and experience in the coaching session creates the triangular space within which we can work and think. I hope to demonstrate the interconnectedness and efficacy of all three aspects.

Domains and systems theory

Halina Brunning (2001) has identified the domains of Executive Coaching that are contemporaneously present during consultations.

These can be seen as:

- *Personal*, comprising the client's personal history and personality;
- *Professional*, encompassing the way in which natural abilities and talents have been developed through training, education, and work experience into skills and competencies;
- *Organizational*, recognizing the impact of the organization on clients and how it influences the way that they take up their roles.

The personal and professional domains of Executive Coaching are self-evident but I would like to expand on the organizational before I present the case study.

Brunning describes the workplace environment as "the stage for the unfolding drama", giving weight to the context in which the client does his or her job. In Open Systems parlance, this would not only be the acting area, but would include the proscenium arch, set, curtains, fellow actors, and the audience. The ability of the actor (or worker in role) to be successful depends on many connected factors. One could include the intentions of the scriptwriter, mindset of the director, and so forth. In other words, a model of understanding organizations as an Open System, where everything is interconnected, is crucial when working with individuals who are a part of that system. The "organization in the mind"[2] of the client, can be as peopled and as busy. Similarly, the managers, staff, clients, service users, etc., may themselves be allocated parts or roles that can play out or repeat the client's own personal internal scenarios.

The organization

An organization is a "formal system, influenced by the internal social structure and subject to the pressures of an institutional environment" (Beishon & Peters, 1972, p. 17).

The primary task of the organization is underpinned by its stated beliefs. These can be found in its mission statement, or stated purpose. They motivate and drive the organization overtly through its structures and management style as it tries to meet its goals, whether for financial gain, public service, research, etc. Employees agree to contribute their skills and labour to serve the stated purpose of the organization in their work contract and are paid so to do.[3]

Second, the organization itself is subject to pressures, constraints and influences beyond its boundaries, by virtue of the society in which it is located. It is subject to the law and influenced by events of the times and the politics of the day. People who comprise "society" work within the organization, bringing their own attitudes and perceptions into the organization and contributing to its culture. These filter between departments and sectors, find their way up from below and descend from management to affect the client in role. The organization is partly the backdrop, but, like the Gestalt concept of "figure and ground", client and organization have a more complicated relationship, often affected by shifting perceptions.

Organizational dynamics can impact on members and saturate them to the point that they become almost too "sodden" to be able to think. An opportunity to work with somebody outside the social system, external to the organization, can provide space for the client to reassert his or her capacity for independent thought as an individual, as well as mobilize personal insight. Viewing work and its complexity from a distance can offer a different perspective of what is going on in the organization. Figure and ground can shift and new configurations can emerge. Clients often prefer to come to my office, rather than to meet me on site, often travelling some distance, although they are busy and under pressure. The physical distance and change of environment can allow more opportunities for perceptual shifts to occur than the pressured and saturated office environment.

Pre-arrival

Negotiating a contract with individual clients in an organization is clearly very different from working with an organizational brief, but there are some similarities. We also need to pay attention to the way in which the contract was initiated and agreed. We recognize that the way in which the working partnership is formed has an impact on the work. When working with an individual within an organizational context, how the client finds the way to your door has relevance to your engagement and the future of your work together. Does the referral come from a more senior manager, who recognizes that the client needs some offline support? This can be done supportively or as a veiled threat to their job security. Is it a personal recommendation from a colleague or a private response to commercial publicity from a well-known firm that specializes in Executive Coaching? Is the work sponsored by the organization or commissioned by the client? If the latter, does the organization require specific outcomes from the work? Even before your first meeting a combination of these factors will have already influenced the client's expectations or possibly have aroused some trepidation.

What clients want

Clients come for coaching with a range of agenda. They may be on a fast track to power and success, either within their present organization or with the intention to advance their career by changing organization. They may arrive full of complaints about their unsupportive company, their obnoxious Chief Executive, their unsympathetic colleagues or employees, unfair competitors, their impossible task, etc. They locate their difficulties right away from themselves and into the environment or others. They hope for some new strategies for changing the behaviour of others and exercising more control over staff and environment. Others may come full of self-doubt and self-blame, looking for some kind of miracle psychic makeover. Full of personal shame, they are convinced that their problems at work are all of their own making. They find it hard to think systemically about the unconscious or sentient life of their organization, and end up taking responsibility for all that goes wrong. In both scenarios, perspective is an issue; the clients are seeing only part of the picture. They benefit from being able to make that perceptual shift so both factors are taken into account.

Mr Thomas's route

I had been recommended to Mr Thomas[4] by another senior manager in an affiliated system. The client chose to contact me, knowing in advance that I had had some experience of working in government systems similar to his own and was personally known to a colleague whom he respected. His expectation, therefore, was that I had some familiarity with the system and that I could probably be trusted. I later understood that a third factor might have been my training as an analytical psychologist. He had arranged the meeting himself, admitting that he had had my name on his "to do" list for nine months before he could "find time" to make the contact. In short, he was well disposed to do the work, but felt some obvious trepidation. After our first meeting, on the agreement of his Chief Executive, we contracted a set of fortnightly meetings. These would become routine monthly meetings for some months to come. I believe that he had been favourably disposed before meeting me, thanks to the recommendation of his colleague. This helped us to establish a working relationship and rapport from the start. He decided to travel down from the north of England for our meetings in London, as his journeys gave him valuable time to prepare and reflect.

My own preparation

In this case study the client came initially with a personal agenda as well as with organizational concerns. Despite being led by the client's immediate concerns, I generally have a mental checklist in my head and in the first session I hope to glean a rough history of the organization, its primary task or purpose, and its products or services, if I don't have prior knowledge. I also need to establish the client's place in the organizational hierarchy.

The client is asked to bring details about their organization, their job description, and an organizational map. The client may be asked to outline their role and responsibilities before explaining their reasons for seeing a consultant. I will sometimes wait for this information if the client urgently needs to explain a crisis or dilemma during the first session. This information can also reveal something of the client's attitude to his workplace, even intimations of the underlying issues, by the manner in which he describes it and through the language used. Because the client's difficulties can be related to, or exacerbated by, the organizational structure, the geography and design of the workplace, the administrative and technical systems that are in place, etc., it helps to have some knowledge of these factors.

Case material

First meeting

> Mr Thomas arrived for our first meeting about forty minutes late. He was flustered but told me that this was normal behaviour and that he was habitually late for all meetings. I felt that he was warning me not to expect too much from him and also that he was feeling chaotic and overwhelmed, and struggling to set boundaries in his working life. He was also concerned about his privacy. He was apprehensive about what others may think if they heard that he had sought coaching. This was despite the fact that his line manager had agreed to the funding for ongoing coaching sessions. I realized that he must be subjecting himself to considerable performance pressure, and was uncomfortable about the implications of seeking coaching, as if he had failed to meet his own expectations.

> Mr Thomas was a senior manager, with a wide, cross-agency brief extending across a large rural county in the north of England. He reported directly to the elected members of the County Cabinet. His line manager was the newly appointed Chief Executive. In his role, Mr Thomas had a wide range of responsibilities for strategy, policy development, and operations, as well as control of the relevant budget. He managed Heads of Strategy, Finance, Administration, and Technology. At our first meeting he described his role and his responsibilities. These were extensive, and, in some cases, rather undefined. It became clear to me, and to him, that there were good reasons for him to take stock and to resume control of his job.

The following issues were raised in the first meeting: poor time management, difficulties prioritizing tasks and in the delegation of tasks to his staff. He described the following problems.

- Most of his time was spent in meetings, sometimes fruitlessly. He chaired most of them, but as he had an unreliable secretary he had to personally ensure that paperwork and reports were distributed beforehand.
- He spent time writing endless local reports and committee items for Members, Partners, and Chief Officers.
- He had to deal with high levels of correspondence and e-mails.
- As a consequence of the work not being done on time, he was constantly dealing with complaints, and placating suppliers and providers of services.
- He felt obliged to deal with these issues personally, fearing that if the Cabinet got to know how inefficient he was his reputation would be in jeopardy.
- The County Council had commissioned new technology, with which there were constant problems; as staff were not trained to use it, it was currently a liability.
- He had vacancies in his senior management posts.
- He was initiating and managing a range of projects, which meant that he was constantly over-stretched and, therefore, inefficient.

Attention to unconscious communication

By the end of this description I felt rather overwhelmed myself and wondered whether I could be any use at all to Mr Thomas. Like him, would my reputation in his organization flounder if I took him on as an impossible task and could not be of any help? On reflection, his difficulties seemed to be as follows. He had created a dependency culture around him, which encouraged his staff to approach him for answers rather than taking up their own authority. He continually tried to spare his staff, taking on their work to free them, and then not being able to deliver. He was always acting down to compensate for staff inefficiencies, even though he was working twelve-hour days and taking work home over weekends. This clearly left him little time to think strategically.

He had also described an uncomfortable and unprofitable relationship with staff, colleagues, and teams. This was hardly surprising, as his discomfort with his own aggression and his fears of being perceived as a bullying manager prevented him from making legitimate demands on their skills and time. His own creativity and efficiency thereby suffered, as he added some of their responsibilities and obligations to his own workload.

I recognized, too, that Mr Thomas was passing on to me not only his own feelings of impotence and sense of a mess impossible to manage, but an organizational dynamic with which I was familiar. I had experienced something similar when I had worked in an affiliated system. Pressured by the government to carry out public services efficiently and cheaply with inadequate resources, and pressured from below by the public to deliver yet more products and services, the organization took a perverse pleasure in the belief that many of its problems were insoluble, despite their best efforts. It was almost as if a large bucket of assorted intertwined junk had been dumped on the table with a triumphant and defiant exclamation of "Well! Let's see you get that sorted!" There was a perverse pleasure in being overwhelmed by the (self-constructed) impossible task.

But Mr Thomas did want a place in which he could think about his work and make some improvements. In this first meeting I had been given some idea of the breadth and responsibility of Mr Thomas's job and also some insight into the way he worked. "I don't work smart," he commented wryly. At the end of the meeting we agreed that some of his difficulties might be related to *how* he managed the work, which might have something to do with his state of mind and his personal history.

At this early stage there was no discussion of how organizational dynamics may affect his work. The time had been taken up with the personal agenda: his anxious concerns about his capacity to do his job.

Influence of the past

In our second meeting Mr Thomas took up where we had left off. A man in his early fifties, he suffered from a number of stress related health problems, including high blood pressure and insomnia. He felt that he was starting to slow down, that all was not well, and that he wanted a change. He lived in a supportive home environment and felt that many of his problems at work were self-generated. He volunteered that he had found personal psychotherapy that he had had in the past very helpful. He was the only child of older parents who were unused to children before his arrival and were strict and demanding. When he was still a child his father had become an alcoholic; his mother suffered from depression and was cold and distant. He had been bullied by his father throughout his childhood and was still deeply angry with his parents. He, too, would go on drunken binges, enjoying the uninhibition that they allowed, and wake up ashamed the next morning, with no memory of the previous night's activities. Drinking to oblivion had been a form of respite. It also increased his sense of shame and self-blame.

He concluded these personal revelations by saying that, despite his difficulties, he really did want to do his job well, as he believed that he could be a positive force for improving the lives of people in his county. He felt that he had to hide his difficulties at work from his superiors, he had to appease his suppliers and providers, and he had to be accessible to his staff at all times. He also felt obliged to lighten their workload at his own expense. All in all, he felt cowed and overwhelmed. When I asked him how he thought that his personal experience was relevant to his attitude to work, we began to discuss links and parallels.

Insight

Without delving too deeply into his personal history, it was clear to me that some of Mr Thomas's behaviour at work was influenced by his childhood. Even as he talked, he began to recognize that his accessibility at work was not merely because he wanted to be an approachable manager. Although he had considerable authority delegated to him by his organization, he was unable to execute it. Authority and tyranny had become confused in his mind. He was determined never to be remotely like his bullying father, and to be seen as a positive rather than a destructive force and thus the cause of harm. He connected this to the problems within his senior staff team. Although they would examine a problem together, agree a strategy and develop a plan, he would not hold them to task, and when he had to evaluate the scheme he would always accept excuses for their failure to execute or complete it on time. He would tend to collude with their excuse of overwork, either by fire-fighting, or by taking on most of the work himself. It was clear that his "soft management" was helpful neither to him nor his staff. One might say that he was persecuting or bullying himself, causing himself stress and ill-health, with an effect not unlike the bullying father who had dominated his childhood and had made him feel so inept. It also emerged that this fear of "harming others" had to do with the sense of his own anger present under the surface, and his fear that it may somehow erupt inappropriately at work. He was allowing his staff to under-perform as he colluded with their justification for repeated failures, which would hardly increase their motivation or their self-esteem. So, the very destructiveness he so feared was indeed finding expression, in its own subtle way, in his management style.

Development

As a result of this discussion Mr Thomas became cheerful and buoyant. This connection between his experience as a boy and his behaviour at work made sense to him and it felt useful. He described a high-powered meeting during which he felt that his work and efforts were being recognized. It had felt gratifying when somebody commented that she wouldn't have Mr Thomas's job for the world. He felt that the feedback from that meeting had made a positive difference. Clearly, he felt seen and understood in our joint work that day and in his meeting: in short, he felt "gratified". Recognition of his suppressed aggression, and an understanding how it affected his work role began to reduce his anxiety in the following weeks. It also meant that he was more in touch with positive experiences at work, such as peer recognition. In response to our earlier discussion, wherein he had described his twelve-hour days, he was embarking on a stocktaking phase and had decided not to work in the evenings or take work home over weekends. He began to think of realistic ways of reshuffling his work agenda and establishing clearer targets for his staff. I felt that he was beginning to focus more on his primary task by delegating less important tasks and prioritizing those which were central to the service provision that was the core of his work and close to his heart.

The process had moved from how personal experience affected his work to his functioning in role at work. He began to think about the challenges of the job and how to meet them. He wanted to discuss the tensions in his team and competition with colleagues. These were to do with management and supervision of staff in the context of the organization—a combination of personal style and organizational dynamics.

By now, instead of trying to present himself as the "accessible manager", he was able to speak of his irritation, and even anger, with some of his staff. This was our focus of work for the next few sessions.

Organizational dynamics

By our third meeting, there was more connection between personal and organizational dynamics. If he could see some of his anxieties as symptomatic of, or a response to, organizational dynamics, he could think about them more strategically. If he was able to recognize them as the drawbacks of a troubled organization, he could take them into account and function differently as a result. This insight helped him to mobilize his personal authority and start to function more effectively in his role. Mr Thomas continued to be more ebullient and authoritative in the sessions, and also at work, where he was forthright about how his district managers were under-performing. He clearly wanted to exercise more leadership: had given some thought to this and had made some decisions to bring about change.

Authority

According to classical management theory (Kast & Rosenweig, 1972, pp. 316–317), an authority which has been legitimized by a central source ensures that the superior "has a right to command someone else and that the subordinate person has the duty to obey the command". This is implied in the notion of official legitimacy, legal in nature rather than social or informally acquired. The person in authority can evoke compliance on the basis of a formal role. Authority belongs to the position, not to the individual. If a subordinate is given responsibility for carrying out a task, he must also take authority for doing so. This mattered to Mr Thomas in the way he was responsible to his CE and the council members, but also in the expectations he had of his own staff.

Part of the whole

Mr Thomas was constantly annoyed with his PA, whose inefficiency and carelessness undermined and embarrassed him in various ways. She failed to set up or cancel meetings, forgot to brief him or provide him with paperwork for meetings, took considerable time off sick, and he was afraid that she would disappear altogether. He assured me that he had always been very thoughtful towards her and tried to take care of her, as she was clearly fragile and could not work under pressure. When asked what that meant, he said that she alternated between panic and resentment. It was not too difficult for Mr Thomas to recognize his own state of mind in this description, and to recognize the similarities between the PA's behaviour and his own inefficiencies.

In fact, he realized that it was common practice in his organization to describe the inefficient staff as fragile, and thus to collude with their behaviour. The staff employed in this part of the public sector were required to manage a paradox: on the one hand, their jobs offered a certain sense of security, on the other hand, the work overload felt crushing and threatened to overwhelm them. So, although there was a prevailing sense among many of the staff that they had an ever increasing and unmanageable workload in response to government directives, there was also job security. People were rarely dismissed; they were merely reorganized into different roles. They remained in the system, recycled and resentful. For Mr Thomas to make this link between his own situation and the organizational culture meant that he was ready to consider making different choices.

Change

Mr Thomas prepared himself to confront the PA constructively and to help her to re-engage. He also paid attention to the state of his management team. Over the next two months he reorganized his senior management team and restructured their roles. This gave him the opportunity to offer redundancy to the one who was most dissatisfied and unco-operative. He recruited for vacant posts and appointed two new senior managers from outside the system. Planning days and regular meetings were incorporated into the new senior management team's working style. He has undertaken an internal review and evaluation and the new team has developed a more creative business plan for the coming year.

He also made some important lifestyle changes: weekend and evening work were now the exception rather than the rule. As Mr Thomas was more able to delegate, he took time off to go away with his family and re-established contact with old friends. He talked of being "ahead of the game". In conjunction with his Chief Executive, he had set his retirement date, and wanted "everything to be ship-shape" when he leaves.

Work in progress

Three-dimensional coaching is not a magic cure-all. There was still much for Mr Thomas to do, and the influences of organizational dynamics continued to impact upon him. He struggled with his negative expectations. He was still reticent about delegating and assigning work, half expecting negative responses or refusal. His tendency to give instructions with a built-in negative supposition was counterproductive: "I don't suppose that you would be interested in . . .", or "I assume you won't want to take on . . .", or "I don't think that you . . .". This confused his staff, both about his wishes and their own obligations. To allow himself clarity, and to be direct with his staff, was an ongoing battle. He recognized the impact of these negative expectations on his management style. This reflective capacity had increased a sense of vigilance and responsibility, rather than leading him to castigate himself, as was his tendency previously. He recognized how *the personal* linked to *the professional* and this realization had improved his professionalism.

He became cognizant with the power of organizational dynamics. He learned how organizational dynamics, even if cumulatively they reinforced his negative expectations of his own staff, affected his capacity for independent thought. He began to understand that sometimes the tensions within the organization itself were also being played out in microcosm in his own department.

As we continued to pay attention in the sessions to our own interaction as coach and client, so Mr Thomas was increasingly able to consider the interplay between himself and his managers, and himself and his own boss.

The work was ongoing and the coaching process had not ended by the time of writing this chapter.

Case summary

This case material comes from eight meetings. In the first session, the client gave an account of the demands of his work role and his difficulties in trying to meet them. In the second session, he connected some of his personal history with the way he takes up his role at work. In the third, he started to recognize how the organizational culture impacts on his work and began to feel that he could behave differently in role. From the fourth, he began to exercise his legitimate authority more effectively. He then continued to develop a process whereby he used the coaching sessions to identify issues that made him anxious. We then scanned his own valencies for certain feelings or behaviours. He considered what influence current preoccupations or anxieties in the organization at large might be having on him and his staff. We considered whether feedback from the coach about dynamics in the coaching session in any way mirrored his work experience. From this time on, the interplay between these aspects emerged alongside new dilemmas and issues that played themselves out in his work environment.

Conclusion

This vignette demonstrates how the three aspects of three-dimensional coaching interact and overlap. First, Open Systems Theory allows the examination of the systemic influences of the environment, within both the organizational boundary and the wider society, on the way client manages a designated role. The culture of my client's organization made it difficult for managers to take up their own authority: incompetent staff were rarely disciplined and seldom dismissed.

Second, with the personal–professional lens we identified how this culture and organizational dynamics resonated with my client's own life experience, which had left him uneasy about his own aggression and his capacity for destructive behaviour. The organizational culture and his own experience combined to undermine his managerial role with difficult staff.

Third, by taking note of how the client and coach related during the coaching sessions, and by being sensitive to the impact of the client on the coach, insight was developed. This dynamic was openly discussed and became useful to the client.

Through the three-dimensional approach he had become both more reflective and more effective in his role. He had improved his work–life balance and started planning his own retirement with a sense of pride and achievement.

Editor's comment

This short case study, which concludes this volume, demonstrates the vital ingredients that make up the distinct and unique characteristics of a systems-psychodynamic approach to executive coaching.

Notes

1. A. K. Rice (1958, 1963).
2. See also a chapter on the "organization-in-the-mind", by Clare Huffington, in this book.
3. Influenced by Beishon and Peters (1972), and Kast and Rosenweig (1972).
4. This is not his real name. The client's consent to this case study has been obtained.

References

Beishon, J., & Peters, G. (Eds.) (1972). *Systems Behaviour*. London: The Open University Press.

Brunning, H., (2001). The six-domain model of executive coaching. *Organizational and Social Dynamics (OPUS)*, 1(2): 254–263.

Kast, F. E., & Rosenweig J. E. (1972). *Organization & Management, A Systems Approach*. New York: McGraw-Hill.

Rice, A. K. (1958). *Productivity and Social Organization*. London: Tavistock.

Rice, A. K. (1963). *The Enterprise and its Environment*. London: Tavistock.

PART IV
A DIRECTORY OF RESOURCES

This section features contact details of organizations, training institutes and private firms specializing in executive coaching delivered from a systems-psychodynamic perspective.

International organizations

International Society for Psychoanalytic Study of Organizations (ISPSO).

ISPSO was formed in 1983 in the USA by a small group of academics and practitioners interested in furthering the psychoanalytic approach to the study of organizations. It has grown into an international society with members from USA, UK, Europe, Canada, Australia, Israel, India, Scandinavia, and Japan.

The aims of ISPSO:

- establishment of a community of thinkers and practitioners who share an interest in examining organizations from a psychoanalytic perspective;
- facilitation of communication and development of ideas, especially the application of research and theory into practice in the psychoanalytic study of organizations across disciplinary, national, and ideological boundaries;
- provision of a public forum for discussion, presentation, and distribution of papers that explore the field of psychoanalytic studies.

Contact details: www.ispso.org

UK organizations

The Grubb Institute

The Grubb Institute has developed an innovative approach to one-to-one consultation called Organizational Role Analysis (ORA). This is an eight-session (two hours per session) consultation using a disciplined and structured method to focus on the participant's experience of leadership in role, exploring the pressure points, opportunities, and dilemmas. The outcome for the participants is a clearer idea of the realities to be addressed and a series of conceptual tools and methods for ongoing transformation of their roles and systems.

Evidence-based Leadership is a three-day programme for leaders who want to work on their experience of leadership in a

group setting. The programme aims to energize and equip participants for action. Working with the Grubb framework of Context,
System, and Purpose, participants are able to develop skills in finding, making, and taking roles to serve the purpose of the systems
they lead and manage. Participants report the emerging clarity in
the alignment of personal desire with the purpose of the system in
the broader context.

Contact details:
The Grubb Institute
Cloudesley Street
London, N1 0HU.
Tel: +44 (0)20 7278 8061
Fax: +44 (0)20 7278 0728
E-mail: info@grubb.org.uk
Web: www.grubb.org.uk
The Grubb Institute is a registered charity.

The Tavistock Consultancy Service (TCS)

The Tavistock Consultancy Service (TCS) offers Senior Executive
Coaching to senior people in organizations. This takes the form of
a series of confidential meetings in which those in leadership roles
can think about their leadership style, the experience, knowledge,
skills, areas for development, and planning for their own futures
and that of their organizations. The TCS also provides a sounding
board for leaders as they work on ideas about developing the organization, and offers expertise where it is needed.

The distinctive competence we bring to senior executive coaching is in "working below the surface": helping clients to bring into
focus the less apparent feelings and responses in themselves and in
others that may be influencing their decisions and actions.

All our coaches are psychologists with additional training in
business, group dynamics, and organizational behaviour. They
bring considerable experience of working in and with many different kinds of organizations as executive coaches, organizational
consultants, change agents, and facilitators, as well as providing
skilled support for organizational and leadership development
roles.

TCS is uniquely situated within the Tavistock & Portman NHS Trust, which has a national and international reputation for quality and excellence in consultancy, training, research, and clinical work.

The general objectives of senior executive coaching are to help clients to develop greater confidence in exercising authority as a manager or leader, enhanced ability to use the full range of their experience, increased flexibility in assessing situations and judging their own responses, and clearer understanding of the strengths and limitations of their style of managing and leading.

Our clients report that coaching has helped them to manage complex organizational change more effectively, to identify stakeholder issues earlier, minimizing impact on the organization, to inspire and empower higher levels of performance in others, to manage personal well-being and work–life balance, and to unlock their true potential.

Executive Coaching Development Programme

The Tavistock Consultancy Service runs an Advanced Course in Executive Coaching. The course is designed to further participants understanding of the task of executive coaching from both systemic and psychodynamic perspectives.

The programme brings the Tavistock Consultancy Services unique "below the surface" approach together with many years of experience in both psychotherapy and in senior executive coaching with blue chip, public and voluntary sector clients. The programme is intended for professionals who wish to widen and deepen their understanding of the coaching task and its place within organizational development.

Successful completion of the course leads to a Tavistock Accredited Certificate in Executive Coaching. The course is externally examined through Exeter University.

Contact details:
Tavistock Consultancy Service
Tavistock Centre
120 Belsize Lane
London, NW3 5BA
Tel: +44 (0)20 7447 3737

Fax: +44 (0)20 7447 3738
Email: tcs@tavi-port.nhs.uk
Web: www.tavistockconsultancyservice.com
TCS is a registered trademark of the Tavistock Consultancy Service.

The Tavistock Institute

Coaching: we see executive coaching as an organizational development activity, capable of generating ideas that can drive strategy and can contribute to organizational learning.

- Coaching at senior level, working with executives to deliver corporate objectives by addressing business and organizational frameworks along with personal and interpersonal issues;
- conceptualizing, designing, and evaluating leadership programmes, which align with business imperatives;
- providing in-house training and consultancy in coaching and mentoring as a core management competence, and supporting coaches in their activities through peer group, or individual consultation.

Clients: current clients include Chief Executive Officers, Directors, Senior Managers in government, not for profit, professional service firms, industry, and commerce.

Contact details:
The Tavistock Institute
30 Tabernacle St
London EC2A 4UE
Tel: +44 (0)20 7417 0407
Web: www.tavistockinstitute.org

Managing Consultants: Executive Coaching and Development
Karen Izod, as above, or direct line: +44 (0)1483 455 668
E-mail: k.izod@tavinstitute.org

James Mackay, as above, or direct line: +44 (0)20 8889 2736,
E-mail j.mackay@tavinstitute.org

OPUS

OPUS—an Organization for Promoting Understanding of Society, was founded in 1975 and is a registered educational charity and company limited by guarantee. Its name reflects its aim: to encourage the study of conscious and unconscious processes in society and institutions within it. OPUS undertakes research, organizes conferences, promotes study groups called "listening posts", and publishes bulletins and papers.

OPUS has over 200 Associates, many from outside the UK. OPUS Associates are mainly professionals from a range of disciplines. OPUS also sponsors the international journal *Organizational & Social Dynamics*, which has a subscription base of nearly 500 throughout the world. In addition, OPUS organizes the Annual International Conference "Organizational & Social Dynamics".

OPUS Consultancy Services provides consultancy regarding individual, organizational, and societal dynamics. OPUS primarily uses an experiential approach to learning, drawing on action research and group relations learning. Two fundamental principles guide all of OPUS interventions: a tailor-made design to meet the needs of each client; OPUS consultants are committed to helping clients become more effective in diagnosing their own problems and finding their own solutions through the transfer of skills and insights.

Contact details:
The Director, OPUS, 26 Fernhurst Road, London SW6 7JW
Tel/Fax: +44 (0)20 7736 3844
E-mail: director@opus.org.uk
Website: www.opus.org.uk
membership@OPUS.org.uk

For information about the OPUS international journal *Organizational and Social Dynamics*: contact Director as above.

For submission of papers to the OPUS Journal: contact the Editorial Assistant, *Organizational & Social Dynamics*: E-mail: atbr20906_2@ blueyonder.co.uk

For enquiries regarding Opus Consultancy Services:
Contact Director (as above) or Consultancy Manager at e-mail: consultancy@opus.org.uk

Social Dreaming

Social Dreaming Ltd. is a not-for-profit company limited by guarantee and registered in London.

Social Dreaming starts from different premises than individual, therapeutic dream work. The focus is on the thinking, insight, and cultural knowledge contained in the dream and the participants transform the thinking of the dream by free association and amplification from the culture.

Social Dreaming now takes place in UK, Ireland, Sweden, Finland, Holland, Germany, France, Italy, Israel, Australia, India, Rwanda, and the USA.

The company offers Social Dreaming as an organizational intervention to foster creative thinking and to enhance the future planning of companies, as well as Creative Role Synthesis to enable individuals manage themselves better in their roles.

Contact details: www.socialdreaming.org

Private firms and practitioners

Miranda Alcock

Miranda Alcock Consultancy works with organizations, teams, and individuals; also offers private work with couples and individuals on an ongoing regular basis.

Contact details:
Tel: +44 (0)20 7267 8995

Halina Brunning

Halina Brunning is a Chartered Clinical Psychologist, Executive Coach, and Organizational Consultant in private practice. She offers Executive Coaching and Role Consultation to individuals working in the public, voluntary and corporate sectors.

Her approach to coaching is based on her own tried and tested model, "The Six Domains of Coaching", that gives her clients an opportunity to make new and meaningful connections in various domains of their life and work. This approach to coaching is best suited to people in transition, especially when a different organizational role, new responsibility, or the impact of complex organizational change becomes a challenge.

Halina also offers consultancy to teams, groups, and organizations; she specializes in facilitating team away-day reviews, post-merger culture consultation, and conflict resolution.

Contact details:
E-mail: halina@brunningonline.net
Website: www.brunningonline.net/halina
Tel: +44 (0)20 8540 9609

Angela Eden
Angela Eden works as an organization consultant, a mediator, and an executive coach. She designs single interventions, strategic "away days", and extended organizational change. Her intent is to influence policy, culture, and performance with her clients in statutory, commercial, and not-for-profit organizations.

Contact details:
Tel: +44 (0)20 7267 8293
Mobile: +44 (0)78 507 29838
E-mail: evolve@am-eden.co.uk
Website: www.edenevolution.co.uk

Executive coaching for senior managers and executives

Laurence J. Gould, PhD
Larry Gould is an organizational psychologist who offers individualized Executive Coaching Programmes for Senior Managers and Executives. These Programmes comprise a combination of formal assessments, multi-dimensional feedback from peers, direct reports, and other key participants in the organization, as appropriate, and individual consultation meetings. This process is especially recommended for those who are in a new role, for those whose role is undergoing a major change or shift, for those who are taking up a role in a new unit or organization, and for those who are facing particularly sensitive and complex challenges in the role they occupy. Executive Coaching is also useful for those who are feeling stuck or lacking creativity in their roles and wish to explore the possibilities for renewal and revitalization.

Contact details:
Laurence J. Gould, PhD

175 West 72nd St. #11E-1
New York, NY 10023
Voice Mail: (212) 874–3612
Fax: (212) 873–2041
E-Mail: Largould@aol.com

Michael Jarrett, PhD
Michael Jarrett is an Adjunct Associate Professor in Organization Behaviour at London Business School and a managing partner of Ilyas Jarrett Consulting, a strategic management consultancy.

He works with a team of experienced consultants who specialize in implementing organizational change. They offer strategic implementation tools, strategic workshops for top management teams, change leadership programmes, and executive coaching.

Their work is underpinned by innovative approaches to change as well as leading edge research. Clients include Lloyds TSB, BBC, Swiss Re.

Contact details:
www.ilyasjarrett.com
Tel: +44(0)20 8815 1388

Richard Kwiatkowski
Richard Kwiatkowski has been developing people for twenty years in a variety of contexts. His present work centres on the application of psychology to organizations and individuals and includes team dynamics, assessment, emotions, and culture change.

His coaching and consulting practice has taken him to many parts of the UK. He has given numerous guest lectures and conference talks.

Contact details:
Appointments can be made for private consultations via his PA at Cranfield on +44 (0)12 3475 1122.
E-mail r.kwiatkowski@cranfield.ac.uk or Richard@niip.org.uk

Anton Obholzer
Anton Obholzer, by training a medical doctor, psychiatrist, psychoanalyst and group and organizational consultant, Anton Obholzer has moved into the application of psychological understanding in the management of organizations.

His consultancy covers a wide range of commercial, banking, and public sector organizations, with the main emphasis of work and publications being on "under-the-surface"/unconscious factors causing resistance to change.

He has worked, and is presently engaged, in projects in USA, UK, Scandinavia, Germany, Austria, Holland, France, Italy, Spain, and South Africa.

His work with chief executives and senior management staff takes the form of mentoring, coaching, and role consultancy. The emphasis is on the multiplicity of factors playing a role in personal and institutional creativity. He is also fluent in German.

Contact details:
E-mail aobholzer@hotmail.com

Jane Pooley

Jane Pooley is a qualified family psychotherapist and member of the Tavistock Society of Psychotherapists, The Institute of Family Therapy, and OPUS. She specializes in consulting to senior executives and their teams in the areas of leadership development, executive performance, and interpersonal and influencing skills. She works with organizations to develop and implement guiding principles based on corporate values. Jane facilitates executive, management, team-building sessions, and supervises coaching practitioners.

Contact details:
J Pooley Associates
Saw Mill Cottage
Ayot Green
Welwyn
Hertfordshire AL6 9BB
Tel: +44 (0)17 0739 5006
Mobile: +44 (0)77 1472 0367
Email: janepooley@tiscali.co.uk

Vega Z. Roberts

Vega Roberts is a Senior Organizational Analyst at the Grubb Institute where she offers coaching and organizational role analysis (ORA) to individual managers as well as leadership development programmes, supervision for coaches and consultants, and a range of organizational development interventions. For a more detailed description of ORA and other leadership development activities, please see the entry for the Grubb Institute.

Contact details:
The Grubb Institute
Cloudesley Street
London NW1 0HU
Tel: +44 (0)20 7278 8061
Fax: +44 (0)21 7278 0728
E-mail: v.roberts@grubb.org.uk

Dr Marlene Spero
(Marlene Spero Associates, Executive Development and Consulting)
Dr Spero consults to individuals, groups, and organizations in transition using a socio-psychological approach. She works as an executive coach and has a particular interest in intercultural issues and leadership development and assessment. Her clients include those in retail, finance, banking, health, education, and IT. She has her own practice and is also an associate of the Bayswater Institute.

Contact details:
E-mail: mspero@easynet.co.uk

INDEX